CRITICAL INSIGHTS

Joseph Conrad

CRITICAL INSIGHTS

Joseph Conrad

Editor
Jeremiah J. Garsha
University of Cambridge, United Kingdom

SALEM PRESS
A Division of EBSCO Information Services, Inc.
Ipswich, Massachusetts

GREY HOUSE PUBLISHING

Copyright © 2016 by Grey House Publishing, Inc.

All rights reserved. No part of this work may be used or reproduced in any manner whatsoever or transmitted in any form or by any means, electronic or mechanical, including photocopy, recording, or any information storage and retrieval system, without written permission from the copyright owner. For information, contact Grey House Publishing/Salem Press, 4919 Route 22, PO Box 56, Amenia, NY 12501.

∞ The paper used in these volumes conforms to the American National Standard for Permanence of Paper for Printed Library Materials, Z39.48 1992 (R2009).

Publisher's Cataloging-In-Publication Data
(Prepared by The Donohue Group, Inc.)

Names: Garsha, Jeremiah J., editor.
Title: Joseph Conrad / editor, Jeremiah J. Garsha, University of Cambridge, United Kingdom.
Other Titles: Critical insights.
Description: [First edition]. | Ipswich, Massachusetts : Salem Press, a division of EBSCO Information Services, Inc. ; Amenia, NY : Grey House Publishing, [2016] | Includes bibliographical references and index.
Identifiers: ISBN 978-1-68217-114-1 (hardcover)
Subjects: LCSH: Conrad, Joseph, 1857-1924--Criticism and interpretation. | Conrad, Joseph, 1857-1924--Political and social views. | Adventure stories, English--19th century--History and criticism. | Adventure stories, English--20th century--History and criticism. | Psychological fiction, English--19th century--History and criticism. | Psychological fiction, English--20th century--History and criticism.
Classification: LCC PR6005.O4 Z683 2016 (print)| DDC 823/.9/12--dc23

First Printing

PRINTED IN THE UNITED STATES OF AMERICA

Contents

About This Volume, Jeremiah Garsha	vii
On Joseph Conrad, Jeremiah Garsha	xiii
Biography of Joseph Conrad, Jeremiah Garsha	xxiv

Critical Contexts

Joseph Conrad—Imperial Writings in a Postcolonial World, Joshua Pritchard	3
The Discursive Evolution of Conrad's Critiques: A Historiography of Critical Receptions to *Heart of Darkness*, Taryn B. Cornell	19
Travelling in Shadowlands—Colonialism and the Holocaust in Widmer's and Sebald's Textual Mining of *Heart of Darkness*, Peter Arnds	35
"Solidarity in Dreams": Community, Difference, and Race from *Narcissus* through *Heart of Darkness*, Kieran Dodds	50

Critical Readings

Misogyny or Artistry? Conrad's Revisions of Two Heroines, from Serial to First Edition, Lydia Craig	69
The Conradian Legacy: Portrayal of "Half-made Societies" in Joseph Conrad's *Nostromo* and V. S. Naipaul's *Guerrillas*, Hatice Övgü Tüzün	84
Reading *Lord Jim* in the Twenty-First Century: The Context, the Immigrant, and the Lord, Fouzia Reza and Vikarun Nessa	99
Joseph Conrad's Sense of Individuation in *Almayer's Folly*, Fitrilya Anjarsari	114
Joseph Conrad on the *Titanic*: A Pioneering Spirit of Safety and Life at Sea, Stefania Elena Carnemolla	132
Modeling Modernity, Phillip A. Lobo	146
The Writer Who Foresaw Slow Food: Joseph Conrad and the Morality of Eating, Francesco Buscemi	162
Quantitative Elocutionary Methods: Joseph Conrad's Harmony and Juxtaposition in *Heart of Darkness*, Gerardo Del Guercio	180

The Unreadable Sea: Manliness in Joseph Conrad's *Victory:*
An Island Tale (1915) and "The Tale" (1917), Benjamin Bronnert Walker 194

Heart of Darkness and the Problem of Faith, Charlotte Fiehn 206

Resources

Chronology of Joseph Conrad's Life 223
Works by Joseph Conrad 229
Bibliography 233
About the Editor 237
Contributors 239
Index 245

About this Volume

Jeremiah Garsha

The purpose of this anthology is to explore Joseph Conrad and his writings from a new perspective. It is written in a way that a reader with zero experience or understanding of Conrad's bibliography can easily pick up this volume and understand the core concepts and connections. No previous knowledge of Conrad's personal history or any of his essays, novellas, and novels is required. Yet, critically, this book is also framed in a way that a dedicated Conradian expert will find it well represents the subject matter, while also offering new insight to that well-versed reader.

With exponentially more being written *about* Conrad than the author ever wrote over his forty-year career, it seems, on the surface, like an impossible task to cover in such a small book what entire growing library shelves seek to achieve. Yet, this book accomplishes that goal. It does so through the diversity the collection of chapters offers. Indeed, the greatest strength of this book is in its global reach of subject matter, done through an international collaboration of outstanding authors.

This text brings together established academics with early career researchers who will undoubtedly be the very people who push disciplines in new, uncharted directions. No longer is the world replete in unmarked spaces, but the realm of literature is wide open for analytical exploration. The contributors' diverse backgrounds and scholarly interests allow for readings into Conrad's work and life in ways that are entirely novel. This occurs, in part, due to the unique perspectives each author has brought to the subject.

While there is the inevitable clustering of contributors around Anglo-American institutes of education (for instance, from my own university in Cambridge), the heterogeneity of their groundings, both in terms of academic pursuits and places of origin, underscore the plurality of viewpoints. Like Conrad, many of these authors composed chapters in their second or third language. Authors are drawn from the locales, colonial or metropole, in which Conrad conducted and based his writing. Subaltern actors employ, within these pages, subaltern theory. The historians use Conrad's writings as primary and secondary source material, interchangeably. The chapters herein cover diverse topics in fundamentally original ways. Conversely, I have purposefully selected chapters that overlap, centering, for example, on the same publication in order to showcase the different ways varying perspectives can produce new interpretations from the same source. *Heart of Darkness*, as arguably Conrad's most famous text, is covered from a multitude of angles, with each new visitation revealing critical insight and exemplifying the plasticity of Conrad's world.

When taken as a whole, the homogenization of polyglottal and diasporic viewpoints move beyond standard analysis. The different languages these authors think in, brought together with their geographically diverse backgrounds and myriad of interests, unlock Conrad's texts to the reader. Rather than examine Conrad under a lens of inquiry, this work creates a prism in which Conrad's oeuvre is fractured, elucidating individual threads while bringing about a convergence of understanding to one of the greatest authors of English literature.

Structure

The fifteen chapters in this book demonstrate the wide-reaching impact Conrad's work has had within and outside of scholarly communities. By way of introduction, this volume begins with my own chapter, reading Joseph Conrad's life and works from a world history perspective, while also making the case that world history as a discipline is enriched with a study of Conrad. The volume then moves to a brief biographical sketch of Joseph Conrad, linking his key publications to the events in his life that they capture. This chapter is supplemented at the end of the volume with a "Resources" section. Here the reader will find a clear chronology of the formative events in Conrad's prolific life, as well as a detailed listing of Conrad's novels, individual short stories, and key nonfiction essays. Finally, a bibliography of recommended secondary literature pertaining to Conrad is offered for further reading.

This volume is split into three sections. In the first section, "Critical Contexts," a historical and cultural overview of Conrad is provided in four chapters. The second section of this book, "Critical Readings," is a collection of ten deeper readings into specific Conradian works or themes organized around his writings. In the final section, "Resources," as discussed above, easy-to-follow lists are given in order to help guide the reader through important dates, keep track of and sort through Conrad's most important publications, and understand the difference between Conrad's fiction and nonfiction writings, which admittedly often blur together. A selection of further reading is then provided.

The first four chapters all use *Heart of Darkness* as jumping-off points into a broad range of analyses. Joshua Pritchard illuminates the historical colonial backdrop in which the novella is set, and the postcolonial world in which it has now been received. His chapter builds the foundations required to understand how Conrad's own experience, both prior to his voyage in the Congo and after, impacted the construction of Conrad's narrative. Next, Taryn B. Cornell creates an analytical matrix assessing the critical receptions of Conrad's novella. By examining the changes over time these critiques have undergone, with cross references to shifts in academic disciplines, she underscores that reading and reacting to Conrad tells us as much about the reviewer as it does about the subject. In the third chapter, Peter Arnds laudably examines the intertextuality of colonial atrocities documented by Conrad in two seemingly disconnected Holocaust literary representations. His comparative use of contemporary accounts exploring Nazi inflicted genocide establish philosophical roots in ideas of human banishment and erasure, bringing out critical elements of Conrad's seminal work. The final chapter in this first section provides the requisite jumping-off point to move this volume forward into the critical reading element. Kieran Dodds takes the unprecedented step of combining "Youth," *Heart of Darkness*, "The End of the Tether," and *The Nigger of the 'Narcissus'* to reveal Conrad's inconsistent ideologies regarding community and belonging, which he juxtaposes with a historical view of colonial interruptions. With a sweeping analysis across a wide range of texts and time periods, Dodds supplements and renews Chinua Achebe's infamous critique by bringing new textual evidence within a postcolonial perspective.

The next ten chapters focus on specific texts, with varying methodological approaches. Lydia Craig's first chapter uses a gender analysis to explore the nuanced differences in *Nostromo* and *The Secret Agent* as they underwent corrective revisions during the translation from serial to first-edition books. She unpacks notions of a forced binary space created by nineteenth-century normative values, in which Conrad writes women as symbolic, often nameless objects without agency.

Hatice Övgü Tüzün undertakes a comparative reading of *Nostromo* and the Trinidadian author V. S. Naipaul's political novel *Guerillas*. Her chapter offers a detailed analysis of *Nostromo* and the influence Conrad had in creating Naipaul's vision of pan-postcolonial sites of renewal, where culture and identity could be made as easily as it could be unmade. Within these metaphorical "island" sites, she argues, Conrad and Naipaul created "half-made societies," which were constructed for colonial control and postcolonial reclamation, respectively. Similarly, Phillip A. Lobo looks at the notion of "world-building" found in *Nostromo*. Yet here, his chapter suggests, the making and unmaking impulse has been updated and passed forward to the reader and consumer. Using the example of the videogames, Lobo tests the broad morality of control, creation, and the banality of flattening out spaces, either under colonial administration or continued through postcolonial development.

Fouzia Reza and Vikarun Nessa bring *Lord Jim* into the present. Their chapter uses a rereading of Conrad's novel in light of the current refugee crisis. Jim, as a European, it is argued, is able to occupy the space of an "expat," retaining control and gaining lordship. Conversely, this chapter explores the notion of being an "immigrant," marked by a lack of control and the difficulty of gaining citizenship. Beyond Conrad's text, social media, political rallies, and popular culture are interwoven in a twenty-first-century context.

Fitrilya Anjarsari's chapter looks at notions of psychological development in *Almayer's Folly*. Her chapter stresses Conrad as a travelogue author, suggesting his writings need to be read alongside his contemporary travel writers and the landscapes they tried to reproduce. She investigates Conrad's motivation for using the Malay Archipelago as a backdrop in many of his writings and the way this contributed to an erasure of Malayan agency.

Stefania Elena Carnemolla brings to light some of Conrad's most overlooked writings. Her chapter analyzes Conrad's publications regarding maritime safety, published just after the infamous sinking of the *Titanic*. In these writings, Conrad combined his own sailing experience with his typically sardonic style in order to critique global capitalism's impulse to build "floating hotels" catering to luxury seeking upper-class clients. She argues these writings helped codify international legislation regarding ocean safety that is still with us today.

Francesco Buscemi uses brief passages within Conrad's fictional works and even his wife's published cookbook to argue that Conrad subtly protested against the globalization and industrialization of food and the growing immorality of consumption. Buscemi sees Conrad's writings as the antecedent to the Slow Food movement and his chapter shows that even the smallest sentence in Conrad's writings imparts invaluable insights.

Gerardo Del Guercio's chapter is a microreading of *Heart of Darkness*. By analyzing the frequency and distribution in which key words appear within the text, his chapter combines statistical analysis in a way that reveals Conrad's unconscious motivations surrounding every single word he wrote. In reading Conrad's words out of place, a hidden distinction arises between the narration of Marlow and that of the unnamed narrator within the novella.

Benjamin Bronnert Walker's chapter is a gendered reading of tropes of masculinity within *Victory* and "The Tale." He analyzes Conrad's only work dealing with the First World War to document the continuity, rather than change, in Conrad's definition of manliness during this transformative period. Walker provides a textual analysis of the two stories' use of concealment—both naturally occurring as fog and dark seas and as façades of masculinity—in order to underscore Conrad's male characters' (and perhaps, by extension, Conrad's own) perpetual need to prove themselves.

Finally, this section returns full circle to *Heart of Darkness*. Charlotte Fiehn's concluding chapter in this volume explores the allusions to Christianity within Conrad's text. Using elements of psychoanalysis, her chapter makes the intriguing claim that Marlow, like a converted pilgrim, was drawn through faith to the psychopathic god-like charisma and corrupting control Kurtz exercised over his disciples. Fiehn interrogates the signifiers within Conrad's text to tease out Judeo-Christian overtones.

The intention of this layout is not to suggest that the chapters should be read in a particular order. Nor, as mentioned at the outset, do any chapters require prior knowledge of Conrad's work. Chapters should be consumed in the order that most helps the reader, either before or after reading Conrad's primary texts. Taken together, however, it becomes clear that even though we are less than a decade away from the centennial of Conrad's death, his writings and world is still very much alive.

On Joseph Conrad

Jeremiah Garsha

A World History Perspective

In the paraphrased words of the late Christopher Bayly: "[We] are all world historians now, though many have not yet realized it" (469). To read Joseph Conrad is to immerse oneself in a world history. Conrad's writings are inseparable from the world he inhabited and the worlds he created. His fictional narratives can be just as informative as firsthand historical accounts, but with the added thrill of forcing the reader to play detective, ciphering out what really happened from the invented stories Conrad so eloquently built upon. Yet, that, too, underscores that reading Conrad's work is an exercise in historical inquiry.

The study of history, at its core, is the separation of "events" from the interpretations of the observers that recorded them. In his monumental, though dated, book *That Noble Dream*, Peter Novick documents the history of the notion of "objectivity" as it has changed over time. Novick uses historical contextualization in order to show how the biographical experiences of historians and the times in which they write shape the historical discipline. The notion that any author can ever describe the past (and the very act of writing is already an action taking place in past tense) without adding in unconscious biases is false. Prior to the 1980s, historians clung to the idea, first articulated by the eighteenth-century German writer Leopold von Ranke, that narratives are able to account for events "as they really happened" (Novick 25-26).

Novick's publication has been eclipsed by the historical turn within the discipline to embrace postmodernist theory. Heralded by poststructuralist philosophers, such as Jacques Derrida, Michel Foucault, Gilles Deleuze, and Jacques Lacan, this shift marked an abandonment of the notion that authors can create unbiased accounts of the past. Put simply, all we have are interpretations of inaccessible events in the past. An author is inescapably a product of his or her time and upbringing and writes as much about himself or herself as about the past he or she attempts to record. In short, humans create inaccurate narratives, not objective, hermetically sealed preservations of the past.

Novick's text was published before a second major turn emerged fully formed. Today the historical discipline embraces a turn away from the domineering "master narratives" written with a top-down approach. It has done this by moving globally. The subaltern writings of and by former colonial states and subjects, with their approach of "history from below," have created a new strain of historical analysis. This is a departure from Eurocentric primacy in its attempt to create more encompassing historical narratives.

Bottom-up perspectives are not new elements to the discipline of history. E. P. Thompson's 1963 *The Making of the English Working Class* remains the definitive example of history from below. The more recent turn, however, can be marked by a hybridized attempt to avoid creating the same master narratives that existed in earlier socially and politically charged forms of history. Bayly saw this as a combined approach of "uncovering a variety of hidden meta-narratives . . . [while] chart[ing] the experiences of people without [recorded] history" (8-9). This approach is the essence of world history, a catch-all term that applies the postcolonial movement to narratives of overlooked and misinterpreted subjects by creating truthful accounts of history.

In the opening of his 2016 book, *What is Global History*, Sebastian Conrad (no relation to Joseph) states simply that global history is created to meet the "demand for a more inclusive, less narrowly national perspective on the past" (2). Sebastian Conrad stresses comparative connections through transnational links that "reconfigure the global order" in response to the nondisciplinary move of globalization within the increasingly interconnected world (*Globalisation and Nation* 389). The lens of world history is one that allows old materials to be processed from the "advantages of immense distance and panoptic range" (Fernández-Armesto & Sacks 303). Quixotically, a reexamination of materials from a god's eye view is complemented with an intensely focused localized framework. The boundaries of time periods and geographic space can be collapsed if one looks into the ways local agency reacts to global processes (Wong 84). By zooming into the hyperspecificity, world history creates new areas of multiple connections, yet also highlights differences in a transnational web. World history, using both zoomed-out and micro-focused perspectives is a study of discourses as they cut across national, regional, and international boundaries, while also bringing temporally separated events into consideration (Iriye 213).

Imperial history created and upheld binary distinctions between colonizer and colonized, privileging the agency of European actors and creating colonial nations as backdrops where European history played out. This was the charge of Conrad's most damning critic, Chinua Achebe (discussed in greater detail in Joshua Pritchard's, Taryn B. Cornell's, and Kieran Dodds' chapters in this volume). While it is debatable whether Conrad was indeed the "bloody racist" Achebe painted him as, it is more helpful to view Conrad as a product of his own history. This is not to undermine the quite valid critiques postcolonial scholars have applied to European literature. Rather, it is to suggest simply that Conrad's writings cannot be separated out from Conrad's experiences. If the tools of world history are applied to Conrad's texts, in both a wide-angle scan and zoomed-in focus, Conrad's texts reveal universal truths about the trappings our own histories have on our thoughts and expressions. In this way, to read Conrad through a world history lens is to augment the world history discipline with tools forged by Conrad himself.

Joseph Conrad creates brilliantly crafted narratives. As discussed above, even autobiographical accounts are works of "fiction." The unconscious exaggerations, the prior experiences, and the lens in which information is processed spin all recorded texts into narrativized "stories." No source materials produced by humans can avoid the trappings of revision. Yet, Conrad's texts offer a prescriptive antidote to the ailing approach of searching for "facts" within the world of fiction.

Conrad gives the reader verbs disguised as nouns. His words do more than describe, they animate. His texts create actions, where the prose reaches out into the audience and alters our present world. It is a transformative experience to read one of Conrad's works. This was something to which Conrad was aware. In the author preface to *The Nigger of the 'Narcissus,'* Conrad wrote: "My task which I am trying to achieve is, by the power of the written word, to make you hear, to make you feel—it is, before all, to make you see. That—and no more, and it is everything. If I succeed, you shall find…that glimpse of truth for which you have forgotten to ask" (x). Conrad uses the elements of fictional storytelling in order to represent truth in a way that is far more accurate than a standard narrative.

This author's preface reveals telling markers of the truth Conrad sneaked in below his reader's gaze. *The Nigger of the 'Narcissus'* is an invented story. The writing of it was motivated by, as with all published works, a desire to sell magazines and printed books for his publishers while simultaneously elevating Conrad's future social and economic status. Yet there are curious factual details left in his novel. For instance, why did Conrad choose to use the name of a ship he himself had sailed on? Beyond the alliterative title, using the actual name of an authentic ship grounds Conrad's writing in reality and connects his novel back to his personal memories of this experience. In the preface, Conrad opens with his intention that his book aspires to be a kind of art that "carr[ies] its justification in every line . . . bringing to light the truth" underlying all fictional works of art (vii). Conrad sees artists as being akin to philosophers or scientists, offering up objective representations of truth in the hidden facts of the fictional text.

Yet, within this concealment of fiction layered over Conrad's lived experience, we are shown the typical Conradian emotional distancing techniques. Conrad, more than the majority of authors, created highly personal novels that repackaged his own life into those of his characters. The distancing of invented details proved a protection against revealing too much of himself, a self-confessed and self-fashioned outsider in all his endeavors. This, too, explains why critiques on his publications sent Conrad into bouts of depression coupled with seemingly inescapable writer's block. Attacks on his plot and characters where attacks on his own life. Considering the great volume of writings Conrad produced during his forty-year career, one can only imagine the wealth of materials that would have existed had every publication attempt not been accompanied by forced pauses.

The elements of Conrad within the novel are trivial, yet represent successful uses of writing a fictional narrative that is not true, but is truthful. There are many ways of knowing the past. By reading the novel alongside established facts about Conrad, a world history approach enlightens our understanding of British seafaring experiences at the dawn of the twentieth century. His writings provide the same historical mining opportunities as archival materials. In this way, *The Nigger of the 'Narcissus'* is a work that should be read aside captains' journals, private letters of sailors, recorded sea shanties, shipping manifests, and the many other broad source materials that inform us about the experiences of people who may otherwise be silenced from the traditional historical record.

The Nigger of the 'Narcissus' is an important first text to examine from a world historian perspective because it was such a transformative book to Conrad. Its serialization in 1897 was, according to Conrad in a revisitation of this moment seven years later, "the first event in my writing life which really counted" (*Collected Letters* 115). Moreover, it is a work in which Conrad plays with how much of his own life he wants to reveal within the text. He has the fictional merchant ship *Narcissus* sailing from Bombay to London, just like the voyage Conrad undertook aboard the *Narcissus*. Critically, the protagonist James Wait is dying from tuberculosis, the same disease that killed Conrad's mother and father. Perhaps the fact that Conrad has Wait die within sight of land after enduring the isolation and solitary confinement aboard the capsized ship was Conrad's way of coming to terms with the loss of his parents. The ship that symbolized Conrad's escape from Russian occupation was one in which his parents could not make the transition from their colonized homeland, alluded to by departure from India, the British Empire's crown jewel, to the metropole. The plight of Wait becomes a stand-in for the alienation Conrad felt in his adopted new homeland, and the truth that Conrad's preface sought to reveal within this text was more about Conrad's desire for community and belonging than it was about the second-class subjection of a black West Indian sailor.

Recalling the preface of *The Nigger of the 'Narcissus,'* Conrad's introduction to *Heart of Darkness* states that this account is an "experience pushed a little (and only very little) beyond the actual facts of the case" (qtd. in Sherry 9). Once more, it is clear that Conrad accurately sees fiction as the best medium for capturing an experience that cannot be replicated in standard autobiographical form. Elements of *Heart of Darkness* come from Conrad's journal during his time in the Congo. Yet it is a work of fiction far removed from Conrad's diary. In fact, it was only in 1925 that his diary was published, capitalizing on Conrad's longstanding literary career and the news of his death. With its straightforward and pithy descriptions, "Joseph Conrad's diary (hiteherto unpublished) of his journey up the valley of the Congo in 1890" made for an anomalous read to the typical Conrad audience when it appeared in the British magazine *The Blue Peter*. As is evidenced by the parenthetical statement that readers were encountering a text "hitherto unpublished," the account, with its raw and unpolished sentences, was a trivialized source, only becoming published in bound from in 1978, tacked on to copies of *Heart of Darkness*. This helps explain, in part, why Conrad used his historical records to create stylized versions of his experiences. In wanting to disseminate his story and ideological impulses, Conrad sought to reach the largest audience. A good story will always outsell a true story.

The facts that Conrad supposedly changed "a little (and only very little)" are naturally quite stretched in *Heart of Darkness*. Nevertheless, it is the comparisons, not the contrasts, which make Conrad's writings on African colonialism captivating. From the outset, it appears as though Conrad's anticolonial critiques within his oeuvre are incapable of challenging British colonialism. Whether this was because of a true allegiance to his host country or pragmatically avoided in order to not alienate his Anglophone audience is unknown. But it is clear that Conrad's stories challenged, overtly, Belgian and Dutch colonial systems, while indirectly calling into question the whole European colonial enterprise. The Dutch East Indies and the Belgian Congo, however, were colonies intimately familiar to Conrad, where his firsthand experience, as always, based his world creation in reality.

Like Marlow, Conrad also traveled to "a European city" in order to find work as a merchant sailor. While the Company's headquarters remains concealed in *Heart of Darkness*, the fact that it is a Belgian company is hidden in plain sight. Marlow, like Conrad, worked for the *Société Anonyme Belge pour le Commerce du Haut-Congo*. In 1890, Conrad traveled to the Matadi outpost and prepared to steam upriver. According to Conrad's biographer, Matadi was were Conrad was first "struck . . . by the greed and duplicity of the white bearers of 'civilization' eager for quick profits, and by the chaos and stupidity of many enterprises" (Najder 133). Matadi thus can be seen as the inspiration for and setting of "An Outpost of Progress," the short story that proceeded *Heart of Darkness* and shares the overall theme of an erosion of morality when Europeans exist outside of the society control.

Heart of Darkness begins with two narrators, Marlow and an unnamed voice, in disagreement over the nature of colonialism. Here, both stand in as Conrad at different times in his life. The unnamed narrator is Conrad prior to his Congo voyage, where Conrad remained convinced that his duties under the Company supported "civilization" and not material exploitation (Najder 127). Conrad's diary entries show this, where his chief complaints, at first, have little to do with appalling conditions of subjection and much more to do with Conrad's "perspective [as] a European traveller exposed to discomfort" (Najder 133). During the trek from Matadi to Kinshasa, Conrad recorded a "beastly" incident where he "fell into a muddy puddle," which was entirely "the fault of the man that carried" him through the jungle in a hammock ("The Congo Diary" 126).

Yet the brutal realities of colonial violence were inescapable during this trek. In another entry, Conrad's diary notes the horrid stench of a decomposed Congolese inhabitant, presumably shot by colonial agents (124). In another noteworthy entry, Conrad tells of encountering "another dead body lying by the path in an attitude of meditative repose" (126). From this recollection, Conrad juxtaposes the images of the corpse with that of Marlow in *Heart of Darkness*. As Marlow begins the story within the story, the unnamed narrator describes Marlow seated on the deck of the *Nellie* with one arm lifted "from the elbow, the palm of the hand outwards, so that, with his legs folded before him, he had the pose of a Buddha preaching in European clothes (7). Here, Conrad has shifted from the naïve narrator into Marlow, representing the contemporary and broken mindset of Conrad, shown through the pose of a corpse. It is from this Buddha pose that Marlow tells the crew that within the Belgian Congo there "were no colonists" as the Congo Free State "merely [to] squeeze" the colony of its natural resources. "They were conquerors," Conrad writes, whose "strength is just an accident arising from the weakness of others. They grabbed what they could get. . . . It was just robbery with violence, aggravated murder on a great scale" (7). The young Conrad who was once upset because his porter got him muddy had transitioned into a skeptic of empire's "civilization" justifications. His Congo experience transformed Conrad's attitudes regarding colonialism, and he seeks to do the same to the reader. Just as he transformed from the unnamed narrator to Marlow, Conrad invites the reader to abandon notions that empires are anything other than violent commercial exploitation.

When the short story "An Outpost of Progress," first serialized in 1897, was published in the bound collection *Tales of Unrest*, Conrad had the opportunity to revisit his text and his past. In the "Author's Note," Conrad calls "An Outpost of Progress" "the lightest part of the loot I carried off from Central Africa" (*Tales of Unrest* ix). Andrea White reinterprets this foreword to be Conrad's subtle attack against African colonization, using the scale of exploitation within colonies to map out his small protest against empire (190). Even the title "An Outpost of Progress" is a satirical stab at the supposed civilization mission used by European nations to justify the partition of Africa.

Conrad writes that "other men have found a lot of quite different things [in Central Africa] and I have the comfortable conviction that what I took would not have been of much use to anybody else" (*Tales of Unrest* ix). Conrad, who left Poland and took to the seas due to his quest for adventure had had his fill after his experience in the Congo. The explorers he so longed to emulate now became lumped into the same category as the colonial agents. They are the "men [who] found . . . quite different things," while all Conrad took was an experience as a direct accessory to the enterprise that he longed to share with the world. This allowed him to maintain his "comfortable conviction" of what he called "a very small amount of plunder. All of it could go into one's breast pocket when folded neatly." Yet Conrad is displaying his usual sarcastic shielding that his experience "would not have been much use to anybody else." Conrad needed to share his account as a witness to crimes against humanity. He wrote three published accounts about it. But Conrad could only tell his account through the medium of fiction. Beyond the rhetorical distancing Conrad attempted, such as using two narrators in *Heart of Darkness* to share his journal entries, or to invent characters and dialogue, Conrad used fiction in order to create a narrative of an event that was more accurate in capturing the essence of his experience than his own journal writing while in the Congo. As he continued in the "Author's Note," "the story itself is true enough in its essentials. The sustained invention of a really telling lie demands a talent which I do not possess" (ix).

Conrad's writings, therefore, preserve history in a way that captivates and transforms the audience. He uses his literary talents and imagination in order to create narratives that are somehow more truthful and more accurate than firsthand accounts can offer. The power of his writing is that it can transport the reader into these fictional spaces in a way that conscripts the mind into participation. As Marlow travels up the Congo River, or as Wait suffers trapped inside a capsized ship, Conrad creates a record of experiences that bring world history narratives into his writings. His narrative inventions stand in for lived experiences. The stories not only map the experiences of Conrad's days as a traveling sailor, but also the experiences of those he encountered and wove into his publications. He preserves the narrative of the men (less so of women) he met that would otherwise be lost to historians. He creates lived experiences that "could go into one's breast pocket when folded neatly."

To read one of Conrad's writings is to read a world history narrative. Conrad's life was one of connecting spaces and places across the globe. He was a personification of Europe; a Polish-born Russian citizen of the Ukraine, who thought in French, wrote in English, and applied Polish grammatical constructions that remain within the English literary tradition. Just as world history seeks to create connections out of seemingly disparate times and places, Conrad lived these connections. His very life is a world history. Information and communication technologies have shrunk the long routes of transit Conrad once undertook. Globalization has created international interconnectivity that would have been unimaginable for Conrad. His world was one of partitioned continents and imperial rivalries that culminated in the First World War. Yet Conrad sought to connect experiences, to share his life through his publications, and to give readers truthful insights into historical events. In this way, he created world histories of his own. And for that we are indebted. After all, we, too, are all world historians now.

Works Cited

Bayly, C. A. *The Birth of the Modern World, 1780–1914*. Oxford: Blackwell, 2004. Print.

The Collected Letters of Joseph Conrad: Vol. 3, 1903–1907. Ed. Frederick R. Karl & Laurence Davies. Cambridge, UK: Cambridge UP, 1990. Print.

"The Congo Diary." *Last Essays*. Ed. H. Ray Stevens & J.H. Stape. Cambridge, UK: Cambridge UP, 2010. 123-137. Print.

Conrad, Joseph. *Preface [in, The Nigger of the 'Narcissus']*. Cambridge, UK: Chadwyck-Healey, 1999. *Literary Theory Full-Text Database*. Web. 15 June 2016.

_____. *Heart of Darkness*. Harmondsworth: Penguin Books, 2007. *ProQuest*. Web. 15 June 2016.

_____. *Tales of Unrest*. New York: Penguin Books, 1977. Print.

Conrad, Sebastian. *What is Global History?*. Princeton: Princeton UP, 2016. Print.

_____. *Globalisation and the Nation in Imperial Germany.* Trans. Sorcha O'Hagend. Cambridge, UK: Cambridge UP, 2010. Print.

Fernández-Armesto, Felipe & Benjamin Sacks. "Networks, Interactions, and Connective History." *A Companion to World History.* Ed. Douglas Northrop. Oxford: Wiley-Blackwell, 2012. 303-310. Print.

Iriye, Akira. "Review: Transnational History." *Contemporary European History* 13.2 (May 2004): 211-222. Print.

Najder, Zdzisław. *Joseph Conrad: A Life.* Trans. Halina Najder. Rochester, NY: Camden House, 2007. Print.

Novick, Peter. *That Noble Dream: The "Objectivity Question" and the American Historical Profession.* Cambridge, UK: Cambridge UP, 1988. Print.

Sherry, Norman. *Conrad's Western World.* Cambridge, UK: Cambridge UP, 1971. Print

White, Andrea. "Conrad and Imperialism." *The Cambridge Companion to Joseph Conrad.* Ed. J. H. Stape. Cambridge, UK: Cambridge UP, 1996, 179-202. Print.

Wong, R. Bin. "Regions and Global History." *Writing the History of the Global: Challenges for the 21st Century.* Ed. Maxine Berg. Oxford: Oxford UP, 2013, 83-105. Print.

Biography of Joseph Conrad

Jeremiah Garsha

Józef Teodor Konrad Korzeniowski, known by his pen name Joseph Conrad, was born on December 3, 1857 in Berdyczów, a Polish city, located at that time within the Russian Empire, present-day Ukraine. Since the turn of the nineteenth century, the Kingdom of Poland had been occupied under a partitioned split between the Austrian Empire in the south, the Russian Empire to the east, and the growing Prussian state to the west (Zins 12). Conrad was born to Polish nationalist intellectuals, members of the landed Polish gentry. His father, Apollo Korzeniowski, was a noted writer and translator, whose work as a prominent activist for Polish independence and anti-Russian sentiments frequently invoked government ire. While Conrad had been named Józef after Apollo's father, in a theme of his own inescapable entanglement with literature that followed Conrad throughout his life, his parents called him Konrad, a named taken from the poems *Konrad Wallenrod* and *Dziady*, stories that invoked notions of Polish liberation from Russian, Prussian, and Austro-Hungarian oppression, penned by fellow exiled Polish nationalist and political activist Adam Mickiewicz (Najder 11).

Indeed, the literary tradition was a fundamental component in Conrad's life from the very beginning. Beyond his own publications, Conrad's father translated the English works of William Shakespeare, Charles Dickens, and the French writings of Victor Hugo into Polish. Conrad, homeschooled by his father to read in both Polish and French, became intimately familiar with his father's library, particularly Hugo's *Toilers of the Sea*, in which we can see the nascent roots of seafaring adventurism, and Shakespeare's plays, which brought Conrad to the foundations of the English literary tradition he himself would transform. Moreover, his father introduced young Conrad to Polish poetry, through which issues of nationalism, belonging, and subjugation complemented his schooling with his lived childhood experiences under Russian occupation (Najder 11-12; Peters 1). Naming his chief protagonist and narrative stand-in "Charles Marlow," after the Elizabethan poet and Shakespeare's contemporary, Christopher Marlowe, underscores the deep connection Conrad found in the printed word (Ray 150), while echoing back to his own familial christening of "Konrad."

When Conrad was four years old, his father's outspoken support of Polish independence movements, calls for land reform, and an abolishment of the serf system led to Apollo's arrest. Along with his family, Apollo was exiled, first to Vologda and its extreme Siberian climate and later to Chernihiv, Ukraine. On April 18, 1865, Conrad's mother died from tuberculosis brought about by their harsh living conditions. Conrad and Apollo were able to move out of Russian-occupied Poland and into the Austrian zone. On May 23, 1869, just three month after moving to Kraków, the once historic capital of the Polish Kingdom, Apollo Korzeniowski also died of tuberculosis, contracted while in exile. At age eleven, Conrad was orphaned.

His mother's brother, Tadeusz Bobrowski became Conrad's guardian and attempted to continue the homeschooling Apollo had initiated. Conrad, however, struggled with his education. It is possible that Bobrowski and his hired tutors were unable to replicate the rigors, passion, and bond Apollo had established, or perhaps Conrad's traumatic childhood experiences and attendant physical and mental ordeals made learning difficult. Regardless of the reason, the only subject Conrad excelled in geography (Najder 43). When Marlow muses in *Heart of Darkness* that ". . . when I was a little chap I had a passion for maps" and a fascination with "the many blank spaces on the earth," promising that "when I grow up I will go" to the inviting and uncharted regions of the earth, it is clear that his narrator is merely a stand-in for Conrad's own exploration of himself and his desires (*Heart of Darkness* 11). His physicians diagnosed Conrad's illness as psychosomatic and prescribed physical exercise in open-air conditions. With young Conrad's lackluster academic display, Bobrowski pushed him to learn a maritime trade, which promised rigor and discipline (Najder 44-46). When reflecting back on his youth, Conrad recalled that his "whole being was steeped deep in indolence of a sailor away from the sea" (*A Personal Record* 73). Indeed Conrad's desire to escape political and personal troubles in his colonized homeland, combined with the passions for exploration and navigation he had gathered through books (Peters 2), and now encouraged by his doctors and supported, financially and ideologically, by his uncle culminated in Conrad's decision to move to Marseilles. At age seventeen, Conrad joined the French merchant fleet.

Though Conrad had left any formal sense of schooling behind, his literary upbringing meant that Conrad was prolifically well read, with fluency in French, serviceable knowledge of Latin and German, and enough Greek to read Homer's epic tales of seaborne adventure in the *Iliad* and the *Odyssey* without translation. His intellectual prowess, combined with the financial support of his uncle, enabled Conrad to sidestep work as an entry-level deckhand and train formally as a ship's mate and commander. The noted Conrad biographer Zdzisław Najder argues that it was because of Conrad's unique background of imposed transient migration, mental and physical isolation, and the strength that he found in the portable comfort of books that Conrad reinvented himself as a man of the sea (419). Najder notes that the act of leaving behind social groups, such as family and friends, while also severing language and cultural connections, traditionally creates internal tensions. Yet, in this isolation, Conrad instead found a sense of confirmation in his own self-worth. Najder writes, "throughout almost his whole life, Conrad was an outsider and felt himself to be one" (493). His high intelligence, when coupled with his external Polish looks, set him wholly apart from the traditional ship worker in European ports.

Just as his readings helped prepare and inspire Conrad for a life at sea, so too did life at sea come to dominate Conrad's own writings. Conrad sailed to the West Indies and then South America aboard the *Saint-Antoine*. Dominique Cervoni, *Saint-Antonie*'s first mate, served as the inspiration for the titular protagonist in *Nostromo*. Conrad writes, "Many of Nostromo's speeches I have heard first in Dominic's voice" (*Nostromo* xxii), and in his exaggerated autobiographical account *The Mirror of the Sea*, Conrad transitions Dominic from a living figure to a cloaked and dualistic "piratical and monkish [seafarer] .

. . darkly initiated into the most awful mysteries of the sea" (164). Speculation exists that it is with Cervoni that Conrad engaged in arms trafficking, thus explaining his more unflattering descriptions of Dominic in *The Mirror of the Sea* (Sherry 163-164). The character of Nostromo smuggles silver from Costaguana and weapons to Catholic factions during the Colombian civil war, an event Conrad may have been involved in and alluded to again in the author's notes of *Victory*. Conrad was aboard "an extremely small and extremely *dirty* little schooner . . . [traveling] between two places . . . whose names don't matter" (xii; emphasis added). Conrad's alleged experience in running weapons may have also formed the setting of *The Arrow of Gold*, where the unnamed narrator is involved in smuggling ammunition from Marseilles to Spain during the Carlist wars, a series of violent conflicts over monarchical legitimacy. Such trafficking is an act in which Conrad himself insinuates personal involvement (Hampson 29-30).

In 1878, at the conclusion of Conrad's service with the French merchant fleet, he suffered a gunshot wound to the chest. Scholars continue to debate over whether this was the result of a duel, as Conrad would later claim, or an unsuccessful suicide attempt. Zdzisław Najder, Conrad's definitive biographer suggests the latter, attributing the motivation to chronic depression that would plague Conrad all his life. He concludes, "even [Conrad] himself may have not known the whole truth of his action" (Najder 67). Conrad had racked up substantial gambling debts, which his uncle was later forced to pay off, signaling troubled times. In exploring the melancholic tropes within Conrad's body of work written later in life, it becomes evident that there are certain overlapping characteristics of suicide, from Almayer's overdose in Conrad's first novel to later scenes, such as the murder-suicide in *The Secret Agent* and Heyst's self-immolation in *Victory*; the theme of tragedy—a blend of Shakespearian and classic Greek—mark the essence of a quintessential Conradian movement. Conrad's writings are deeply personal, and his lived experiences are never too far away from his characters' turmoil.

In 1878, Conrad resigned from the French merchant fleet after four years of service. In a re-visitation of his escape from Poland, Conrad still fell under the jurisdiction of the Russian Empire and would have been subject to forced conscription had he stayed with the merchant fleet. Therefore, he moved to England in order to naturalize as a British subject, officially placing him out of Russian reach. With limited English abilities, Conrad joined the British civilian fleet and fully adopted a new homeland. In spite of an initial language barrier and his self-imposed perpetual outsider status, Conrad rose quickly through the ranks of the fleet, eventually gaining captain status.

While Conrad was stationed on the *Palestine*, the ship caught fire and forced Conrad into a lifeboat, an experience he used in the creation of his short story "Youth." Conrad then served as second mate on the *Narcissus*, which sailed to India, and later on the *Vidar*, which allowed Conrad a long stint in Singapore, Borneo, and the Malay Archipelago. There, Conrad encountered the noted trader William Charles Olmeijer; a corrupted misspelling of his last name becomes Almayer of *Almayer's Folly*. Many informants Conrad encountered during his travels became enshrined in Conrad's writings, as did the personal details of his own experiences, including even trivial inspiration, such as preserving the name of the ship Conrad sailed on in *The Nigger of the 'Narcissus.'* The character of Captain Lingard, found most prominently in *Almayer's Folly*, Conrad's first novel, recurs in a trilogy of works and inadvertently concludes Conrad's canonical career with the publication of *The Rescue* in 1920 more than two decades after Conrad wrote it.

Having sailed around Australia and Mauritius in his first role as captain of a ship, Conrad returned to England to write what became his first novel, *Almayer's Folly*. Peculiarly, Conrad chose to write in English, his third language. Because of this, his English syntax is punctuated with French and Polish elements, explaining the particularity and continued popularity of his writings. As Najder postulates, Conrad's trilingualism allowed him to occupy a unique space as an author "brought up in [the] Polish . . . cultural environment" yet a man who thought in French, a "language he spoke with [the] greatest fluency (and no foreign accent) until the end of his life ... [Yet] he wrote in English—the tongue he started to learn at the age of twenty." Conrad was thus thoroughly European, a transnational "English writer who grew up in other linguistic and cultural environments," whose work straddles "the borderland of auto-translation" (Najder ix).

In 1890, Conrad traveled to Africa, steaming up the Congo River and keeping a journal of his experience, out of which he wrote "An Outpost of Progress" and then his magnum opus, *Heart of Darkness*. Witnessing the brutality of colonial atrocities, the journey had a transformative effect on Conrad's outlook and shaped the tone of all his writings thereafter. He returned to England psychologically broken. While Conrad accepted one more first mate position on the *Torrens*, sailing from England to Australia in 1893, by the end of the year, Conrad's seafaring adventures and nautical pursuits were relegated strictly to the written page. In this way, captaining the *Roi des Belges* through the Congo was the high-water mark of his career, both as a sailor and author, yet it was a hauntingly troubled experience that destroyed Conrad's quest for adventure.

In the same year that *Almayer's Folly* was published, under the anglicized nom de plume "Joseph Conrad," Conrad began a relationship with Jessie George. They married two years later in 1896, and Conrad used their honeymoon to compose "The Idiots." A son, Borys, was born in 1898, and as Conrad settled into fatherhood, he birthed his most famous character, Charles Marlow, the narrator of "Youth." Marlow occupies a central element in all his texts, often telling the story to another unnamed narrator, who in turn is recounting the tale to the reader. In this way, Marlow shields Conrad and his highly personalized stories behind the aegis of triplicate distancing, while also replicating Conrad's own thought process, as he translates his French thoughts into English. Calling upon Marlow once more, Conrad debuted *Heart of Darkness* in serialized form beginning in 1899. *Lord Jim*, also narrated by Marlow, followed soon after.

By the time *Lord Jim* appeared in book form, Conrad had gained a noteworthy reputation, but never financial success. Even

Under Western Eyes, a story so intimately close to Conrad's personal history, filled with thematic issues of belonging and betrayal, where the shadow of his father lingered on every page of depictions of Russian domination and revolution, failed to resonate with his contemporary audiences. The text's poor reception caused Conrad to suffer a mental collapse. Yet relief came in 1912, when Conrad gained a global audience with journal articles on the sinking of the *Titanic*, providing Conrad the opportunity to showcase his literary talents mixed with his maritime experience. His collection of short stories *'Twixt Land and Sea* suddenly sold better than any book he had hitherto published. When *Chance* debuted in both serial and book form, Conrad suddenly found the critical and economic success that had escaped him for so many years.

Finally financially stable, in 1914, Conrad and his family visited Poland for the first time in twenty years. When World War I erupted, the Conrads suddenly became trapped in a hostile country. The British citizenship that allowed Conrad to escape Russian reach meant that Austro-Hungarian forces could arrest Conrad as an enemy combatant (Peters 14). Traveling through warring nations, Conrad made his way back to England via Vienna and Italy. While the war had direct and indirect influences in Conrad's life, only his short story "The Tale" reflects the personal issues of responsibility and guilt that the hostilities brought to Conrad's mind. With the war's conclusion, Conrad was able to finally finish *The Rescue*, a manuscript he had been writing off and on for twenty-three years. It was as if the end of European hostiles freed Conrad to return to issues of colonialism in the Dutch East Indies. Published in book form in 1920, *The Rescue*'s critical and commercial success surpassed *The Arrow of Gold*, released the previous year. Conrad then began work on what he envisioned to be a short story, which ultimately spiraled into the novel *The Rover*. Though a commercial hit, the novel was unpopular with literary critics, a psychological blow that dramatically slowed Conrad's progress on *Suspense*. In 1924, Conrad was offered knighthood, which he declined. On August 2, 1924, while still working on the *Suspense* manuscript, Conrad felt chest pains. Assured by his physician that he was in good health, Conrad went to sleep. He woke up the next morning feeling recovered, before collapsing and dying of heart attack. He was sixty-six years old.

Works Cited

Conrad, Joseph. *Heart of Darkness*. Ed. Robert Kimbrough. New York: W.W. Norton & Company, 1988. Print.

_____. *The Mirror of the Sea: Memories and Impressions*. London: Dent, 1946. Print.

_____. *A Personal Record: Some Reminiscences*. New York: Cosimo, 2005. Print.

_____. *Victory: An Island Tale*. London: Dent, 1948. Print.

Hampson, Robert. *Conrad's Secrets*. Basingstoke, UK: Palgrave Macmillan, 2012. Print.

Najder, Zdzisław. *Joseph Conrad: A Life*. Trans. Halina Najder. Rochester, NY: Camden House, 2007. Print.

Peters, John G. *The Cambridge Introduction to Joseph Conrad*. Cambridge, UK: Cambridge UP, 2006. Print.

Ray, Sid. "Marlow(e)'s Africa: Postcolonial Queenship in Conrad's *Heart of Darkness* and Marlowe's *Dido, Queen of* Carthage." *Conradiana* 38.2 (Summer 2006): 143-161. Print.

Sherry, Norman. *Conrad's Western World*. Cambridge, UK: Cambridge UP, 1971. Print.

Zins, Henryk. *Joseph Conrad and Africa*. Nairobi: Kenya Literature Bureau, 1982. Print.

CRITICAL CONTEXTS

Joseph Conrad—Imperial Writings in a Postcolonial World

Joshua Pritchard

Introduction

> The conquest of the earth, which mostly means taking it away from those who have a different complexion or slightly flatter noses than ourselves, is not a pretty thing when you look into it too much. What redeems it is the idea only. An idea at the back of it; not a sentimental pretence but an idea; and an unselfish belief in the idea—something you can set up, and bow down before, and offer a sacrifice to....
> (Joseph Conrad, *Heart of Darkness* 6)

These are some of the first words that Charles Marlow speaks aboard the *Nellie* as it rests at anchor on the river Thames. Part of a longer diatribe about the brutal realities of imperialism and colonialism, these words set the scene for a disturbing voyage into the heart of Africa. Conrad's condemnation of the colonial endeavor is relatively unique for a time when most of Europe scrambled to seize as much of the world as they could. Focused on imperialism's frontiers where the interactions between colonizer and colonized were most evident and damaging to both groups, Conrad's writings force discussion about difficult topics. Racism, forced labor, cultural superiority, religion, and trade all make prominent appearances within his fiction and remain the subject of debate even today.

In order to explain why Conrad grapples with these subjects, it is crucial to understand both the broader context within which he was writing, but also Conrad's own personal encounters and experiences with life on the colonial frontiers. In much the same way Marlow's narration provides context for his own perspective on the events that unfold in *Heart of Darkness*, so too does the relationship between Conrad's life and the world in which he lived. Significantly, this contextualization explains why the narratives that Conrad produced during his lifetime have become more significant for the contemporary world. This chapter explores both of these topics to provide insights into their visibility in Conrad's writings, focusing principally on the locations, characters, and themes of his work with regards to European colonial imperialism.

Russian Imperialism and Conrad's Childhood

Although not openly discussed in Conrad's own words until the autobiographical accounts penned later in his life, there are traces of a disdain for imperialist rule throughout his bibliography. One element in explaining this attitude can be found in the brutal realities of life for Conrad and his parents under Russian imperialism. In 1861, Apollo and Ewa Korzeniowski were forced into exile by Russian authorities with their infant son, Józef Teodor Konrad Korzeniowski. Conrad's father was charged with "clandestine revolutionary activity" for his involvement with a committee that later orchestrated the failed 1863 January Uprisings; a short-lived but violent guerrilla insurrection against mandatory conscription by the Imperial Russian Army within the Polish-Lithuanian Commonwealth. Due to these convictions, Conrad's family lost all of their lands to the Russian Empire.

With the exile of his family for their Polish nationalism and the deaths of both parents by the time he reached the age of twelve, Conrad faced the stark realities of what imperialism meant for those it subjected. As one scholar noted in a review of the autobiographical work *A Personal Record*, "Conrad was unable to grapple with 'the oppressive shadow of the great Russian Empire' whilst struggling to counteract the emotional impact of the loss of both parents due directly to Russian tyranny" (Szyzypien 17). Conrad refused to engage with his childhood or the national identity he inherited at birth until he was in his fifties—*A Personal Record* is one of the very few works that sees Conrad directly address his roots. Furthermore, Conrad refused to work with Russians under any circumstances, even when these Russians were themselves victims of the Russian state (8).

When considering Conrad's childhood heroes, however, an interesting disparity occurs. According to his own recollections as recorded in the posthumously published collection, *Last Essays*, the young Conrad was infatuated with the unmapped regions of the world. Moreover, he was an ardent admirer of those men who ventured deep into Africa, Asia, and the Pacific to lay bare unexplored and unclaimed regions of the world. These idols of British Victorian imperialism—David Livingstone, Mungo Park, Captain James Cook—shaped Conrad's views of a world he had not yet seen and had a tremendous impact on the path he followed (*Last Essays* 10). Ironically, Conrad sought refuge from the personal legacies of Russian imperialism in the exploits of those imperial agents, a contradiction that contributed to Conrad's conflicted depictions of European practices of colonialism in his writings. Conrad's desire to go to sea from an early age was a response to this internationalized thinking. For Conrad, Austria-Poland, to which he had returned shortly before his father's death, presented too small a world for a man who had lost himself in 'all the glories of exploration" (*Heart of Darkness* 7).

Marseille and the Caribbean

In a broader context, Conrad's arrival in Marseilles in November 1874 at the age of sixteen was indicative of a much larger trend occurring both in Europe and across the increasingly connected world. In the following century, 60 million people left Europe for a better life overseas, principally in the New World; 3.6 million people emigrated from Poland alone (Wesseling 17). Such migration was unprecedented in human history, greatly impacting the economic, social, and political spheres of both the lands these people arrived in and the nations they left behind. Conrad found inherent interest within these international movements, and his perspective of the world was shaped in part by this understanding of migration. As Andrea White explains, "as an early modern, he sensed the current of a world-wide disruption of peoples and ideas, of exiles and rootlessness. . . . [Conrad's] writing acknowledges and even participates in the decentring of monolithic unities and traditional hierarchies" (197).

Finding employment with the French shipping firm *Delestang et Fils*, Conrad spent the next four years learning his trade as a seaman on merchant vessels. His time working out of Marseille inspired *The Arrow of Gold*, a semi-fictional, semi-autobiographical account published in 1919 about a gunrunner for the Spanish Carlist cause. Although Conrad's own involvement with gunrunners for the Carlists has been questioned (Ziejka 61-64), the repeated mentions of such escapades in *Some Reminiscences* and *The Mirror of the Sea*, as well as *The Arrow of Gold*, highlights the apparent influence of the cause on Conrad. Carlism was a complex movement revolving around a number of different issues, but one central principle was support for regional autonomy within the nation; an ideal that would have appealed to Conrad in light of his own childhood experiences. Even if he himself did not engage in active support for the Carlists, the decision to give such an option to the characters in his work demonstrates a deeper-held conviction.

Three voyages to the Caribbean were made during Conrad's time in Marseille and left a lasting imprint in his literary mind. At least three characters, as well as numerous locations, can be traced back to these trips. The first mate on Conrad's third voyage to the Americas, Dominic Cervoni, makes a prominent appearance in *The Mirror of the Sea* as the hero of that same name, and Cervoni can also be seen as the foundation for Nostromo and Peyrol in *The Rover*. It is also entirely possible that during that third voyage, Conrad visited South America, the setting for his later novel, *Nostromo* (van Marle 94).

The nautical focus of much of Conrad's writing is another familiar theme developed from his experiences in Marseille and subsequent years employed in the British Merchant Service. A large part of the sense of reality in his narratives comes from his own familiarity with seamanship. The actions of the captain or crew in response to problems or decisions with their ships are given a notable place in the narratives themselves. Whether it is in *An Outpost of Progress*, where the delayed arrival of the company steamboat leads to the tragic events between Kayerts and Carlier, or the abandonment of the distressed *Patna* in the novel *Lord Jim*, "for the reader of Conrad's voyage tales some knowledge of the seamanship is essential for understanding crucial points of the action" (Foulke 247). Although Conrad's time at sea was only just beginning, the trans-Atlantic voyages he made and the initiation into the camaraderie of sailors greatly influenced the development of Conrad's characters, themes, and settings.

The Malay Novels, the British Merchant Service, and New Imperialism

In 1878, Conrad joined the British Merchant Service, at the time one of largest merchant navies in the world and responsible for supporting the world's most expansive colonial empire. By the time of Conrad's first voyage, the British Empire controlled "10 millions of square miles, or about one-fifth of the 50 millions of square miles composing the habitable globe," as well as 315 million inhabitants—almost 20 percent of the estimated global population at that time (Temple 469).

These rough figures are indicative of the unprecedented scale and rate at which European powers colonized the world towards the end of the nineteenth century. Termed "New Imperialism," to distinguish it from the archaic colonial empires that had conquered the Americas in the fifteenth and sixteenth centuries, this new process was driven by a multitude of factors outside of the scope of this chapter. They can be best summed up in the four "C's" —Commerce, Christianity, Civilization and Conquest (Pakenham xxiv). Between 1850 and the early 1900s, a Second Industrial Revolution occurred in Britain and across the European continent, creating new manufacturing processes and products. This "Technological Revolution" saw an influx of existing technologies, such as railroads, steam ships, and the telegraph, due to reduced costs and improved manufacturing. As the historian John Darwin succinctly noted, the Second Industrial Revolution gave Europeans "the means to colonize far faster and on a far larger scale than was previously possible. It gave them the means to penetrate new markets and crush old competition.... Above all, it enhanced their capacity to project their physical power over far greater distances and at much lower cost" (493). For a Europe that was facing an ever-increasing population and an economic system dependent on continued expansion, these technological advancements provided a temporary escape in the form of colonial empires and overseas markets.

As the Americas had already been colonized for centuries, European "New Imperialism" turned its attentions to Africa and Asia. The rise of steamships made what had been, in the 1850s, a three- to four-month journey from Europe to Asia now possible in three to four weeks and placed the distant locales firmly within the potential grasp of European powers. It is no coincidence that for a young Polish seaman recently enlisted in the BMS, this region of the world dominated his years of service and the themes and locations of his first novels.

In 1881, serving aboard the *Palestine*, Conrad found himself adrift in a lifeboat after his ship sank. His first steps on Asian soil were when this lifeboat safely reached an island off Sumatra in the East Indies. He recorded his experiences in 1898 in a short story entitled "Youth," with the *Palestine* renamed the *Judea*. His 1883 voyage aboard the *Narcissus* out of Bombay laid the framework for his incisive novel *The Nigger of the 'Narcissus.'* The main character of the novel, Jimmy Wait, was based on a shipmate during that voyage named Joseph Barron, who similarly died at sea. These characters were not drawn from Conrad's memory simply for convenience. As Miriam Marcus writes, James Wait's purpose is to function "as a disturbing presence, as the site on which contemporary ambivalence about race is registered and engaged - but only with the greatest difficulty" (40). Conrad creates these characters to force discussion about the nature of the accepted social thinking, to the extent that the title itself—*The Nigger of the 'Narcissus'*—became the focus of much debate between Conrad and his publishers in America who were reluctant to publish the book under that title, not because of the offensive nature of the word but because they believed a book about a black man would not sell in the United States (Johnson 110).

In 1887, Conrad spent six months travelling through the islands around Java and Borneo. One particular ship played a huge part in shaping the themes of his writing; the *Vidar*, an Arab-owned steamer. His encounters with the multitude of different local societies throughout the Dutch East Indies as well as with his fellow European traders had a profound impact on Conrad's worldview. Furthermore, these interactions provided Conrad with the material he required for his first series of Malay fiction that included *Almayer's Folly* and *An Outcast of the Islands*. The titular Kasper Almayer was a characterization of a European trading agent named Willem Carel Olmeijer, whom Conrad met in 1887 at Berau in Borneo. The area around Berau itself was the basis for fictional Sambir. As Conrad himself claims "if I had not got to know Almayer pretty well it is almost certain there would never have been a line of mine in print" (*Personal Record* 87).

This statement belies a deeper implication regarding Conrad's intent in writing about these narratives. Even before Conrad's infamous journey up the Congo River in 1890, he had begun to see behind the facade of European imperialism to the harsh truth that accompanied interactions between European and native on the colonial frontier. Amongst the four "C's" behind imperial ambitions, there were inherent contradictions between Civilization and Commerce. Colonization was presented to the world as a means of raising up to European levels all the people of distant lands who could not become "civilized" by themselves. A Darwinist view of racial groups dominated debates about "progress"—conveniently for those supporting colonization, this progress led to "Europeanized" ideas of civilization founded on the notion of a hierarchical superiority of the white race. European colonial powers subsequently leaned upon the argument that one of the benefits of colonialism was the contact between racially superior white Europeans and the "uncivilized," heathen non-Europeans. As the character Kurtz argues in *Heart of Darkness*, each company station along the river into the hinterland "should be like a beacon on the road towards better things, a center for trade of course, but also for humanizing, improving, instructing" (44).

The preferred depiction of the colonial encounter was that of the civilized white man converting, against much struggle, the uncivilized native. Frederick Selous—a British gentleman explorer intrinsically involved in the colonization of Southern Africa—succinctly summarizes this point of view in his autobiography; "the ways of the civilized man are not the ways of the savage, who, there can be no doubt, would rather put up with all the ills from which we consider we have freed him, than be subject to the restraints of a settled form of Government" (xiv). "Progress" had to be imposed on those who could not discover it for themselves and it fell to the white man to do so. Rudyard Kipling described this notion as "The White Man's Burden," and this was the supposed "redeeming idea" behind colonialism that Conrad writes of through Marlow in *Heart of Darkness*. Trade was the tool through which this "civilization" was to be spread, but it is apparent that from as early a point as his time in the BMS, Conrad quickly grew disillusioned with this theory. The flawed depiction in his novels of these individual traders who are supposed to represent the "superiority" of the European colonizers makes clear his critical stance.

Both *Almayer's Folly* and *An Outcast of the Islands* provide a fundamental reprove of European imperialism by rejecting the notion that the supposed superiority of Europeans gave an entitlement to colonize the world. Written in part before Conrad's fateful voyage to the Congo, *Almayer's Folly* emphasizes that despite the admiration provided to the paternalistic Lingard by the local population, it is only part of a nuanced relationship that sees white men described as bringers of ruin and greed, arriving "with prayers on their lips and loaded guns in their hand" (115). The novel goes further in condemning the self-perceived superiority of European civilization through the actions of Nina, the daughter of the Dutch trader, Kaspar Almayer. Rejecting the usual binary portrayal of the civilized whites and uncivilized natives, the mixed-race and well-educated Nina rejects her European father in favor of her native mother. She denounces European culture as being racialist, morally absent, and exclusive in those it benefits, all of which elucidates the flaws in the Darwinian notions of "progress" that accompanied and buttressed European colonialism and trade. In *An Outcast of Islands*, Aïssa similarly condemns Willem's homeland as "a land of lies and evil from which nothing but misfortune ever comes to us—who are not white" (144).

In both of his first two novels and the majority of his later work, Conrad's characters undermine the typical racial roles they were expected to play in the colonial encounter. This rejection of racial stereotypes is particularly fascinating for the subtlety with which he accomplishes it. Conrad's indigenous characters—whether the persistent and tenacious Babalatchi or the critically-minded Aïssa— are recognized for the merits of their own heritage and culture rather than their comparative status to the European. Conrad gives the "colonized" a voice and an agency that was largely absent from comparable works of the period by making space in the traditional narrative of "good" European versus "bad" native.

Conrad's depiction of the European traders in his first two novels arguably came from what Conrad witnessed onboard the *Vidar* in the rivers of Borneo. Away from the prosperous port cities and the well-travelled trade routes, the practices of colonialism and imperialism were much more brutal than European literature typically portrayed. On the frontier of colonial trading, "instead of the efficient, benevolent bearers of civilization's torch, [Conrad] saw men cut off from and nostalgic for Europe, and drunk on power, their presumed racial superiority, and alcohol" (White 184). Conrad was not the only one to recognize such things—Karl Marx, for example, noted that "the profound hypocrisy and inherent barbarism of bourgeois civilization lies unveiled before our eyes . . . in the colonies, where it goes naked" (88). Yet it is in his depictions of colonialism that Conrad stands apart. His emphasis that colonialism was not a top-down implementation that remained untouched by the realities of situations on the ground provided the basis for his condemnation of colonial exploitation. On the pages of his work, colonialism became a more personalized endeavor shaped as much by individuals as it was grand, overarching schemes. Conrad had seen individuals to be flawed in their execution of the "Civilizing Mission," and this theme becomes even more apparent in what is arguably his most famous novella, *Heart of Darkness*.

Africa and the "Heart of Darkness"

For Conrad, and for many in Europe, Africa would become the focal point for a growing criticism of unchecked colonialism. After all it was in Africa, not Asia, that "European imperialism was at its most spectacular" (Wesseling 147). In less than twenty years, the "Scramble for Africa" produced over thirty new colonies and protectorates, covering 10 million square miles and containing 110 million subjects. It is unsurprising that it was in Africa that the worst aspects of colonization and imperialism rose to the fore. European powers that had previously been colonial outposts controlling only thin enclaves along the coasts of the continent, suddenly turned their attentions towards the interior and quickly seized control (at least on paper) of huge swathes of the hinterland. Only two African countries remained independent—Liberia and Ethiopia. In many instances, individuals played a significant part in founding colonies with little assistance from the metropole. George Taubman Goldie in Nigeria and Cecil Rhodes in Southern Africa established gigantic chartered territories under the banner of business first and empire second. In Europe, empire building was depicted as nothing more than a simple formula that could be repeated in any situation—conquest (whether through a military or commercial negotiations), annexation and finally administration.

The Congo Free State was no exception. Ruled as a private fiefdom by Leopold II, King of the Belgians, the area of land claimed and granted to him at the Berlin Conference in 1884–85 was eighty times larger than the Belgian nation itself. As was the case in most of the other colonial empires, it was the accountants who ran the show. In the Congo, profits overcame any considerations for basic human rights or even the lives of the indigenous Africans. The Belgian government was forced to annex the colony in 1908, as international condemnation grew over the treatment of the Congolese people by Leopold II. Estimates indicate that the actions of Leopold II led to a population decrease of up to 13 million people within two decades. The population was decimated through murder, starvation, exhaustion, exposure, disease, and a low birth rate. Although not unique in terms of the nature of colonial rule, the scale of this genocide shocked the international community, including those in other colonial metropoles (Vanthemsche 41)

It was into this brutal environment that Conrad ventured in 1889, his first experience of the African hinterlands coming when he was already in this thirties. Conrad's time spent in the Congo provided him with even more evidence for his indictments of imperialism. Although he himself likely had little involvement with the ivory trade or the people who suffered most from it, Conrad had a multitude of sources he drew upon to understand the barbarity occurring in the region. Traders and missionaries made up the majority of these, but it was a British consul named Roger Casement whom Conrad met whilst in the Congo that provided the most fuel to the author's fire. A report produced by Casement in 1904 is regarded as a key factor in turning British public opinion against colonialism in general as well as leading to the annexation of the Congo Free State by the Belgian parliament in 1908 (Zins 63). In many regards, Conrad's *Heart of Darkness* also contributed to this shift in public opinion, providing a brutal insight into what colonialism meant for those on the frontier and those who carried "civilization" to the world.

There can be little doubt that much of the appeal from Conrad's work is due to the flawed characters brought to life in his publications. Figureheads of the colonial enterprise were not exempt from his critical eye. *The Inheritors*, a cautionary tale about moral corruption in a future world, uses villains who strongly resemble Joseph Chamberlain and Leopold II. Yet it was the officials working for these leaders and operating on the ground who take center-stage in the majority of Conrad's narratives and give a face to imperialism. In both *Heart of Darkness*, and its precursor, *An Outpost of Progress*, the motivations of the white men in Africa is an insightful reflection of the individuality with which colonization was realized and a rejection of hegemonic European colonialism. The unsuccessful painter who had built Kayerts' and Carlier's station, went to Africa because he was "weary of pursuing fame on an empty stomach" (*Outpost of Progress* 1). Kayerts found himself at the station because he was attempting to earn a dowry for his daughter. Similarly in *Heart of Darkness*, when Marlow asks the unnamed white man with whom he travels from the Company Station to the Central Station why he is there, he gets the scornful reply, "To make money, of course. What do you think?" (25). The Eldorado Exploring Expedition was there to "tear treasure out of the bowels of the land [. . .] with no more moral purpose at the back of it than there is in burglars breaking into a safe" (39). Marlow himself is there for adventure, a now realized childhood desire to go to "the biggest, the most blank space on the map" (7). The Russian harlequin on the riverbank desires to "see things, gather experience, ideas; enlarge the mind" (76). How Kurtz found himself in the most remote of outposts is never made clear, although the reader is led several times to believe Kurtz had a desire to educate the Africans in order to trade more fruitfully.

But as much as their motivations for being in the African hinterland are heterogeneous, their actions whilst there are not. A contemporary review of *Heart of Darkness* by Edward Garnett ended with the statement that the novella offers an "analysis of the deterioration of the white man's morale, when he is let loose from European restraint, and to make trade profits out of the subject races" (Murfin 99). In a letter to *Blackwood's Magazine*, in which *Heart of Darkness* first appeared as installments in 1899, Conrad stated that the motivations behind that novella were "the criminality of inefficiency and pure selfishness when tackling the civilising work in Africa" (Murfin 100). The descent of these men into savagery is Conrad's perception of what imperialism means for those involved on a fundamental level. If white men were supposed to be bearers of civilization, then the "burden" was one that the white man could not necessarily carry. Conrad goes to great lengths to depict these incursions by colonial powers into the lands and lives of those being colonized as anything other than benevolent and advantageous to those involved because of this individuality.

Conrad's Relevance Today

Although tainted by the language and perceptions of the time, for instance his talk of "cannibals" and "niggers," and traced with hints of justification for elements of the colonial enterprise, Conrad's handling of the native peoples is peculiarly positive for the time in which he was writing. He neither condemns them as bestial "subhumans," nor tries to redeem them as "noble savages." He presents them as holders of a human past, a past that remains a part of all people and that can come out away from the restrictions of European civilization. In the "Author's Note" prefacing *Almayer's Folly*, Conrad sees the distant settings and characters of his narratives as a space that should not diminish the ways in which European readers could relate to all those involved. "There is," he implores, "a bond between us and humanity so far away . . . I am content to sympathise with common mortals, no matter where they live" (viii). In his critique of imperialism, he ends up subverting the binary of racial hierarchy that dominated literature at the time—the "civilized" white man and the "savage" native. In both of his early Malay novels, and later works like *Nostromo* and *Victory*, Conrad does much to permit the non-European an identity outside of the European perception. As Gene Moore argues, "Conrad was one of the first Western writers to give voice to the claims and aspirations of non-Western peoples" (237).

This discussion highlights one of the significant reasons why Conrad's writings remain relevant over a century after they were first penned. As Edward Said explains, Conrad's writings and narratives are bound to a specific time and a specific place; the imperialistic world of the late nineteenth and early twentieth centuries. *Heart of Darkness*, for instance, forces the reader to see the world through the eyes of an individual of that period and for whom the depicted views, which today seem antiquated and offensive, are normal. The language and rhetoric used, combined with the first-person narration of Marlow, makes it impossible to step out of this time-frame or to approach the narrative from an abstract perspective. Yet despite this, Conrad ensures that the practices of imperialism are questioned throughout, in ways which do not detract from the dominant viewpoints of the time. Said reiterates this, stating that "Conrad's way of demonstrating this discrepancy between the orthodox and his own views of empire is to keep drawing attention to how ideas and values are constructed (and deconstructed) through dislocations in the narrator's language" (29). In *Heart of Darkness,* Marlow is markedly inconsistent in his telling of his voyage up the Congo. At times he is critical of imperialism, praising only the idea behind it. At other times, he is a fully-fledged advocate of the civilizing mission. This is a reflection of Conrad's own uneasiness with the realities of colonialism.

However, this is not enough for some critics. The Nigerian author Chinua Achebe, for one, contends that "Conrad was a thoroughgoing racist" (176) and decries Conrad's work for perpetuating a neo-imperialist and Eurocentric view of the colonial encounters. Others have denounced *Nostromo* and *Heart of Darkness* for taking what should be a story belonging to those who suffer most in it—the land and the people of that land—and appropriating it from a Western perspective. Mukhtar Chaudhary for example has condemned the apparent categorization of characters based upon racial features, writing that "the human hierarchy in Conrad is, in descending order in value and worth, the British, the Continental European, and the rest" (41). *Lord Jim* is similarly denounced for containing "what may fairly be called a defence of traditional Western cultural values and practices" (Ducharme 4). This debate seems unable to resolve itself, with broad camps staking claims to Conrad's memory.

Nevertheless, it must be recognized that Conrad's writings did much to undermine the traditional Eurocentric histories that were ascribed to colonized nations and peoples. By today's standards, his criticisms of the imperial endeavors may seem relatively tame. Yet they were largely unmatched in the ways that they made the reader aware of the moral ambiguities of imperialism during the period his first novels were published. In a world that is frantically trying to right the wrongs of older generations, history becomes a casualty when it does not fit the current zeitgeist. Elements of history that people disagree with are removed at the risk of offending. They are discarded or hidden from the public eye and public discussion. Conrad's writings offer an alternative. His texts are not only reflections of a period of history that has left a lasting legacy on the modern world, but his unique personal perspective as a victim of imperialism during his childhood and an indirect perpetrator of it during his time in the British Merchant Service, ensures that the nuances of the encounters on the imperial frontiers are available for generations who can only struggle to understand the social norms of a world a century ago. In this regard, Conrad's work is invaluable for those attempting to understand the realities of imperialism and colonialism of the late nineteenth century and becomes even more so with every passing year.

Works Cited

Achebe, Chinua. "An Image of Africa: Racism in Conrad's 'Heart of Darkness.'" *Massachusetts Review* 17.4 (1977): 782-794. Print.

Chaudhary, Mukhtar. "Race as a rhetorical construct in Joseph Conrad's fiction." *Abhath Al-Yarmouk, Literature and Linguistics Series* 21.2 (2003): 41-77. Print.

Darwin, John. *After Tamerlane: The Rise and Fall of Global Empires, 1400–2000.* London: Bloomsbury Press, 2007. Print.

Ducharme, Robert. "The Power of Culture in *Lord Jim.*" *Conradiana* 22.1 (1993): 3-10. Print.

Emerson, Rupert. "Colonialism." *International Encyclopedia of the Social Sciences.* Vol. 3 New York: Macmillan Reference, 1968. Print.

Foulke, Robert. "Sea." *Joseph Conrad in Context.* Ed. Allan H. Simmons. Cambridge, UK: Cambridge UP, 2014. Print.

Johnson, William A. "'To my readers in America': Conrad's 1914 preface to *The Nigger of the 'Narcissus.'*" *Conradiana* 35.1&2 (2003): 105-122. Print.

Jones, Adam, *Genocide: A Comprehensive Introduction* (London, 2006).

Knowles, Owen. "Conrad's Life" *The Cambridge Companion to Joseph Conrad.* Ed. J. H. Stape. Cambridge, UK: Cambridge UP, 2006. Print.

Marcus, Miriam. "Writing, Race, and Illness in '*The Nigger of the 'Narcissus.'* The Conradian. 23.1 (1998): 37-50. Print.

Marx, Karl. "The future results of British Rule in India." *On Colonialism.* Moscow: Progress, 1968. Print.

Moore, Gene M. "Conrad's Influence." *The Cambridge Companion to Joseph Conrad.* Ed. J. H. Stape. Cambridge, UK: Cambridge UP, 2006. Print.

Ross C. Murfin, ed. *Heart of Darkness*. By Joseph Conrad. New York: St. Martin's Press, 1996. Print.

Selous, Frederick, *Sunshine and Storm in Rhodesia: Being a Narrative of Events in Matabeleland*. London: Nabu, 1896. Print.

Szyzypien, Jean M. "Joseph Conrad's 'A Personal Record': Composition, Intention, Design: Polonism." *Journal of Modern Literature* 16.1 (1989): 3-30. Print.

Temple, Richard. "The General Statistics of the British Empire." *Journal of the Statistical Society of London* 47.3 (1884): 468-484, Print.

van Marle, Hans, 'Lawful and Lawless: Young Korzeniowski's Adventures in the Caribbean', *L'Époque Conradienne* 17 (1991): 91-113. Print.

Vanthemsche, Guy. *Belgium and the Congo, 1885–1980*. Cambridge, UK: Cambridge UP, 2012. Print.

Wesseling, H. L. *The European Colonial Empires, 1815–1919*. London: Harlow, 2004. Print.

White, Andrea. "Conrad and Imperialism." *The Cambridge Companion to Joseph Conrad* Ed. J. H. Stape. Cambridge, UK: Cambridge UP, 2006. Print.

Ziejka, Franciszek. "Conrad's Marseilles." *Yearbook of Conrad Studies (Poland)* 7 (2012): 51-67. Print.

Zins, H.S. "Joseph Conrad and British critics of colonialism." *Pula: Botswana Journal of African Studies* 12.1&2 (1998): 58-68. Print.

The Discursive Evolution of Conrad's Critiques: A Historiography of Critical Receptions to *Heart of Darkness*

Taryn B. Cornell

The Analytical Value of Historiographies

This chapter presents a historiographical analysis of a wide range of critical responses to Joseph Conrad, surveying prominent reviews of his work throughout the twentieth century. Due to the novella's distinctive and fascinating reception, this chapter will focus specifically on *Heart of Darkness*, which depicts the journey of Marlow, a ferryboat captain, to retrieve the infamous ivory trader Mr. Kurtz from colonial Congo. As an overview of key pieces responding to *Heart of Darkness*, a broad survey of the literature examines not only the ways in which academics have understood Conrad's work, but also the disciplines from which they hail. While Conrad was an author of considerable repute, his critics and champions proceed from a plethora of disciplines, including politics, history, psychology, and art, as well as literature. This interdisciplinary backdrop has stimulated diverse interpretations of Conrad's writings.

Historiographies are an underappreciated tool in an analytical arsenal. Far more than a basic literature review, a historiography offers the opportunity to intertwine critical lenses that would be of significant value to the study of Conrad's oeuvre, specifically regarding Africa. Building on a survey of significant critiques, this chapter identifies interpretive trends within the body of critical literature, seeking to analyze the continuities and changes evident in scholars' stances on Conrad's work over time. By identifying the internal logics of these positions, it explores the discursive evolution of popular interpretations to *Heart of Darkness* over a century.

This chapter then contextualizes the resulting periodization. Academia does not exist in isolation: academics are necessarily a product of their temporal context—including when they engage with a period outside of their own, as modern scholars of Conrad necessarily do—and thus invite interest as subjects of study themselves. By historicizing the intellectual, cultural, and geopolitical environment of their work, this chapter demonstrates how Conrad's critics are reflections of the social changes and academic pressures of the late nineteenth century to present day. Accordingly, this chapter provides a critical insight into the relationship between academics' methods of analysis for Conrad's works and the normative framework promoted by their own historically particular milieu.

Ultimately, it is argued, the historiography of critical receptions to Joseph Conrad has followed a markedly different path than what one might expect for a novelist. Few authors can claim to have incited responses across several disciplines, feeding into contemporary and future sociopolitical movements and causing shifts in theoretical paradigms far beyond their time. Conrad's *Heart of Darkness* has done just that. From its inception as an anti-colonialist novella, it underwent a staggering range of reviews. Journals, books, and edited volumes, like this one, have been dedicated to a variety of responses, from alternative interpretations of his works to the psychoanalysis of his motivations through the text. As Owen Knowles noted in his introduction to the 2007 Penguin edition, "there is now virtually an interpretation of the story [of *Heart of Darkness*] to suit every predilection—the psychoanalytic, philosophic, political, post-colonial and gender-based" (xx). This chapter seeks to unpack, evidence, and historicize such a claim.

Early Critical Responses and Their Limitations

First serialized in *Blackwood's Magazine* in 1899, *Heart of Darkness* did not receive any significant critical responses until its 1902 publication in book form (Murfin 99). Early receptions to its publication primarily centered on its aesthetic value as a novella. Its portrayal of adventure, of breakdown, and of the human condition was explored in depth, with particular focus on the final scenes, in which Mr. Kurtz's fiancée, known only as his "Intended," is informed of his death. Unsigned reviews from 1902 praised Conrad's unique style and his "power of conveying atmosphere"—a literary talent in which "Mr. Conrad has few equals" (qtd. in Armstrong 310). The general consensus leaned towards a celebration of his skills in storytelling, and *Heart of Darkness* was often mentioned as the most impactful of the trio in which it was published (short stories *Youth* and *The End of the Tether* forming the other two).

At the time of its publication, Conrad had established himself as a critic of colonialism, and *Heart of Darkness* provided an accordingly unflattering account of imperial missions in the Congo. During the late Victorian era, in the midst of the so-called "Scramble for Africa" that saw European states race to carve out territories in the continent, such depictions were certainly progressive. Many of Conrad's contemporaries thus responded to the anti-imperialist message in *Heart of Darkness* as much as they lauded its literary value. Upon its publication in 1902, Edward Garnett, for example, summarized the novella as "an impression, taken from life, of the conquest by the European whites of a certain portion of Africa," masterfully written to force the reader to reflect on the story of "two Continents in conflict, of the abysmal gulf between the white man's system and the black man's comprehension of its results" (qtd. in Armstrong 307-308).

Such undertones were by no means unanimously perceived, however. In another unsigned review from 1902—which Conrad himself called "fairly intelligent"—the critic argued, "It must not be supposed that Mr. Conrad makes attack upon colonisation, expansion, even upon Imperialism," rather that he presented the reader with stories that "show the impact upon an undaunted spirit of what is terrible and obscure; they are adventure in terms of experience" (qtd. in Armstrong, 309-310). Another critic from the same year declared, "The reviewer deliberately abstains . . . from any attempt at analysis of a story like 'The Heart of Darkness'," implying others who attempted to do so had done it injustice, and issuing a warning that Conrad "demands thoughtful attention [from his readers]" (qtd. in Armstrong 312).

Admired by some, the ambiguity of his meaning was frustrating to others: a 1903 review by poet laureate John Masefield lamented how the narrative—even if expertly written—risked "becoming somewhat rhetorical" in parts where it was "most unconvincing" and "reminds one rather of a cobweb" (qtd. in Armstrong 313). This sentiment was later echoed by novelist E. M. Forster, who asserted that "What is so elusive about [Conrad] is that he is always promising to make some general philosophic statement about the universe, and then refraining with a gruff disclaimer" (qtd. in Armstrong 315). Nevertheless, it is clear that even Conrad's earliest critics noted the wider applicability of the novella and its potential implications, while simultaneously praising him as a novelist who "enriches English literature" (Edward Garnett, qtd. in Armstrong 307).

Notably absent from the typical early refrains, however, was any consideration of race. While this would be heavily criticized later—on which, more will follow—it should come as little surprise. The very word "racism" did not exist until the 1930s, and even the earlier concept of "racialism"—referring to the "belief in the superiority of a particular race leading to prejudice and antagonism towards people of other races, *[especially] those in close proximity*"—was not wholly relevant to colonialism (Firchow 4, emphasis added). As Peter Firchow later noted, a sense of "threat to one's cultural and racial integrity or economic well-being" was certainly lacking at the time of Conrad's writing, given the distance between the colonies and Europe, and even the earliest ideas of these concepts referred to twentieth-century encounters in multiracial areas of Europe (Firchow 4-5). Unlike the imperial mission, therefore, racism was not considered a topic of anxiety, or even contention; rather, the concept of white racial superiority was a normative assumption of the period in which Conrad's works were written.

The exception to this can be witnessed in Edward Garnett's aforementioned review. Garnett praised Conrad for "the acutest analysis of the deterioration of the white man's *morale*, when he is let loose from European restraint, and planted down in the tropics . . . to make trade profits out of the 'subject races'"—to which Conrad directly responded with heartfelt gratitude, having earlier confirmed his intention to expose "the criminality of inefficiency and pure selfishness when tackling the civilizing work in Africa" (qtd. in Armstrong 308; Murfin 100). Despite the mention of race, even Garnett's response was focused more on imperialism and the European condition, accepting at face value the portrayal of Africans in *Heart of Darkness*. Indeed, he went on to claim that "There is no 'intention' in the story, no *parti pris*, no prejudice one way or the other; it is simply a piece of art . . . [depicting] the white man in uncivilised Africa" (qtd. in Armstrong 308).

While comprehensible, early critics' silence on Conrad's treatment of race was not necessarily defensible: as Chinua Achebe later charged, "That this simple truth is glossed over in criticism of his work is due to the fact that white racism against Africa is such a normal way of thinking that its manifestations go completely undetected" (788). The critics' normalization of white racism should, however, be understood in context. In the midst of the colonial project, a foresight of postcolonialism was necessarily inconceivable. It was thus possible for early critics to understand Conrad's depictions of Africa as progressive while failing to remark upon, or even to notice, his problematic representations of Africans themselves (on which, more will follow).

Evolving Critical Receptions: From Form to Freud

From Conrad's death in 1924, the disciplinary range of critical responses to his works expanded dramatically. That is not to say that analyses from a literary standpoint were nonexistent: indeed, one of the more famous critiques of *Heart of Darkness* came from F. R. Leavis in 1948. While acknowledging that "*Heart of Darkness* is, by common consent, one of Conrad's best things," Leavis agreed with Forster's exasperation at the elusive meaning of *Heart of Darkness* and roundly criticized Conrad's "adjectival insistence upon inexpressible and incomprehensible mystery" (204). Rather than such repetition forming a motif complementary to his narrative, Leavis contended that "the actual effect is not to magnify but rather to muffle" (205). By contrast, Ian Watt argued for Conrad's deliberate creation of "literary impressionism," building on the earlier ideas of Ford Madox Ford, and likened *Heart of Darkness* to works by artists such as impressionist painter Claude Monet (169-173). Watt contended that Conrad sought to symbolically address "the problematic relation of individual sense impressions to meaning," injecting a level of uncertainty into his narrative that demands the reader to fill in the blanks (174). As Watt's use of impressionist art demonstrates, the twentieth century bore witness to the evolution of multidisciplinary critical receptions that responded to more than *Heart of Darkness*' value as a literary piece alone. Freudian psychoanalyses were primary illustrations of this, exemplifying how temporal pressures form strong influences on critics' responses.

Following the work of infamous psychotherapist Sigmund Freud, psychoanalyses of texts became a fashionable approach in the mid-twentieth century for academics in a range of fields. Albert J. Guerard presented a comprehensive example of this in 1958, using a close analysis of the language and literary devices employed in *Heart of Darkness* as evidence for various aspects of Conrad's personality. Through his extensive examination of the use of time and consciousness, for example, Guerard concluded that the novella is a metaphor for Conrad's exploration of his own psychology, further suggesting that the African setting is little more than incidental to the true purpose of the story: "the journey within" (1). As he commented, "In Freudian theory, we are told, such preoccupation [with darkness] may indicate a fear of the feminine and passive. But may it not also be connected, through one of the spirit's multiple disguise's, with a radical fear of death, that other darkness?" (Guerard 47). Ultimately, Guerard argued that Conrad's eponymous darkness refers to "the temptation of atavism," or the lure to revert to our ancient or primitive condition, that is omnipresent throughout the human experience (38). Such an approach was heavily attacked by subsequent academics.

Changing the Terms of the Debate: Chinua Achebe and Postcolonial Critiques

In the background of African states achieving independence from imperialism, as well as global civil rights movements gaining widespread publicity through new forms of media, academia likewise focused on postcolonial theories, critiques, and reassessments beginning in the 1960s. Considering original interpretations of

Heart of Darkness as an indictment against colonial practices in the Congo, postcolonial critiques found predictably compelling purchase with the novella. Indeed, they dramatically changed the terms of the debate in which modern reviewers now operate.

First delivered as a lecture in 1975 and published in 1977, Nigerian novelist Chinua Achebe wrote what arguably remains the most influential—and controversial—response to *Heart of Darkness*. Titled "An Image of Africa," Achebe rejected wholesale the popular favor the book enjoyed and memorably condemned Conrad as "a bloody racist" (788). He charged Conrad with a series of hypocritical, destructive acts of racism, portraying Africans in his novella as little more than props even as he claimed to denounce European exploitation. If Conrad indeed used the Congo River as "merely a setting for the disintegration of the mind of Mr. Kurtz," as Guerard and others psychoanalytically argued, by doing so, he necessarily constructed "Africa as a metaphysical battlefield devoid of all recognizable humanity, into which the wandering European enters at his peril" (Achebe 788). What was unique about Achebe's polemic was its explicitly political and social purpose in its own era, yet addressed through the exploration of a work of fiction written almost a century earlier. While he acknowledged the normality of racism in the nineteenth century, he contended that "even after due allowances have been made for all the influences of contemporary prejudice on his sensibility, there remains still in Conrad's attitude a residue of antipathy to black people which his peculiar psychology alone can explain" (Achebe 789).

Conrad himself was not the only object of Achebe's ire; he also condemned a catalogue of previous critics—notably the psychoanalysts—for "[following] every conceivable lead (and sometimes inconceivable ones) to explain Conrad. . . . And yet not even one word is spared for his attitude to black people," leading to his damning conclusion that "[they] must regard the kind of racism displayed by Conrad as absolutely normal" (790). He further extrapolates the source of this prejudice out, denouncing "the willful [*sic*] tenacity with which the West holds [its stereotypical image of

Africa] to its heart" (Achebe 793). Indeed, Achebe criticizes the very study of the novella as proof of the West's enduring racism:

> Whatever Conrad's problems were, you might say he is now safely dead. Quite true. Unfortunately his heart of darkness plagues us still.[1] Which is why an offensive and totally deplorable book can be described by a serious scholar as "among the half dozen greatest short novels in the English language," and why it is today perhaps the most commonly prescribed novel in twentieth-century literature courses. (790)

It is difficult to overstate how dramatically Achebe's response overhauled academic analyses of *Heart of Darkness*. It is perhaps unsurprising—given such a comprehensive condemnation of Conrad, his works and all those who read them—that critical receptions after 1975 were made to speak to Achebe's accusations, if not to respond directly to his charges of racism then at least to defend their own ongoing interest. Yet even those who seek to disregard Achebe's analysis are compelled to engage with it, so crucial a cornerstone to analyses of Conrad's writings it has become, and it remains a significant influence upon modern interpretations of *Heart of Darkness*.

The "Image of Africa" Debate

In the years immediately following Achebe's diatribe, scholars of *Heart of Darkness* became seemingly more preoccupied with responding to the "Image of Africa" debate than to the novel itself. Initial outrage led to equally emotive endorsements of his allegations, the most notable of which was written by Frances B. Singh. Aligning herself with Achebe's review, Singh evaluated the treatment of black people by the two main characters—Marlow and Kurtz. Exploring the metaphorical significance of the book's title, she concluded that "Marlow uses the unknown, remote, and primitive Africa as a symbol for an evil and primeval force"—and, all the more problematically, that "the story also carries suggestions that the evil which the title refers to is to be associated with Africans, their customs, and their rites", as "they have the power to turn the white man's heart black"

(Singh 271). Singh also rejected the common counterargument that Marlow's motives may not be Conrad's. While she conceded the anti-imperialist undertones of the novella, Singh also pointed to a range of his other works that challenged the assessment of Conrad's outlook as liberal, concluding that his ultimate ambivalence "ironically [turned] a story that was meant to be a clear-cut attack on a vicious system into a partial apology for it" (280).

Responding critiques of this approach have been numerous, but are united in a common call for contextualization. For some, the consideration of Conrad's historical context was sufficient to dismiss Achebe's indictment altogether as irrelevant and itself grounded in a temporal bias. Such scholars asserted that Conrad should not be considered racist but instead should be recognized as progressive for his context. The work of Edward Said was particularly eminent within these types of responses. Working to invalidate Achebe's concerns, he cautioned against "blaming the Europeans sweepingly for the misfortunes of the present" (Said 20). Indeed, Said seemed to disregard Achebe's point entirely when claiming that *Heart of Darkness* "does not give us the sense that [Conrad] could imagine a fully realized alternative to imperialism [because] the natives he wrote about in Africa, Asia, or America were incapable of independence" (28). Furthermore, he also demanded recognition of the context in which postcolonial theorists criticized Conrad, mentioning Achebe directly as an example of when "the formerly silent native speaks and acts on territory taken back from the empire"—referring to scholars from newly independent states reading and responding to colonial literature about themselves (Said 34).

Nevertheless, Said argued quite convincingly for the need to appreciate Conrad in his own era: "As a creature of his time, Conrad could not grant the natives their freedom, despite his severe critique of the imperialism that enslaved them" (34). A perhaps more nuanced version of this retort came from Peter Firchow. Firchow carefully addressed the topic of race by arguing again for the need to take Conrad in his context—one in which, as noted earlier, the very word "racism" was yet to exist (4). Exploring the linguistic origins of concepts that critics like Achebe have levied against Conrad—

including "race," "racism," "colonialism," and "imperialism"—Firchow in fact defended Conrad's stereotypic depictions of Africans as tending "to be subtler and more balanced that that of most other writers of the period," even attempting to reflect "multinational, multiethnic experience" (7).

Other scholars sought to balance the debate by simultaneously acknowledging Conrad's problematic characterizations while also contextualizing their construction. Though coming to terms with Achebe's accusations, such reviews have also defended Conrad's enduring relevance for scholarly attention. Hunt Hawkins' noteworthy article, first written in 1982 and updated for the fourth Norton Critical Edition in 2006, is one such example of a more balanced response to the "Image of Africa." While he agreed with many of Achebe's points of contention—stating, for example, that "Achebe is quite right that much of *Heart of Darkness* dehumanizes Africans"—Hawkins also looked beyond the novella to Conrad's other works in order to question "how thoroughgoing" Conrad's racism was for its time (366; 374). Hawkins noted that "Racism in Conrad's time was endemic" and that aspects of such prejudice are certainly visible in his writings as a result (373). Yet, despite the fact that he employs "the temporal evolutionary trope in *Heart of Darkness*," Hawkins found strong evidence that "rather than using this trope to support imperialism, Conrad uses it to do the opposite" (369).[2] He pointed, in the novella, to the particularly damning portrayals of Europeans, who were frequently described as violent and exploitative, and he also endeavored to recognize where the humanity of his African characters were afforded respect (Hawkins 369-372). In this way, Hawkins directly responded to Singh's charges of the evil influence of Conrad's Africans on Mr. Kurtz, instead arguing "that Kurtz's corruption comes not from Africans but from Europe and from Kurtz himself," while appreciating the problematic nature of many of Conrad's characterizations (371).

Such attempts at a compromise can be further witnessed in Patrick Brantlinger's work. Brantlinger analyzed the "impressionism" and "schizophrenic" nature of Conrad's writing, criticizing interpretations that saw *Heart of Darkness* "as only racist (and therefore imperialist), or as only anti-imperialist (and therefore antiracist)" (256). Instead, he rejected this binary and argued compellingly for the possibility of racism and anti-imperialism coexisting in the novella. *Heart of Darkness* may indeed criticize the empire and its architects—and that was undoubtedly impressive given the almost complete lack of other anti-colonial fiction before the First World War—but "its anti-imperialist message is undercut by its racism, by its reactionary political attitudes, by its impressionism" nevertheless (Brantlinger 274). While Brantlinger seemed to agree with many of Achebe's issues with Conrad's racism, he also viewed the complexity and contradiction of his anti-imperialism as a hallmark of the novella's enduring value, rather than its failing:

> [The] real strength of *Heart of Darkness* does not lie in what it says about atrocities in King Leopold's Congo. . . . There are few novels, however, which so insistently invoke a moral idealism they do not seem to contain and in which the modernist will-to-style is subjected to such powerful self-scrutiny. (274)

The Intersection of Race and Gender

These academic debates intersected with sociopolitical movements at a crucial point in history. With the successes of women's movements and rise of feminism in the second half of the twentieth century, gendered lenses also came to the fore of academic analyses. The twentieth century saw a dramatic shift towards a focus on identities—first on Conrad himself and the psychoanalytic and later on postcolonial theory and race—which led to new attention on gender and the use of female characters in *Heart of Darkness*. Indeed, the internal logics of postcolonial and gender critiques are cut from the same cloth: as Torgovnick noted, "Few periods in history have been more concerned than modernity with the articulation of the psychological subject and the cultivation of the individualistic self" (157).

Building on the focus on identity present in postcolonial critiques, then, feminist critics of Conrad focused on the intersection of his treatment of women and race in *Heart of Darkness*. Two key reviews, both written in 1990 at a time when feminism was taking on an increasingly political form, re-examined the portrayal of female characters in the novella and accused existing critiques of "[operating] from within the same system of gender values and notions of the political as Conrad himself" and, by doing so, silenced "important issues raised by the text that are political in a different sense" (Torgovnick 143). Examining the construction of masculinity and power and the West's obsession with the "primitive," Marianna Torgovnick particularly concerned herself with Mr. Kurtz's black mistress and the challenge she presented to the Western taboo of miscegenation (interracial procreation). Torgovnick argued that she was Conrad's ultimate representation of the "native" and likened the taboo of their relationship to "fantasy sites," such as head-hunting and ritual slaughter (153). Indeed, she contended that Conrad's portrayal of women in *Heart of Darkness*—as "fantastic, collective ('women are all alike'), seductive, dangerous, deadly"—was the very same as his depiction of the primitive: "the associations are not rational but 'intuitive,' the underside of the rock of Western objectivity and aesthetics" (Torgovnick 156).

Jeremy Hawthorn similarly viewed Kurtz's black mistress as the primitive foil to his white Intended's civilization. Both women, the two main female characters in a story largely occupied by men, were argued to be symbolic constructions in *Heart of Darkness* rather than created as characters in their own right. With images of gender inextricably bound up with ideas of race and culture, Hawthorn argued that Conrad used the women to promote a more nuanced portrayal of the European vision of Africa. Conrad did not use the black/white binary in the way one might expect from a novelist of his era: "[undercutting] simple symbolic associations . . . to disabuse the reader of the belief that good and bad can be straightforwardly defined," the idealized Intended was depicted "as weak, unhealthy and corrupted" by Marlow's lies, embodying "a sort of living death" through her exposure to evil (Hawthorn 407-408). In juxtaposition, "the powerful life of the African woman is, like the wilderness reflected in her, passionate and fecund"; Kurtz's mistress represented "a concentrated life that contrasts with the sterility seen in a European idealism cut off from reality" (Hawthorn 409).

While Conrad may have employed these characters to serve an anti-imperialist message, he nevertheless relied on a well-worn, stereotypical binary for women—"devoted and chaste" versus "sensual and sexual"—and, by doing so, engaged in "the process whereby women are dehumanized by being divided into spirit and body and are denied the full humanity that requires possession of both" (Hawthorn 409). Both Mr. Kurtz's Intended and his mistress are only ever named as such. Devoid of individual agency, their existences are defined by their relationship to Kurtz and the Western institution of marriage, using signifiers of temporal promissory ("Intended") or promiscuity ("mistress") linked solely to him. With a total of three female characters in the novella and a portrayal of women appositely one-dimensional for a work written in the nineteenth century, gendered readings of *Heart of Darkness* tended to incite a level of "repulsion" from their reviewers in much the same way as Achebe's disgust at its portrayal of race (Torgovnick 145).

The Continued Relevance of Conrad's Works

The fact that this volume has been published in 2016, almost one hundred years after Conrad's death, speaks to the ongoing academic fascination and analytical value of his oeuvre. Far from being confined to English students' reading lists, Conrad has incited impassioned receptions in a broad range of disciplines. This chapter has demonstrated the discursive evolution of popular responses to his work, ranging from the immediate, social liberalist responses to more typical literature critiques, from psychoanalysis to feminism, culminating in modern attempts to save his reputation from obscurity by responding to Achebe's review. Regarding the persistent lure of *Heart of Darkness*, Owen Knowles perhaps summarized it best:

> "Come and find out" (15). The African jungle's teasing invitation to Marlow is also projected to the story's readers ... the history of *Heart of Darkness* criticism vividly indicates how the invitation has been taken up by successive generations and how, in the process, the work has undergone constant renewal. (xxxi)

By no means claiming to be fully comprehensive, this chapter has demonstrated that the historiography of key critical receptions to Conrad's *Heart of Darkness* has taken a unique form. As one should expect, the temporal context of his critics was crucial to the normative framework they promoted, and *Heart of Darkness* has enjoyed a particularly broad range of disciplinary relevance. From the outset, Conrad's reviewers acknowledged the wider implications or applicability of his work outside of the realm of literature. Early critics responded to his unfavorable portrayal of colonial Congo in the aftermath of the 1880s "Scramble for Africa" at a time when anti-colonialism was fashionable among the liberal-minded. Later critics built on the academic popularity of Freudian techniques of analysis to present psychoanalytical studies of Conrad's own character through his depiction of others. Yet it was not until Achebe that the stagnating debate on his presentation of imperialism—in whose favor consensus had largely been reached—was opened up and sharply contrasted with his treatment of race. That another author's response has had such a significant impact is remarkable; it would be inconceivable now to study *Heart of Darkness* without also engaging with Achebe as a prominent contributor. The "Image of Africa" debate continues to influence modern responses and further promoted gendered critiques of Conrad's treatment of women as feminist movements in the late twentieth century to the twenty-first collided with postcolonial theory. Paradoxically, in light of Achebe's objections, the "Image of Africa" debate has broadened the disciplinary horizons under which the novella remains relevant temporally.

That Conrad's work has divided popular opinions over the years—from his treatment of identities to metaphysical debates over the true meaning of *Heart of Darkness*—is perhaps his most enduring strength. His critical receptions continue to demonstrate the wide-ranging impact of literature, encouraging students from a variety of disciplines to appreciate the interlocution of fiction and reality, maintaining his novella's relevance over a century later. Such continued scholarly interest in his work serves both to validate and to perpetuate its position as an ongoing fixture in the popular canon of English literature, encouraging those asking, "should we read *Heart of Darkness*?" to continue answering, emphatically, "yes" (Miller 39; Armstrong xvii).

Notes

1. Note the lack of capitalization and italics here; implying Achebe is not referring to the title of the book but rather to Conrad himself.
2. Referring to the colonial concept of a linear progression of civilization, which placed white Europeans at the pinnacle of human achievement and black Africans at the "primitive" bottom. The logic behind the so-called "white man's burden"—or the need for the white man to help the black man "evolve" from his primordial state—was often used in justificatory narratives for the morality of imperialism.

Works Cited

Achebe, Chinua. "An Image of Africa." *Massachusetts Review* 17.4 (Winter 1977): 782-794. Print.

Armstrong, Paul B., ed. *Heart of Darkness*. 4th ed. New York: W. W. Norton & Company, 2006. Norton Critical Editions Ser. Print.

Brantlinger, Patrick. *Rule of Darkness: British Literature and Imperialism, 1830-1914*. Ithaca, NY: Cornell UP, 1988. Print.

Conrad, Joseph. *Heart of Darkness and The Congo Diary*. London: Penguin, 2007. Print.

Firchow, Peter Edgerly. *Envisioning Africa: Racism and Imperialism in Conrad's* Heart of Darkness. Lexington: U of Kentucky P, 2000. Print.

Guerard, Albert Joseph. *Conrad the Novelist*. Cambridge, MA: Harvard UP, 1958. Print.

Hawkins, Hunt. "*Heart of Darkness* and Racism." *Heart of Darkness*. 4th ed. Ed. Paul B. Armstrong. New York: W. W. Norton & Company, 2006. 365-375. Norton Critical Editions Ser. Print.

Hawthorn, Jeremy. "The Women of *Heart of Darkness*." *Heart of Darkness*. 4th ed. Ed. Paul B. Armstrong. New York: W. W. Norton & Company, 2006. 405-415. Norton Critical Editions Ser. Print.

Knowles, Owen. "Introduction to *Heart of Darkness*." *Heart of Darkness and The Congo Diary*. London: Penguin, 2007. xiii-xxxviii. Print.

Leavis, F. R. *The Great Tradition: George Eliot, Henry James, Joseph Conrad*. London: Faber and Faber Limited, 1948. Print.

Meyer, Bernard C. *Joseph Conrad: A Psychoanalytic Biography*. Princeton, NJ: Princeton UP, 1967. Print.

Miller, J. Hillis. "Should We Read *Heart of Darkness*?" *Conrad in Africa: New Essays on* Heart of Darkness. Ed. Attie de Lange & Gail Fincham with Wiesław Krajka. New York: Columbia UP, 2002. 21-39. Print.

Murfin, Ross C., ed. *Heart of Darkness*. By Joseph Conrad. New York: Bedford/St Martin's. 1996. Case Studies in Contemporary Criticism Ser. Print.

Said, Edward W. *Culture and Imperialism*. London: Vintage Books, 1994. Print.

Singh, Frances B. "The Colonialistic Bias of *Heart of Darkness*." *Heart of Darkness*. 3rd ed. Ed. Robert Kimbrough. New York: W. W. Norton & Company, 1988. 268-280. Norton Critical Editions Ser. Print.

Torgovnick, Marianna. *Gone Primitive: Savage Intellects, Modern Lives*. Chicago: U of Chicago P, 1990. Print.

Watt, Ian. *Conrad in the Nineteenth Century*. Berkeley: U of California P, 1979. Print.

Travelling in Shadowlands—Colonialism and the Holocaust in Widmer's and Sebald's Textual Mining of *Heart of Darkness*

Peter Arnds

Urs Widmer's novel *In the Congo* (*Im Kongo*, 1996) and W. G. Sebald's philosophical travelogue *The Rings of Saturn* (*Die Ringe des Saturn* 1995) both draw on Joseph Conrad's *Heart of Darkness* (1899). What unites Widmer and Sebald is the attempt to talk about the Holocaust through the representation of atrocities committed under colonialism in Conrad's seminal novel. Their texts are, however, radically different in incorporating Conrad's story. Having translated *Heart of Darkness*, Widmer's text approximates Belgian-style colonialism with the myth of Swiss neutrality. Modeled in parts on Conrad's short novel, *In the Congo* operates in a satirically provocative manner while never losing sight of the seriousness of its historical backgrounds—nineteenth-century colonialism, Switzerland's involvement with Nazi Germany and the Mobutu regime, and the dire realities of Swiss immigration policies.[1] It is the story of Kuno, a male nurse in a Zurich retirement home, who travels to the heart of the Congo jungle in search of his former friend Willy. Willy runs a very successful beer brewing company there, and Kuno is sent on a mission by Anselm Schmirhahn, the owner of the brewing empire in postcolonial Congo and a former Nazi collaborator, to find out why all of a sudden the monthly checks have stopped. After arriving in Kinshasa, Kuno, like Conrad's Marlow, travels up the Congo River in a boat called the *Perle des Afriques*. When he arrives in Kisangani he finds his former friend Willy, who had eloped thirty-seven years earlier with Kuno's first love Sophie. He does not recognize them because both have turned black. On returning to Zurich, Kuno notices that he has also become a black man, now trying to enter the Swiss fortress. Ironically, however, he wins the love of his life, Nurse Anne, who never liked him as a white guy. Together, they immigrate to Zaire, a place far from Conrad's heart of darkness but their place of light as Kuno takes over the brewing company from Willy and lives there happily ever after with Anne.

In its conflation of the sacred and the profane, the novel is magical realist. Serious contexts such as Switzerland's insistence on neutrality in the face of Nazi atrocities, the collaboration of some of its entrepreneurs with the Third Reich, contemporary immigration policy and Switzerland's involvement in postcolonial exploitation of places like the Congo, blend easily with Widmer's very own brand of humor in scenes such as the one in which Kuno asks Anne to marry him and she tells him that he can wait "bis Sie schwarz sind."[2] Any translation of this rather untranslatable German phrase, which literally means "until you are black" but figuratively translating into "until the cows come home" or "in your dreams, pal," must inevitably lose its humor, which is so closely linked to the plot of the novel, because she actually does fall in love with him upon his return to Zurich as a black man.

Because *In the Congo* is loosely modeled on Conrad's *Heart of Darkness*, the reader immediately senses that Kuno corresponds to Marlow as Willy does to Kurtz. Widmer's characters and African setting, however, are stripped of the colonial horrors described in great detail by Conrad. Widmer, on the other hand, lightens them up with a great deal of jocularity and carnivalesque activity—by eros and fetishes, monstrous tribal leaders and dictators who defy any realistic description, so that we are continuously reminded of Napoleon's famous words after returning from Russia and just having lost over half a million men to the winter that "*du sublime au ridicule il n'y a qu'un pas* (from the sublime to the ridiculous, there's but one step)." In this regard, as we shall see, Widmer's text mining of Conrad is quite different from Sebald's.

Nonetheless, Widmer does evoke links between the past and the present, between colonialism and postcolonialism, between Hitler and Mobutu, and between the random killing of colonial subalterns and the treatment of immigrants today, whose deportation to their home countries may entail certain death. Moreover, Widmer's text does, to an extent, reveal echoes from Conrad's, especially in the scene of the river passage from Kinshasa to the interior. Conrad's description of the jungle with its aura of primordial times and its "[t]rees, trees, millions of trees, massive, immense, running up high. . . . We were traveling in the night of first ages. . . . We were wanderers on a prehistoric earth"[3] reverberates in Widmer: "Trees, trees, where there was no water there were trees. Gigantic trees bent over the water, seemed to want to throw themselves into it, but have not done so since primordial times" (Widmer 127). Both share descriptions of human life hidden in the jungle and the potential threat emanating from it: "The bush was swarming with human limbs in movement, glistening, of bronze colour" (Conrad 73); "now and again when we were close to the river bank I thought I could see black skin flash up and indistinct shapes fleeting by" (Widmer 127). Conrad's aura of despair, the drums behind the curtain of trees, the howling of natives, followed by unbearable silence, the immensity and impenetrability of the forest, its beauty and terror, all this is also part of Widmer's scenery of which Kuno says: "Such beauty I had never seen, nor such terror" (Widmer 127). Last but not least, the blind shooting that goes on everywhere to subdue the natives, Europeans randomly "shelling the bush" (Conrad 41) is also picked up in the Swiss novel: "Once I shot a series of bullets into the forest without hitting anything" (Widmer 200).

Conrad's jungle, where the colonists are killing off those 'superfluous men' of whom Hannah Arendt speaks,[4] no doubt inspired Widmer not only for his African forest, where he who kills the fastest is master (Widmer 134), but also for his descriptions of the Swiss border forest at the beginning of the novel. The latter is associated with the Jewish refugees trying to escape Nazi Germany and being turned away by the Swiss immigration authorities, a refusal that entailed certain death in the gas chambers; and yet the narrator says, one did not know whether those running through the forest had come to murder or were trying to flee from being murdered (Widmer 9). Later, he goes on to tell us, the immense forest had disappeared (Widmer 11), an allusion to postwar Switzerland's deliberate obliteration of unwelcome memories of the past.

A direct line runs from here to the forest that Kuno enters in Zaire, a place that holds the memory of the "extermination of whole peoples" (Widmer 47) both under colonialism and in postcolonial times under Mobutu, who is also a character in this novel. Colonial genocide is a central topic in Conrad's story. He describes it in horrid detail, especially at the beginning of Marlow's river journey. Waiting for the steamboat to be repaired at the Central Station, he is shocked to find the dying natives described as enemies or criminals when, in fact, they are just mere shadows of their former selves, slowly dying from starvation and being worked to death:

> They were dying slowly—it was very clear. They were not enemies, they were not criminals, they were nothing earthly now—nothing but black shadows of disease and starvation, lying confusedly in the greenish gloom. Brought from all the recesses of the coast in all the legality of time contracts, lost in uncongenial surroundings, fed on unfamiliar food, they sickened, became inefficient, and were then allowed to crawl away and rest. These moribund shapes were free as air—and nearly as thin. (Conrad 44)

It is passages such as this one that may have influenced Widmer for his backdrop of colonial crimes revealed now and again, as in the words by one of his natives that his fetish "had not even helped my grandfather. He had worked for the white men and when he was at the end of his tether they watched him starve" (Widmer 163). Although such passages may get drowned out by much of the humor in this novel, Widmer's jungle is not just a jocular horror cabinet, where *eros* and *thanatos* are the daily order of things, but repeatedly it stands in for Switzerland itself. Then and now, he seems to suggest, his country shuts its eyes to atrocities outside its borders. When in the tribal reunions that are held every year a fake chieftain is discovered, he is immediately killed. Could this be an innuendo to Switzerland's deportation in 1986 of 'fake' refugees from Zaire who used Angolan passports to be allowed to stay in Switzerland and who were, upon being returned to their home countries, most likely being tortured to death? At the time, rumors of atrocities were not believed by the Swiss government, especially because they were denied by Mobutu himself.[5]

Widmer follows Conrad in juxtaposing the tortured individual in his loneliness in the state of nature where *homo hominem lupus est* (man is a wolf to man) with the sovereign positioned above the law, colonial masters such as Kurtz, whose insanity culminates in his absent-minded plea to "[e]xterminate all the brutes" (Conrad 78), and whom Widmer uses as a model for postcolonial rulers such as Hitler or Mobutu. In both texts, we can observe that symmetry Agamben points to between the *homo sacer*—humans cursed and abandoned by society as undesirable—and the sovereign.[6] Both the *homo sacer* and the sovereign find themselves in that state of exception where the habitual law of the community has no hold. Both are what the Germans call *vogelfrei* (as free as birds), free from the social contract in the sense of being excluded from the communal bond based on human rights, "as free as air" as Conrad puts it in the passage cited above. One of Widmer's excluded humans is the Tamil, who awaits his deportation from Switzerland and whose fear of being killed at home induces him to commit suicide with a poisonous mushroom. The text suggests that turning away refugees is a Swiss tradition, especially in the 1930s and 40s. Kuno refers to the horrors of the Holocaust (Widmer 70) when his father and Berger, two inmates of the retirement home Kuno works for, glorify the work they used to perform for the 'Line Wiking,' an intelligence unit during the Second World War that informed the Allied Forces about German military operations. Berger, whose production of high efficiency lenses attracts the Nazis' interest making him their collaborator, allows Widmer to debunk the myth of General Guysan of Switzerland's noncollaboration with Nazi Germany and invincibility due to its geographic location as an Alpine fortress.[7]

One of the most memorable scenes in the book is the encounter between Berger and Hitler, in which the latter is so impressed with the Swiss man that he gives him his private telephone number, assuring him that he can call for help at any time. When interrogated later by the Gestapo about his activities in the Wiking intelligence unit, Berger avails himself of Hitler's number and gets away unharmed. This scene then repeats itself between Kuno and Mobutu, the lion ruler, as the brewery is being attacked by Mobutu's army and Kuno can only stop the ambush and get away by using his ultimate fetish, the telephone number Mobutu had given him earlier. By way of such parallel scenes, Widmer clearly links the past to the present, the entrepreneurial links between Switzerland and Nazi Germany with those between Switzerland—the beer is a postcolonial product replacing the quest for ivory and rubber in the colonial period—with Mobutu's Congo.

Mobutu the lion man parallels Hitler as wolf man. Hitler himself strongly identified with that animal, not least because of his first name's Old Germanic origin meaning, 'Noble Wolf'.[8] Therefore, it is not Willy, Kuno's former friend who had once eloped with Sophie to run the brewing company in the jungle, but rather these tyrants who ultimately recall Conrad's Kurtz, the despot in the heart of darkness, that remarkable man, according to Marlow, but nonetheless someone whom civilized society has abandoned and who therefore becomes one with all his victims, the natives abandoned by humanity: "He was shamefully abandoned" (Conrad 87). In his state of abandonment, Kurtz's death is then a twofold one: before he dies physically, he is already considered dead by the European community, which has given up on him. This is very different for Widmer's Willy, whom Kuno visits to inquire why the monthly payments to Anselm Schmirhahn have stopped and who then returns to Europe and hands over the company to Kuno, to whom the Congo becomes a terrestrial paradise.

Widmer's forest in the Congo is mostly a healthy place echoing Jean-Jacques Rousseau's concept of an escape from the maladies of European over-civilization, while the troubled Swiss border forest, still untouched in Kuno's childhood, after the war is largely in decline and being deforested as the receptacle of Swiss guilt. Widmer is playful, however, with the theme of race, especially in the scene when Kuno finds himself transformed into a black man in a matter of two days and, as such, returns to Switzerland. When the Swiss immigration officer asks him for the purpose of his visit, he says that his father is dying, which prompts the border official to the question: "In Switzerland?" Kuno's answer: "People die everywhere" (Widmer 176). In its tone of voice, Widmer's humorous novel is consequently very different from Conrad's, as it is from the apocalyptic aura the German-born author W.G. Sebald, who taught at the University of East Anglia, habitually employs in his texts.

Sebald's travelogue *The Rings of Saturn* about the barren but historically rich landscape of South East England also engages with Conrad's text. He reconstructs the life of Teodor Józef Konrad Korzeniowski/Joseph Conrad when hiking through the Suffolk town of Lowestoft, where Conrad once worked on a cargo ship. As part of his exploration of the destruction of the world, its species, and humanity—a central theme arching across most of his work—Sebald follows Conrad's upbringing in Poland under Russian colonial rule, the deaths of his exiled father and mother, to his indictment of colonial conditions in Belgian Congo, where, like his protagonist Marlow, Conrad travelled up the Congo River. Finally, Sebald also describes the encounter with the Irish Roger Casement, to Conrad the only honest man he ever met in an Africa[9] (Sebald 126) that was completely corrupted by colonialism. Casement's fight against the crimes of colonialism in Belgian Congo, South America, and Ireland until his execution then become the focus of the latter half of Sebald's fifth chapter.

The intertextuality between Sebald's *The Rings of Saturn* and Conrad's *Heart of Darkness* is intense in their shared theme of wandering through the smooth space of a superficially empty landscape: "Little was marked in the interior of this part of the world, no railway lines, no roads, no towns, and as cartographers would often embellish such empty spaces with drawings of exotic beasts . . . they had rendered the Congo . . . as a snake coiling through the blank, uncharted land" (Sebald 117). Although Sebald's walk is circular and Marlow's passage along the river is linear, both seem to be lost in a labyrinth of trails and passages. Conrad's biblical reference to this primordial and still undisclosed place is hard to miss, and yet the snake also represents one rhizomatic line in the labyrinth of the river landscape whose center, very much in parallel to the mythical labyrinth of Knossos, is occupied by demons. As Kurtz, this example for the worst of colonialism, is, as it were, the Minotaur at the center of Conrad's text, this text in turn then fills the demonic center of Sebald's text—literally the center of the narrative as it is chapter 5 out of 10, from where it is linked thematically and linguistically to other moments of historical horror. Conrad himself is viewed as a messenger from the underworld, the hell of colonialism. Conrad's experience of colonialism begins during his childhood, which was filled with the trauma of losing both parents due to the harsh conditions experienced during Apollo Korzeniowski's exile in Vologda, the Russian Empire's heart of darkness.

With some of the passages from *Heart of Darkness* directly copied or retold, Sebald's textual mining follows Conrad's text far more closely than Widmer's. Wandering in *The Rings of Saturn* happens under the sign of Saturn, the planet of melancholy, and it occurs in a landscape that bears all the signs of an apocalypse and seems alien to Sebald. Despite his many years of employment at the University of East Anglia outside Norwich, the author/narrator often feels like a stranger in this part of the world, where the native population eyes him suspiciously, a mistrust very much in line with the old fear of nomads and itinerants as being somehow in cahoots with the forces of the underworld.

Impressions of mobility and immobility alternate for Sebald as they do for Marlow. Central to the act of walking is also the contrastive experience of joy and terror—the joy of escaping urban gravity and being liberated by the wide open spaces of East Anglia and the terrors of planetary destruction he encounters in this landscape, the terror also of getting lost—recalling Conrad's "you lost your way on that river as you would in a desert" (Conrad 61)—to the point of becoming completely immobile. Here the "endlessly winding paths" (Sebald 173) of the Dunwich Heath entangle the wanderer and lead him around in circles, preventing him from moving in any direction. In Conrad's story, too, we read about the "paths, paths everywhere; a stamped-in network of paths spreading over the empty land" (Conrad 47), and we hear about Kurtz's aimless wanderings through the jungle in search of ivory, a motif Conrad models on his encounter with Roger Casement, who would disappear into the jungle for weeks on end in the company only of two bulldogs and a carrier (Conrad 83 n.12; Sebald 126).[10]

The sensation of complete immobility within his circular mobility evokes nomadism in the classical sense. According to Gilles Deleuze and Félix Guattari the nomad does not really move but "clings to the smooth space left by the receding forest"; he is without a real home, unlike migrants who become reterritorialized and find new homes.[11] What the two French philosophers have described for the nomad is precisely Sebald's experience on the Dunwich Heath: the related phenomena of treelessness—especially after a storm in 1987 almost all the trees of the area got destroyed—and homelessness, where "going native" is impossible as the local people—the natives as it were—do not understand him, although he speaks their language well. Instead he experiences a complete lack of deep roots (Deleuze's *arborescence*) in a place where only "the yellow roots of nettles creep onwards in the soil" (Sebald 181). This is an apt image for the Deleuzian *rhizome* as tubers with shallow roots, and here the vertiginous wanderer is surrounded not only by the ubiquitous destruction of plant and animal life but by the horrors of the war machine, one of the principal features of the Deleuzian nomadology, and by images of the brutality and futility of colonialism.

This futility of colonialism is captured primarily in the image of shelling the empty bush, a motif Sebald takes directly from *Heart of Darkness*. His narrative analytically presents us with King Leopold's exploitation of the Congo thinly disguised as an enterprise meant to open up this territory to the world while also leading the 'savages' into the light of civilization. King Leopold is described as the sovereign with unlimited power, and in comparison with Widmer's text, we can see a continuity between the colonial tyrant and postcolonial rulers such as Mobutu, a mimic man engaging in the kinds of genocidal practices that colonialism once taught the Congo.[12] Conrad himself, Sebald tells us, witnessed precisely what he has Marlow describe, the ruthless treatment of the starving natives—those *Schattenwesen* (shadow creatures or shadow beings) who are as free as air (Sebald, original, 146; Conrad 44), being worked to death, at which point they are then allowed to crawl away into some pit and left to die. Sebald integrates Conrad's expression "as free as air" into his web of atrocities suffusing the text, primarily however linking it to the subtext of the Holocaust. After all, 'as free as air' not only evokes the German expression of 'vogelfrei' for the *homo sacer*, but specifically also the ashes and smoke spilling forth from the crematoria of the concentration camps, which always loom behind the wanderings in Sebald's texts.

Like Marlow's journey, Sebald's walk is one that takes place in the shadowlands of human destruction and the destruction of humans. Sebald shares Conrad's pessimism regarding the loss of any hope in the benevolence of human endeavor: "I looked around, and I don't know why, but I assure you that never, never before, did this land, this river, this jungle, the very arch of this blazing sky, appear to me so hopeless and so dark, so impenetrable to human thought, so pitiless to human weakness" (Conrad 83). This aura of hopelessness and despair fills the book all the way to its final image of the plight of nineteenth-century weavers, who experience the melancholic spirit of Saturn *ad extremis* as their work drives them into insanity. The title of the book, *Rings of Saturn*, thus refers not only to the narrator's melancholic circular wanderings but quite literally also to the image of the rings of silk spun by a certain type of moth, the *saturnia carpini*, the progenitors of the weavers' saturnine spirit of lethargy, their heightened sensation of torture by "looms . . . reminiscent of instruments of torture" (Sebald 282). Like Conrad's story, Sebald's narrative reveals the links between *travel*, *trouble* and *travail*, between destructive labor, torture, anguish, madness, and finally death: it does so for the weavers and a host of other persons in in this nineteenth-century climate of despair, including literary figures like the German poet Friedrich Hölderlin (1770–1843), whose search for the deep root of words sent his mind into madness. Madness has a close relationship with wandering, the madman's mind that travels too much[13] but also the traveler who can be driven mad, as in the case of Kurtz: "But his soul was mad. Being alone in the wilderness, it had looked within itself, and by Heavens! I tell you it had gone mad" (Conrad 94). Kurtz's madness, however, is largely the result of the 'unsound methods' of colonialism that he has implemented, which make him want to leave. In the end, however, he is incapable of doing just that and in staying has to "forget himself amongst these people—forget himself—you know" (Conrad 84).

In view of the atrocities of various ages contributing to the gradual destruction of the planet, forgetting is a keyword in all three narratives. These journeys unearth the forgotten. In doing so, Sebald carefully interweaves the fates of individuals like the Irish revolutionary Roger Casement, who, after first visiting colonial Congo, devotes his entire life to revealing colonialism's atrocities, with other forms and temporal layers of oppression, such as the destruction of a species like the herring:

> At last the catch is unloaded and we see the work in the halls where women's hands gut the herring, sort them according to size, and pack them in barrels. Then (so says the booklet accompanying the 1936 film), the railway goods wagons take in the restless wanderer of the seas and transport it to those places where its fate on this earth will at last be fulfilled. (Sebald 54)

Sebald's use of words here, of 'Güterwagen' (railway goods wagons) or 'ruheloser Wanderer' (restless wanderer, evoking also the homelessness of the Jewish diaspora), links the destruction of herrings to the Holocaust. This linkage is then made more explicit through the photo Sebald has added to his text[14] showing mountains of dead herrings, an image that stands in direct relation to the photo of the camp victims of Bergen Belsen. [15] This proximity of the extermination of an animal species and the genocide of humans is also supported by the torturous experiments conducted on herrings in order to investigate their survival capacity. And "alles spielte sich ab in wüster *Finsternis*" (everything happened in darkness) (Sebald 70) says the narrator of the yearly killing of 60 billion fish, reminding us also of Conrad's *Herz der Finsternis* (Heart of Darkness). It is a figure that sets in parallel the millions killed in Belgian Congo[16] with the millions killed in the Nazi camps.

After they die, the herrings begin to glow for days, with their scales the color of snow or *ash* (my italics, Sebald, Hulse's translation, 73) thus revealing the secret of their slaughter. Their glimmering ties in with the shadow figures of the Congo—"gradually, emerging from the dark, Marlow reports, the glimmer of a pair of eyes is directed upon me from beyond" (Sebald, original, 146; my translation, as Hulse shows little fidelity to the original here): "Evidently no one cared to stop these black shadows (*Schattenwesen*) when they crept off into the bush. They are free now, as free as the air that surrounds them and into which they will slowly dissolve" (Sebald 120). In turn these *Schattenwesen* (literally, shadow creatures or shadow beings) evoke the Muselmänner of the Nazi camps, those victims caught between life and death. [17]

It is words like 'Schattenwesen' (shadowy apparitions) 'Asche' (ash) or 'in Luft auflösen' (dissolve in air) that are the *Knotenpunkte*, the nodal points of the different lines along which Sebald's walk around East Anglia reveals various atrocities in the gradual destruction of the planet. The dividing line between humans and animals is thin in these descriptions. The liminality Sebald explores between the species ultimately also serves the purpose of pointing out the mechanisms of abjection in colonialism and totalitarianism in which to facilitate killing humans these were perceptually reduced to the level of animals, for it is no doubt easier to ignore one's empathy with animals than with humans. Marlow's words that "the worst of it [was] the suspicion of their (the natives') not being inhuman" (Conrad 63) finds a contrastive echo in Sebald's comment that those responsible for the mass killing of herrings console themselves with the thought that physiological condition of herrings protect them from fear and pain, but that "in truth we know nothing of the herrings' feelings" (Sebald, original, 75).

Indeed, Sebald's *travel* along the trails connecting these atrocities is full of *trouble*. While the poetics of wandering reflect the circularity and melancholy inherent to the rings of Saturn, Sebald's politics of wandering lie specifically in the potential of walking itself in bringing hidden or forgotten truths in their historical connectedness to light. His walk stirs a temporary remembrance, a fleeting emergence of what resembles the truth about the past and its repetition in other forms in the present, before these contexts cloud over again by non-travel, receding into the shadowlands of human oblivion.

Notes

1. I have shown this in more detail in Peter Arnds, "Into the Heart of Darkness: Switzerland, Hitler, Mobutu and Joseph Conrad in Urs Widmer's novel *Im Kongo*," 329-342.
2. Urs Widmer, *Im Kongo*, 18. The translations from this text are my own. All subsequent quotations from this text are marked by page numbers in brackets.
3. Joseph Conrad, *Heart of Darkness and Other Stories*, 63. All subsequent quotations from this text are marked by page numbers in brackets.
4. Cf. Hannah Arendt, *The Origins of Totalitarianism*, 150: "Older than the superfluous wealth was another by-product of capitalist production: the human debris that every crisis, following invariably upon each period of industrial growth, eliminated permanently from producing society. Men who had become permanently idle were as superfluous to the community as the owners of superfluous wealth."
5. Cf. Adolf Muschg, *Die Schweiz am Ende. Am Ende die Schweiz*, 93.
6. In *Homo Sacer*, Agamben points to the ambivalence of the medieval wolf man, who in being expelled to a life outside of communal law is uniquely tied to the sovereign, whose power to abandon individuals equally positions him outside of that law. This symmetry between the sovereign beast and the persecuted *vargr* (wolf/outlaw) or *Friedlos* (man without peace, that is, in a permanent state of war) reflects the wolf in his dual perception of the powerful hunter versus the hunted pest. There can be no sovereignty without abjection, a fact also recognized by Jacques Derrida in his *Séminaire: La bête et le souverain* (*The Beast & the Sovereign*), his lecture series about the wolf in culture held at the École des Hautes Études en Sciences Sociales (EHESS).
7. Cf. Tom Bower, *Nazi Gold* (New York: Harper Collins, 1997) 36: During the Second World War the Swiss government created a myth "whose hero was General Henry Guisan. . . . Under Guisan's plan of national defense, in the event of German invasion, there was to be nominal resistance along Switzerland's frontiers while the army retreated to the Alps, abandoning the bulk of the population and

industry. Based in that natural fortress, the Swiss would repel the enemy. When the German invasion did not materialize, Switzerland's rulers referred repeatedly to a miracle, the miracle of General Guisan, the brave commander whose bold strategy had outfaced the mighty Nazis and saved the nation."

8. Athalwolf/Adulfr; Cf. R. G. L. Waite (1993) *Hitler: The Psychopathic God*, 163-6.
9. W. G. Sebald, *Die Ringe des Saturn*, 126; *The Rings of Saturn*. Trans. Michael Hulse. Subsequent quotations are to the translation by Hulse (except where I mark it as my own) and indicated by page number in brackets.
10. Cf. Frederick R. Karl and Laurence Davies (eds.), *The Collected Letters of Joseph Conrad*. Vol. 3 (Cambridge, UK: Cambridge UP, 1986) 101-2
11. Gilles Deleuze and Félix Guattari, *A Thousand Plateaus. Capitalism and Schizophrenia*, 381.
12. Cf. See Homi K. Bhabha's chapter "Of mimicry and man: The ambivalence of colonial discourse," in *The Location of Culture*, 85-92.
13. In German, mad, or *verrückt*, literally means being displaced from somewhere, from one's home in traveling, which is why in earlier ages, when travel was not the norm, insanity was associated with dislocation.
14. on page 71 of the German version
15. on page 78-79.
16. According to Adam Hochschild's much-contested claim that 10 million people may have died in this nearly forgotten 'holocaust,' cf. Adam Hochschild, *King Leopold's Ghost: A Story of Greed, Terror, and Heroism in Colonial Africa*, 280.
17. Giorgio Agamben, *Remnants of Auschwitz: The Witness and the Archive*, 44-5: The Muselmänner were the living dead in the camps, who had given up on life but were not yet dead; the term is derived from "the Arabic word muslim: the one who submits unconditionally to the will of God."

Works Cited

Agamben, Giorgio. *Homo Sacer. Sovereign Power and Bare Life.* Stanford, CA: Stanford UP, 1995. Print.

_____. *Remnants of Auschwitz*: *The Witness and the Archive.* New York: Zone Books, 2002. Print.

Arendt, Hannah. *The Origins of Totalitarianism.* San Diego/New York: Harvest, 1973. Print.

Arnds, Peter. "Into the Heart of Darkness: Switzerland, Hitler, Mobutu and Joseph Conrad in Urs Widmer's novel *Im Kongo.*" *The German Quarterly* 71.4 (Fall 1998): 329-342. Print.

Bhabha, Homi K. "Of Mimicry and Man: The Ambivalence of Colonial Discourse." *The Location of Culture.* London/New York: Routledge, 1994. 85-92. Print.

Conrad, Joseph. *Heart of Darkness and Other Stories.* London: Wordsworth Editions, 1996. Print.

Deleuze, Gilles & Félix Guattari. *A Thousand Plateaus. Capitalism and Schizophrenia.* Trans. Brian Massumi. Minneapolis: U of Minnesota P, 1987. Print.

Derrida, Jacques. *The Beast and the Sovereign.* Vols. 1 & 2. Trans. Geoffrey Bennington. Chicago/London: U of Chicago P, 2009. Print.

Hochschild, Adam. *King Leopold's Ghost: A Story of Greed, Terror, and Heroism in Colonial Africa.* New York: Houghton Mifflin, 1998. Print.

Karl, Frederick R. & Laurence Davies, eds. *The Collected Letters of Joseph Conrad.* Vol. 3. Cambridge, UK: Cambridge UP, 1986. Print.

Muschg, Adolf. *Die Schweiz am Ende. Am Ende die Schweiz.* Frankfurt am Main: Suhrkamp, 1990. Print.

Sebald, W. G. *Die Ringe des Saturn.* Frankfurt/Main: Fischer, 2002. Print.

_____. *The Rings of Saturn.* Trans. Michael Hulse. London: New Directions, 1999. Print.

Waite, Robert. G. L. *Hitler: The Psychopathic God.* New York: Da Capo Press, 1993. Print.

Widmer, Urs. *Im Kongo.* Zürich: Diogenes, 1996. Print.

"Solidarity in Dreams": Community, Difference, and Race from *Narcissus* through *Heart of Darkness*

Kieran Dodds

Conrad's 'Pseudo-Humanism'

This article proceeds with a critical consideration of four of Joseph Conrad's texts: *Youth, Heart of Darkness, The End of the Tether*, and *The Nigger of the 'Narcissus'* (henceforth *'Narcissus'*). These works are analyzed with the goal of extracting Conrad, and in particular Conrad's politics, from his protagonists; their existential to-and-fro between belonging on the one hand, and standing alone and apart on the other, reveals something of the author. Sharing a close chronology and, crucially, an imperial centrality, it is a sample of Conrad's early fiction that sharply illustrates both his insight and inconsistency. And while by no means the only setting in which Conrad grapples with community and difference, the colonial encounter is integral to understanding how these relate to race, and the profound implications this has for any Conradian political philosophy.

In these imperial stories, Conrad articulates a once dominant, now deeply dated humanism that privileges European voices over those belonging to Africa, his mystical "East," and elsewhere away from the colonial metropole. This argument, of course, borrows from Chinua Achebe's classic case that *Heart of Darkness*, with its appropriation of Africa as a "foil in Europe, a place of negations," belongs not to the pantheon of "permanent literature" (783). Where it differs slightly is in its assertion of a Conradian *humanism*, however troubling its applications. In each of the four texts, Conrad is keen to stress that multiple and binary communities exist within one definite humanity: in *Youth*, "West" and "East"; in *Heart of Darkness*, civilization and savagery; in *The End of the Tether*, "the white and the brown" (162); and in *'Narcissus,'* ultimately, the "Nigger" and the rest of the crew. Conrad sets his tales in moments of interplay between these communities and asks what this means for the European self and European solidarities. They are in this way "pseudo-humanist," to take the term of Martiniquais author and activist Aimé Césaire (176), both acknowledging a common humanity and privileging a particular human or humans.

Conrad's work is a "struggle with himself" (Said, "Claims" 5) that remains mostly unresolved. His novelty lies in the inner workings of that struggle, in how he *tries* to resolve, by way of colonial autobiography, the competing claims of individual human and abstract humanity. That these are in tension with one another is for Conrad an ordinary, even necessary, thing; again, this is a theme of his work whatever the setting. The colonial encounter in which Conrad participated, however, crystallizes the apparently irreconcilable difference of European and non-European cultures and communities—even if Conrad famously went further than most contemporaries in refusing to cast the two as "enemies" (*Heart* 43). When these binary communities are forced together—the "negro in the British forecastle" (*'Narcissus'* 9) or the "silent Malay" among "overhanging" white men (*Heart* 140-141)—the reader is left with a still heightened and unsettled tension. As Tim Christensen has argued, Conrad's characters of color are "fundamental but paradoxical" (28) to his narratives; they stir his European characters to individual introspection and simultaneously define and undermine their ideal community. It is this problematic pseudo-humanism that is left: Conrad's communities are made and unmade by difference, his preferred political solidarity collapsing into pessimism and self-interest in the imperial arena. In short, this is an essay that charts Conrad's often confused navigation of private and public, of Self and Other—and concludes that it is only through the lens of the author's imperial subjectivities that we find an uncomfortable resolution.

"[Tiring] of the Sea": Chronology in Conrad's Imperial Stories

Although *Youth, Heart of Darkness*, and *The End of the Tether* were published together in one volume, Conrad was quick to deny that the three "[laid] . . . claim to unity of artistic purpose" (*Prefaces* 71).

'Narcissus,' he went further still, stood with *Nostromo* "apart and by [itself] in the body of my work"; the "only bond between them" was the time of their writing (71). Conrad's deliberate minimization of time and place, however, is difficult to understand. When read together, these stories reveal a chronology of discovery if not a completely coherent narrative. The commonalities between the four, including *'Narcissus,'* are striking enough that they cannot be explained away by the reader's difficulty in disentangling authorial intent from published form. Where in *Youth* there exists a romantic individualism and personal naïveté, this gives way in *Heart of Darkness* to emergent, imperfect communities and a creeping interrogation of imperialism's inner logic (albeit from within the narrow parameters of that logic). By the volume's third story, that logic is just barely intact, Conrad playing with power dynamics so that its white figure of authority relies entirely on the subaltern sailor for his livelihood. *'Narcissus'* situates itself somewhere between these stories, but with echoes of each; original in some ways, it is in others foundational to understanding Conrad's attitudes to community, difference, and race.

In *Youth*, Conrad presents a nascent political philosophy centered on the individual, imperfect as he (the gendered pronoun is appropriate) must be. The story of an ill-fated ship's voyage to a mystical and unknown Orient, it revolves almost solely around the crew—the "men of the East" appear only on the penultimate page (Conrad, *Youth* 27) —and, in particular, the young Marlow, later to appear in *Heart of Darkness* and other Conrad stories. Conrad's character is immature and easily influenced, "[living] the life of youth in ignorance and hope" (12), but he is not worthy of the reader's condemnation. In fact, his wide-eyed "simplicity of heart" (4) serves as a welcome counterpoint to the "[ghostly]" Newcastle skipper (10) and hardened Liverpool shiphands (17). Already this highlights Conrad's tendency for essentialization. In this instance, it is a mostly harmless regionalism that plays on English class stereotypes, as opposed to the racist Othering of the colonized. However, Conrad is also here hinting at the possibilities and constraints of collective organization. Early in the tale, his protagonist thrives on the camaraderie of the ship, noting the shared emotion of having all "forgotten how it felt to be dry" (8). The living sea at first binds the men together. And yet he is at his happiest when tragedy strikes and the vessel sinks, liberating him from his squadron and compelling the young man to sail independently: "[I remember] the feeling that I could last for ever, outlast the sea, the earth, and all men" (25). For Conrad, youth and its attendant outlook is "silly," but also "charming [and] beautiful" (23). The contradiction between the necessity of the collective and the temptations of solitude—still unclear, it seems, in Conrad's mind—is immediately set out for the reader.

Heart of Darkness represents a significant progression in Conrad's politics, where single-minded adventure transforms itself into an interrogation of both the individual's place within the imperial project and indeed the virtue of that collective project. The novel's opening, for example, is not dissimilar to that of *Youth*: Marlow is excited about "the mystery of an unknown earth! . . . The dreams of men, the seed of commonwealths, the germs of empires!" (Conrad, *Heart* 32). There is, to start with, a similar externality of perspective and a sense, later partially challenged, of automatic European entitlement. And yet this is immediately qualified with Marlow famously casting a comparison between the rivers Thames and Congo: "And this also . . . has been one of the dark places of the earth" (33). Although the takeaway from *Heart of Darkness* is clearly not that empire is morally unjust and ought to be dismantled, there is nevertheless a much greater and still growing degree of introspection from Marlow as to its relative merits. More importantly for Conrad, empire is the perfect setting to explore not quite the "breakup of one petty European mind" in Kurtz (Achebe 788), but greater existential questions about the human need for "solitude and solidarity" and the "contradictions between radical individualism and social cohesion" (Lord 3). *Heart of Darkness*, as with all these stories, is concerned with individual belonging in the context of competing communities. As Conrad writes of Kurtz, "Everything belonged to him—but that was a trifle. *The thing was to know what he belonged to, how many powers of darkness claimed him for their own.* That was the reflection that made you creepy all over" (76-77, emphasis mine).

It is with the aging Captain Whalley in Conrad's third volume, *The End of the Tether*, that the author's developing chronology is illuminated most clearly. A once successful sailor whose luck "had been simply marvellous" (Conrad, *End* 115), Whalley is brought to despair by the dual misfortune of a capitalist crisis in banking and the loss of his sight. Concealing his reliance on the subaltern Malay Serang to sail his ship, Whalley's fellow white sailors come to realize his disability and plot to sink the vessel for insurance money. Whalley chooses to remain on board and drowns, having long ago "declared himself formally tired of the sea" (112) and its "loneliness" (114). The most interesting aspect of the text is its inversion of expected power dynamics. In his old age, Whalley is almost entirely dependent on the Serang—the "pilot-fish" to the captain's "whale" (162-163)—to survive. To the rest of the (white) crew, the nature of this relationship was "repugnant to [the] imagination, shocking to [their] ideas of honesty . . . [and their] conception of mankind" (163). Conrad is here knowingly radical. His overturning of order calls into question the ship's entire lifeworld, teasing not only an equal relationship between "the white and the brown" (162), but a relationship in which "the brown" is invested with significant power and responsibility. Again, this only goes so far: Whalley, the tale's tragic hero, still subscribes to the view that imperial subjects ought to be "[checked] by superior force . . . held in trust from God" (187), while the fate of the silent, stereotyped Serang is deemed unimportant at the novel's end—unlike the "carking care of poverty" and "hard struggle for bread" suffered by Whalley's distant daughter (219). It does however bring into focus the emergent sense of community among Conrad's characters. Captain Whalley, despite his world-weariness, is most often defined by his relationship to others. There is, therefore, a definite political trajectory to these stories. Whalley's ideal of solidarity, while unfulfilled, follows on from the carefree individualism of *Youth* and the imperfect interrogation of empire present in *Heart of Darkness*.

Written and published just prior to this trilogy, *'Narcissus'* is at once bound to and separate from it, representing perhaps Conrad's most explicit treatment of community and its political place. It is unusual in including as its protagonist an articulate Other: Wait is a black West Indian man serving on a British ship who with his very first words—"I belong to the ship" (Conrad, *'Narcissus'* 32)— asserts his rights. The contrast between the eponymous Wait and *The End of the Tether*'s "silent" (141) and "placid" (148) Serang is stark. In setting his story thus, Conrad is concerned more with race than empire (the two are, of course, intimately and inextricably connected). This allows Conrad to play with the very meaning of community: its constituents, its political desirability, and also its weaknesses. And in this sense, *'Narcissus'* is a worthy companion to each of the hitherto discussed tales. Indeed, its differences, especially Wait's prominence, illuminate and allow for a more explicit treatment of the themes broached elsewhere in Conrad's work. This is laid out as early as the preface, the author noting that "[Wait] is nothing: he is merely the centre of the ship's collective psychology and the pivot of the action" (9). Which is to say, surely, that Wait is also everything, the "common bond" (173) that ties a fragile community together. It suggests that Conrad sees a dialectical relationship between individual and collective, the implications of with which the author struggled.

Community: Reification and Rupture

In an 1898 letter to the Scottish socialist politician and author R. B. Cunninghame Graham, Conrad wrote:

> There is no morality, no knowledge and no hope; *there is only the consciousness of ourselves* which drives us about a world that whether seen in a convex or a concave mirror is always but a vain and floating appearance. (Conrad, Graham, & Watts 70-71, emphasis mine)

While echoing the character Heyst's insistence in Conrad's later novel *Victory* that "he who forms a tie is lost" (215), this passage also seems to directly contradict the raft of scholarship emphasizing Conrad's political allegiance to community and solidarity. Avrom

Fleishman, for instance, sought to demonstrate the philosophical debt owed by Conrad to the nineteenth-century organicist movement, whose thinkers thought individual agency to derive from the collective. Here, however, Conrad strikes a Nietzschean or even Wagnerian tone. This is the author's great political paradox. On the one hand, he is suspicious of personal and political relationships stretching beyond the self, determined, in the words of one author, "that every human connection must carry the heaviest of costs" (Gorra xvii). On the other, he sees solidarity as a human virtue of enormous emancipatory potential. The character of James Wait in *'Narcissus'* is said to speak to:

> the latent feeling of fellowship with all creation—and to the subtle but invincible conviction of solidarity that knits together the loneliness of innumerable hearts, to the solidarity in dreams, in joy, in sorrow, in aspirations, in illusions, in hope, in fear, which binds men to each other, which binds together all humanity—the dead to the living and the living to the unborn. (12)

If this circle can indeed be squared, it is in these four stories. Race and empire were the prisms through which the author looked to resolve this personal and political contradiction.

In spite of Marlow's famous challenge to empire—"[the] conquest of the earth, which mostly means the taking it away from those who have a different complexion or slightly flatter noses than ourselves, is not a pretty thing when you look into it too much," (Conrad, *Heart* 34) —Conrad could not quite envision a global south independent of imperialism. *Heart of Darkness*, Edward Said writes, while a "[scrupulous recording of] the differences between the disgraces of Belgian and British colonial attitudes," did not challenge the underlying assumption of a "world carved up into one or another Western sphere of dominion" (*Culture* 27). A sure reason for this is Conrad's intimate involvement in the imperial project, from which his stories take inspiration. *Youth*'s Beard and Mahon are named after some of the author's former shipmates, while the *Narcissus* is a vessel on which Conrad also sailed. *Heart of Darkness*, of course, was loosely based on the author's expedition to the then Congo Free State and central Africa. These facts led Said to elsewhere claim that Conrad was in *Heart of Darkness* "hiding himself within rhetoric" (*Joseph* 5), his prose a product of bitter experience. There is therefore a narrative certainty and uncertainty to the works. Conrad is certain of the *idea* of empire, and what this means for the formation of community. He identifies the tension between an empire's, and indeed a state's, need to incorporate and differentiate the subjects under its control—later a major point of analysis for historians (Cooper 2005) and political scientists (Mamdani 1996) alike. But he is uncertain of his own positionality: is Conrad an actor, an observer, or both? In *Youth*, for instance, "the East spoke to [Marlow], but it was in a Western voice" (26); his understanding is compromised, perhaps fatally, by his own background. The everyday details of empire therefore pass his narrators by: "the beaten nigger groaned *somewhere*" (Conrad, *Heart* 53); "[the] hurt nigger moaned feebly *somewhere* nearby" (54); "[an] athletic black belonging to *some* coast tribe"; "the . . . pilgrims buried *something* [Kurtz's body] in a muddy hole" (98, emphasis mine). Empire was an essential part of Conrad, but it was also an elusive one. As such, it proved the perfect testing ground on which to reflect and reform his political philosophy.

A matter on which Conrad rarely wavered was an aspiration to humanity for imperial subjects—an aspiration that resulted, ironically, in his caricature of competing and unequal communities. Writing in an introduction to Alf Garnett's study of Ivan Turgenev, Conrad revealed that his appreciation of the great Russian novelist sprang largely from his "essential humanity": Turgenev's characters, "fortunate and unfortunate, oppressed and oppressors are human beings, not strange beasts in a menagerie of damned souls knocking themselves about in the stuffy darkness of mystical contradictions" (Conrad, Foreword viii). It is an approach Conrad looked to mirror in *Heart of Darkness*. For all that "damned souls knocking themselves about in the stuffy darkness" reads like a blurb to Conrad's work, it is obviously true that he insisted strongly on Africans' "humanness." Marlow's insistence that the Congolese chain-gangs he encountered were "men—men, I tell you" (Conrad, *Heart* 44) was, in the context of the brutality of Belgian imperialism in that country, more radical than it ought to have been. However, Marlow immediately casts these very same men as "[black] shapes" and "black shadows" (44) whose age was indeterminable and motives unfathomable to white men (45). In doing so, Conrad creates a community that is both alike and apart from his own. Achebe's criticism, that it was the "lurking hint of kinship, of common ancestry" (783) that was most worrisome to Conrad, holds true.

Even in *Youth*, by far the most individualized of these tales, Marlow describes a community of "Eastern" men who despite their (admittedly slight) differences are at one:

> I saw brown, bronze, yellow faces, the black eyes, the glitter, the colour of an Eastern crowd . . . A wave of movement passed through the crowd from end to end, passed along the heads, swayed the bodies, ran along the jetty like a ripple on the water, like a breath of wind on a field – and all was still again. (Conrad, *Youth* 27)

It is a story framed almost entirely externally to empire, concerned far more with Marlow and the white crew of the *Judea* than with this united crowd. And the crowd is clearly defined by its racial composition, its "blaze of vivid colour" (Conrad, *Youth* 27). Nevertheless, the author feels compelled to assert that these men are "beings," which is to say human: "This was the East of the ancient navigators, so old, so mysterious, resplendent and somber, living and unchanged, full of danger and promise. And these were the men" (27).

Heart of Darkness continues this thread, a so-perceived perverted community of uninhibited Congolese men—to whom Kurtz attaches himself—serving to complicate already fraught questions of self and solidarity. Like the men of the "East," the faces of the "black fellows" are "like grotesque masks . . . but they had bone, muscle, a wild vitality, an intense energy of movement, that was as natural and true as the surf along their coast" (Conrad, *Heart* 41). The collective pronoun is significant, but so too is the recurrence of movement as a metaphor for sameness. As Marlow watched the swaying bodies in Java cohere together, so too he observes on the

Congo River, "deep in the tangled gloom, naked breasts, arms, legs, glaring eyes,—the bush was swarming with human limbs in movement, glistening, of bronze colour" (73). This oneness among the colonized contrasts sharply with Marlow's lingering suspicion of dependency. Of Kurtz's Russian admirer, he observes that he "crawled [before Kurtz] as much as the veriest savage of them all" (86). Servility, he seems to suggest, is an un-European and therefore deeply unappealing trait; to be a decent man is to stand on one's own. Kurtz, the "lone white man turning his back . . . setting his face towards the depths of the wilderness" (60), again problematizes this picture. A man with the courage to face down his existential angst, he is an object of Marlow's appreciation (he, too, had "struggled with himself" (94). However, Kurtz's turning to the "wilderness" and away from the Enlightened, rational individual is so disturbing to Marlow as to call into question whether solidarity is desirable or even possible: "No eloquence could have been so withering to one's belief in mankind as his final burst of sincerity" (94). Conrad concludes with the figure of Kurtz's fiancée, whose veneration of Kurtz is telling: "'What a loss to me—to us!'—she corrected herself with beautiful generosity; then added in a murmur, 'To the world'" (104). There is more than a hint of irony to Marlow's recall here; her world is a narrow one and community an afterthought, so abstract ("'the world'") as to be meaningless. The final words Marlow invents for Kurtz—his fiancée's name—are similarly trite. His real epitaph, "'The horror! The horror!'" (97), is however a genuine and violent expression of collective as well as individual suffering. They show that for all Conrad is preoccupied with the self, appeals to solidarity are never far behind.

Their battle for predominance and their contradictory—one might charitably argue dialectical—relationship continues to play out in *The End of the Tether*. Whalley's longing for companionship, whether in the form of his daughter, his comrade Van Wyk, or shipmates from his younger days, exists alongside an aged cynicism. As Andrew Bennett has shown, the Captain's blindness serves as a metaphor for this struggle: "it puts the sailor apart at the same time that it aligns him with all of humanity: the desire to see for the seaman makes him both exemplary and unique" (139). But Bennett, accepting like Said the autobiographical element to Conrad's work, also looks to explore Conrad's "literary blindness." The author, in other words, is in existential dialogue with the reader through his characters; Conrad is himself looking for answers, about self, solidarity, difference, community.

In *'Narcissus,'* he comes closest to finding them. Here, the sailors share much in common with the imperfect communities of Conrad's previous tales:

> Men in black jackets and stand-up collars, mixed with men barefooted, bare-armed, with coloured shirts open on hairy chests, pushed against one another in the middle of the forecastle. The group swayed, reeled, turning upon itself with the motion of a scrimmage, in a haze of tobacco smoke. All were speaking together, swearing at every second word. (*'Narcissus'* 19)

Russian Finns, Scandinavians, Irish, and British move together as one, their degree of difference subsumed by a shared purpose in sailing the *Narcissus*. The arrival of Wait, and his immediate assertion of belonging, therefore represents a great communal rupture; his illness is described by one as an "infernal spell which that casual St. Kitt's nigger had cast upon our guileless manhood!" (Conrad, *Narcissus* 54). And yet his presence also serves to reify that community of sailors. In becoming ill, he enables the very solidarity that his race in this context threatens: the visits he receives, in which the crew "seemed to leave behind a little of [their] own vitality, surrender some of [their] own strength," create "the indestructible thing!"—solidarity—for which, in the preface, Conrad declares to be looking for himself (165). On Jimmy's death, this limited solidarity, contradictory and constantly in competition with men's cynical calculations and doubts, is washed away with his body: "a common bond was gone; the strong, effective and respectable bond of a sentimental lie" (173).

At the heart of Conrad's work is the "conflict between organic solidarity and skeptical individualism" (Eagleton 134). This is both a strength and a weakness. In taking seriously "disintegrative individualism," Conrad perhaps tries to make the case for "human solidarity" stronger, Eagleton argues (134-135). However, his conviction toward the individual is so pervasive, even in his expressions of ideal communities, that the reader might be left wondering whether "he who forms a tie" is not "lost" after all. Ursula Lord is right, therefore, to cast the question as "solitude *versus* solidarity" [emphasis mine]; both do battle across novels, novellas, short stories, and even letters—and leave contradictions in their wake. Again, it is in *'Narcissus'* where the battle almost reaches a state of truce. Christensen correctly argues that through the black body of Wait, Conrad arrives at a community with an "imaginary consistency" (28); the individual marked out by his difference—his race—"enables an ideal community to be imagined" while "[preventing] the attainment of such a community" (35). The individual, then, tends to prevail in Conrad—even if he and his characters imagine and wish it to be otherwise.

Postcoloniality, 'Made to the Measure'

Conrad's difficulty in realizing community among his characters arises largely, in postcolonial phraseology, from his "pseudo-humanism." This phrase is taken from Aimé Césaire's *Discourse on Colonialism*, in which he famously compares the Nazi horror in Europe to the suffering that Europe itself visited on the global south through colonialism. The implication here is not that European fascism is dangerous to so-called enlightened humanism but that it is this very humanism from which Nazism springs: "At the end of formal humanism and philosophic renunciation, there is Hitler" (Césaire 37). Although Césaire means by this to attack a certain strand of European, and especially French, intellectual—the passivity of "metaphysical [ethnographers]" and "chattering [Nietzscheans]" like Lévi-Strauss and Foucault (Ciccariello-Maher, 146)—his criticism can apply equally to artists and authors. One can avoid comparing Conrad to Hitler while maintaining Césaire's argument that "no one colonizes innocently" (39). This leaves no room for the likes of Marlow. Conrad's sympathetic colonizer is for

Césaire a misnomer, for whom there can be no worthy conception of solidarity at all.

The unique environment of the *Narcissus*, with its power weighted in so many different directions, allows for a more explicit articulation of the pseudo-humanist position than solely along the River Congo. As in *Heart of Darkness*, the author simultaneously affirms and denies an imperial subject's complete humanity. Creighton certainly speaks for Conrad when he remarks of Wait, "the man's a man if he is black" (137). But a fuller picture is provided by the character Donkin: "watching the end of that hateful nigger, [he] felt the anguishing grasp of a great sorrow of his heart at the thought that he himself, some day, would have to go through it all—just like this—perhaps!" (Conrad, *'Narcissus'* 171). This is a perfect illustration of Achebe's criticism of *Heart of Darkness*. What troubles the white crew is precisely Wait's humanness and the fear that they might one day suffer as he has. And yet Wait is not human as the white crew are human. Yes, he is marked by his difference—crudely cast as a "hateful nigger"—but he is also unequal in that his purpose is an instrumentalizing one; his suffering is not important in and of itself, but only in so far as it foreshadows the suffering of certain privileged others. This mirrors the way in which his character is used as a tool in the making and unmaking of an ideal Conradian community.

As Gayatri Chakravorty Spivak has pointed out, Conrad's hoped-for solidarity is complicated due to his working in binaries. Her own contention that "[to] be human is to be intended toward the other" (Spivak 73) in fact reads like Conrad's "feeling of unavoidable solidarity" (*'Narcissus'* 14). Spivak's solidarities are however finely distinguished from *collectivities*, which contain both progressive and regressive potential, and *planetarities*, more utopian and inclusive social forms belonging to the future. *Heart of Darkness*, she finds, is a written representation of dichotomous collectivities, of European civilization and African savagery. It is true that the collectivities share in humanity, but there is no presumption of equality—surely a key component of solidarity. In other words, Conrad's is an unequal, or pseudo-, humanism, deficient in its analysis of difference. This applies to gender as it does race: *Heart of Darkness*, notes Nina Pelikan Strauss, "[discloses] less the human Id . . . than a certain kind of male self-mystification," which "cannot be affirmed in a humanist criticism without embarrassment to both men and women" (135).

The crux of these analyses is not that the universal—the "human"—is itself a reactionary concept, but rather that it is falsely laid claim to by Conrad. The author's progressive aspiration to fraternity retreats into naked individualism when he essentializes and instrumentalizes his characters of color. Jacques Derrida, in his study of friendship and fraternity, finds there to be multiple models of such relationships: a "secret-private-invisible-illegible-apolitical" friendship that recognizes the differing experiences of men and women, white and black; and a "manifest-public-testimonial-political" friendship that works through the law and, therefore, must necessarily deny difference and assert universalist principles (277). Their relationship is however dialectical rather than adversarial, since both are contingent on human equality. Conrad's fatal flaw is in denying this equality, in stressing a humanity of the similar-but-different, of the human-but-lesser. In this equation, fraternity, community, and solidarity are unrealizable. As Césaire charged of Roger Caillois, Conrad imagines a humanism of sorts but not a "true humanism—a humanism made to the measure of the world" (73). Césaire's humanism is driven by an appreciation for what Jane Hiddleston calls "our universal vulnerability [and] mutual respect . . . [and] the desire to celebrate humanity as the sharing of differences" (102). Conrad's humanism, on the other hand, treats difference as a threat to the very formation of a political and human community. It is therefore "narrow and fragmentary, incomplete and biased"—as Césaire writes of the philosophy of European 'pseudo-humanism' (77).

Works Cited

Achebe, Chinua. "An Image of Africa." *The Massachusetts Review* 18.4 (1977): 782-94. Print.

Bennett, Andrew. "Joseph Conrad's Blindness." *Ignorance: Literature and Agnoiology*. Manchester, UK: Manchester UP, 2009. 132-153. Print.

Césaire, Aimé. *Discourse on Colonialism*. Trans. Joan Pinkham. New York: MR, 1972.

Christensen, Tim. "Racial Fantasy in Joseph Conrad's *Nigger of the 'Narcissus.'*" *ARIEL: A Review of International English Literature* 37.1 (2006): 27-43. Print.

Ciccariello-Maher, George. "European Intellectuals and the Colonial Difference: Césaire and Fanon beyond Sartre and Foucault." *Race after Sartre: Antiracism, Africana Existentialism, Postcolonialism*. Ed. Jonathan Judaken. Albany: State U of New York, 2008. 129-154. Print.

Conrad, Joseph, R. B. Cunninghame Graham, & Cedric Thomas Watts. *Joseph Conrad's Letters to R.B. Cunninghame Graham*. London: Cambridge UP, 1969. Print.

Conrad, Joseph. Foreword. *Turgenev: A Study*. Ed. Edward Garnett. London: W. Collins Sons, 1917. v-x. Print.

_____. *Heart of Darkness: And Other Stories*. Ware, UK: Wordsworth Editions, 1999. Print.

_____. *Prefaces to His Works: With an Introd. Essay by Edward Garnett and a Biogr. Note on His Father by David Garnett*. Freeport, NY: Haskell House Publishers, 1971. Print.

_____. *The Nigger of the 'Narcissus.'* Garden City, NY: Doubleday, 1914. Print.

_____. *Victory*. New York: Penguin, 1996. Print.

Cooper, Frederick. *Colonialism in Question: Theory, Knowledge, History*. Berkeley: U of California P, 2005. Print.

Derrida, Jacques. *Politics of Friendship*. London: Verso, 1997. Print.

Eagleton, Terry. *Criticism and Ideology: A Study in Marxist Literary Theory*. London: NLB, 1976. Print.

Fleishman, Avrom. *Conrad's Politics: Community and Anarchy in the Fiction of Joseph Conrad*. Baltimore: Johns Hopkins, 1967. Print.

Gorra, Michael Edward. Introduction. *The Portable Conrad*. By Joseph Conrad. New York: Penguin, 2007. ix-xlii. Print.

Hiddleston, Jane. "Aimé Césaire and Postcolonial Humanism." *The Modern Language Review* 105.1 (2010): 87-102. Print.

Lord, Ursula. *Solitude versus Solidarity in the Novels of Joseph Conrad: Political and Epistemological Implications of Narrative Innovation.* Montréal: McGill-Queen's UP, 1998. Print.

Mamdani, Mahmood. *Citizen and Subject: Contemporary Africa and the Legacy of Late Colonialism.* Princeton, NJ: Princeton UP, 1996. Print.

Said, Edward W. "The Claims of Individuality." *The Edward Said Reader.* Ed. Moustafa Bayoumi & Andrew Rubin. London: Granta, 2001. 3-13. Print.

——————. *Culture and Imperialism.* London: Vintage, 1994. Print.

——————. *Joseph Conrad and the Fiction of Autobiography.* New York: Columbia UP, 2008. Print.

Spivak, Gayatri Chakravorty. *Death of a Discipline.* New York: Columbine UP, 2003. Print.

Straus, Nina Pelikan. "The Exclusion of the Intended from Secret Sharing in Conrad's "Heart of Darkness." *NOVEL: A Forum on Fiction* 20.2 (1987): 123-37. Print.

CRITICAL READINGS

Misogyny or Artistry? Conrad's Revisions of Two Heroines, from Serial to First Edition
Lydia Craig

Accusations of misogyny have pursued Joseph Conrad's works since their publication. Conrad's critics fault descriptions and dialogue seemingly expressing his deep personal distrust of women, at best interpreted as chivalrous condescension and, at worst, blatant sexism as demonstrated by his famous narrator Charles Marlow. I argue that Conrad's literary depictions of male and female interaction relates to his interest in the dramatic tension resulting from failed sexual and romantic encounters between two distinct, opposing personalities. In order to support my claim that Conrad equally prioritized and even more sympathetically portrayed his female characters, I will examine two later novels, *Nostromo: A Tale of the Seaboard* (1904) [hereafter *Nostromo*] and *The Secret Agent: A Simple Tale* [hereafter *The Secret Agent*] (1907) that demonstrate significant revisions to the heroines' personalities and appearance in the serials, presenting previously overlooked textual evidence of Conrad's literary attitudes towards both genders. I contend that these revisions work to highlight the ways in which a female character either affects or fails to affect male characters in the novel, clarifying the harm caused to a woman's domestic happiness by male blindness in *Nostromo* and justifying a woman's tragic belief in two men's devotion in *The Secret Agent*.

Women Motivating Men
Critical reception to Conrad's famous character Marlow typifies the interpretive confusion caused by Conrad's general portrayals of men and women and these characters' conflicting statements regarding each other. Instead of being the musings of a misogynist as some critics argue, Marlow's extremely vocal perspectives on the female sex in works such as *Heart of Darkness* (1899) and *Chance* (1913) may, in fact, reflect the nineteenth century's sharp divide between

men and women in regards to life experience and moral perspective, a divide that Conrad not only realizes, but commonly exploits to create friction within his plots.[1] Approaching the subject from a feminist perspective, Nina Pelikan Straus insists that Marlow's racist and sexist complicity in Kurtz's imperialist world prompts him to ignore his "masculinist vulnerability" (186). John G. Peters claims that instead of reiterating "dominant nineteenth-century cultural ideas about women," Marlow seeks refuge in the sheltered, delusional female perspective as a refreshing alternative to the imperialist project's harsh masculine truths that he must confront as a man (88-93). While Gordon W. Thompson agrees that throughout both early and late works, Conrad deliberately separates male and female characters into two distinct and separate worlds, he believes Conrad's purpose is to explore human themes:

> Conrad wanted his readers to take seriously 'the claims of the ideal'—the possibility of transcendent truth—and he usually embodied this possibility in stereotyped female characters; Conrad wanted his readers to take equally seriously the possibility that this world is without higher meaning and all claims of the ideal are illusions—and this possibility is played out in the fates of his male characters. (444-445)

Incorporating Thompson's concept of "the possibility of transcendent truth" into my argument, I assert that women function in Conrad's novels as embodied symbols of what should be; what cannot be due to human folly; and, therefore, the vital thing that is impossible for male characters to grasp. Though the specific "what" changes across the novels, the disjuncture between the male and female characters not only strikingly conveys Conrad's perception of the human failure to connect, but also accurately reflects, on a global scale, his awareness of the late nineteenth century's gendered spheres.

In order to create dramatic tension, Conrad frequently relies on what Lissa Schneider has termed his particular understanding of "Aristotelian strictures of drama . . . the need for the representation of theme, fall, catastrophe, denouement" (49-50), which in his works derives from the reaction to or influence of female characters on males. Women represent the draw, the impetus that motivates already flawed male characters to stray out of their own sphere and directionally progress either towards them or away from them. Writing to William Blackwood in 1897, Conrad outlined a tentative, ultimately abandoned plot for *The Rescue* (1820), explaining his understanding of how descriptions of romantic interactions should function in his narrative to mediate between characters and reader:

> ... all the effect must be produced in the working out—in the manner of telling. . . . The human interest of the tale is in the contact of Lingard the simple, masterful, imaginative adventurer with a type of civilized woman—a complex type ... Lingard ... not the woman—is the principal personage. That's why all the first part is given up to the presentation of his personality. It illustrates the method I intend to follow. I aim at stimulating vision in the reader. If after reading the *part 1st* you don't see my man then I've absolutely failed and must begin again—or leave the thing alone. (Conrad, *The Collected Letters*, 381)[2]

First, when reading a romantic interaction between genders, the reader must be stimulated by the personality contrast resulting from a clash of "types." In Conrad's hypothetical instance, the woman, despite not being the main character, is nevertheless fully formed and interesting in her own right, "a complex type." Secondly, the reader must be provided with a full "presentation" of these characters prior to seeing this clash, or in Conrad's opinion, the whole novel fails. The third fact suggested by Conrad's methodology is the importance of stimulating imaginative "vision" through description, without which his characters are literally invisible to the reader.

Mrs. Gould's Revenge on the Silver

Conrad cared deeply about the revision process, treating each first edition as a second opportunity to write a more artistic draft for a "more selective, scrutinizing, and long-term readership" than that of the "ephemeral" serial publication (Watts 101).[3] This revision often adjusted the power dynamics between male and female characters in accordance with his contextual vision of what that precise relationship should symbolically accomplish. Suffering from a breakdown and chronic writer's block, Conrad struggled to complete *Nostromo* throughout its serialization between January 29 and October 7, 1904 in the British periodical *T.P.'s Weekly*. Accordingly, as Frederick R. Karl concludes, "the shortened ending of the serial is a direct result of the need to forego artistic considerations in favor of a quick ending" (Karl 141). However, when revising the manuscript for the first British edition published in 1904 by *Harper & Bros*, Conrad added several scenes and expanded the ending in addition to other revisions, many of which represent significant changes to the persona and actions of the main female character, the unhappily married Mrs. Emilia Gould.

Set on the eve of the Sulaco revolution in the fictional South American country of Costaguana, the politics of the story hinge around the circumstance that the Englishman Charles Gould, owner of the San Tomé mine, has allowed his passion for silver to exceed his love for his excellent wife. An admirable specimen of a domestic goddess, Mrs. Gould epitomizes attractiveness and courtesy with her "little figure" further minimized by the "heavy mass of her hair and the long train of her gown" (Conrad, *Nostromo*, First ed. 164). By using the patronymic "Gould" (pronounced "gold"), Conrad stresses her superior, but disregarded worth in contrast to the silver. Meanwhile, madly in love with the fascinating Antonia Avellanos, French revolutionary and journalist Martin Decoud pursues political ambitions in Costaguana, proclaiming his romantic "passion" to be his chief motivation in supporting independence (169). Flaunting his passionate love as a stark contrast to her own situation, Decoud uses Mrs. Gould's awareness of her rivalry with the silver mine to enlist her aid in his *coup d'etat*, which involves stealing her husband's silver and bearing it away in a ship with the heroic sailor Nostromo as accomplice:

> "Mrs. Gould, are you aware to what point he has idealized the existence, the worth, the meaning of the San Tomé mine? Are you aware of it?" He must have known what he was talking about. The effect he expected was produced. Mrs. Gould, ready to take fire,

gave it up suddenly with a low little sound that resembled a moan. (Conrad, *Nostromo*, First ed. 169)

Consequently, she colludes in Decoud's theft to regain her husband's affection, making her crime one of passion rather than of politics.

While Mrs. Gould's marital situation never satisfactorily resolves itself, her portrayal in the first edition increases her decisiveness and strength of character. In the serial, Mrs. Gould deduces that Nostromo is involved with the younger of two local sisters from family friend Dr. Monyghan's typically caustic remark that he fancies Linda "would not be sorry" to see Giselle married (Conrad, *Nostromo* 4: 455). Concerned for "that child," she insists that "Nostromo must be spoken to!" and tells the doctor to "tell him to come and see me" (4: 455). When the doctor expresses doubt that Nostromo would comply with Mrs. Gould's order, she immediately retreats, seeks refuge in domesticity, and renounces future involvement:

> "No, no! I forbid you!" Mrs. Gould cried hastily. "I-I think I'll send for the girls—or for the father himself."
> "It would be much better. Old Viola shall know how to take care of his honour." Mrs. Gould meditated. She had the fate of these girls very much at heart. But to-morrow . . . would be very full, with a two-o'clock dinner party. . . .
> "I shall ask the Garibaldino [Linda's father] to come and see me the day after," she thought to herself. . . . Perhaps the best thing would be to say nothing at all to anybody. (Conrad, *Nostromo* 4: 455)

This passage has been drastically emended in the first edition to portray Mrs. Gould in a bolder, more maternal light, confident in her own ability to tactfully defuse a bad situation.

> "I feel I have a duty towards these girls," said Mrs. Gould, uneasily. "Is Nostromo in Sulaco now?"
> "He is, since last Sunday."
> "He ought to be spoken to—at once."
> "Who will dare speak to him? . . ."

> "I can. I will," Mrs. Gould declared. "A word will be enough for a man like Nostromo . . . He must put an end to all this by marrying Linda at once," pronounced the first lady of Sulaco with immense decision. (Conrad, *Nostromo*, First ed. 409-10)

Mrs. Gould braves unpleasantness to protect the girls from public censure, appealing to Nostromo's gallantry by using her social prominence and femininity, instead of pleading social duties to avoid conflict as her character did in the serial.

Furthermore, by giving Mrs. Gould a lengthy internal dialogue in the first edition, Conrad clarifies the reasons for her fundamental estrangement from Charles Gould and adds two new components, self-awareness and the specter of adultery. While Mrs. Gould has formerly supported Charles's business interests and maintained his home, his physical absence from the domestic sphere has resulted in her childlessness and inability to fully experience womanhood, a thought that causes her "a great wave of loneliness." She reflects with pathetic clarity on her husband's emotional neglect: "And it came into her mind, too, that no one would ever ask her with solicitude what she was thinking of. No one. No one, but perhaps the man who had just gone away. No; no one who could be answered with careless sincerity in the ideal perfection of confidence" (Conrad, *Nostromo*, First ed. 411). Dr. Monyghan being the "man" in question, Mrs. Gould apparently has perceived his silent adoration and craves the human companionship it could provide, though she clings to her morality. Having now concocted her own acute rationale as to why her marriage has failed, her husband's "material interests" (412), she realizes her great mistake has been marrying an individual motivated and inspired by something other than herself, leaving her with "no one."

Mrs. Gould's vindictive relationship with the silver intensifies in the first edition, which parallels her physical barrenness with the fruits of her husband's labor in his late father's mine, a site of business and patriarchal heritage. She twice takes revenge, first helping Decoud steal the silver and then guaranteeing that its whereabouts remain unknown. In the serial, she merely decides not to ask a dying

Nostromo where it is: "'Oh, no! No!' exclaimed Mrs. Gould, in a low voice. 'Isn't it lost and done with? Isn't there enough treasure without it to make everybody in the world miserable?'" (*Nostromo* 4: 456). However, in the first edition, she internalizes her extreme surprise at its mention before making the same exclamation aloud: "Frankness personified, she remembered with an exaggerated horror that for the first and last time of her life she had concealed the truth from her husband about that very silver. She had been corrupted by her fears at that time, and she had never forgiven herself" (*Nostromo*, First ed. 439). More aware of her motivations, Mrs. Gould suffers extreme, if slightly insincere guilt, before maintaining her fixed purpose. Beside Nostromo's bed in the serial version, she confides, "I, too, have been guilty of deception about that very silver," and rejects his offer to reveal its location by saying, "No, Capataz [. . .] Let it be lost forever" (*Nostromo* 4: 457). Conrad changes her confession in the first edition to the more passionate declaration, "I, too, have hated the idea of that silver from the bottom of my heart," and lengthens her decisive rejection of the treasure: "No, Capataz. No one misses it now. Let it be lost for ever" (*Nostromo*, First ed. 442). In speaking for her husband, who doubtless "misses" the silver very much, Mrs. Gould specifically deprives Charles of any agency over his mine's produce, just as he has deprived her body of children.

Finally, delicate but meaningful changes to the scene between Nostromo's distraught lover Giselle and Mrs. Gould depict the latter as utterly and consciously miserable, reawakening the fearful temptation of future adultery. In the serial Mrs. Gould attempts to comfort Giselle, saying, "Console yourself, child. Very soon he would have forgotten you, living by his side, for his treasure," a statement described as "the first and only movement of cynical bitterness in her life" (*Nostromo* 4: 457). In the first edition, this is a "moment," not a "movement," which is "worthy of Dr. Monygham himself" (*Nostromo*, First ed. 443). Like him, Mrs. Gould has been unable to achieve the vital human connection to the opposite sex and projects her own misery onto Giselle's situation. An additional exchange takes place between the women:

"Console yourself, child. Very soon he would have forgotten you for his treasure."
"*Señora*, he loved me. He loved me," Giselle whispered despairingly. "He loved me as no one had ever been loved before."
"I have been loved too," Mrs. Gould said in a severe tone.
Giselle clung to her convulsively. "Oh, *señora*, but you shall live adored to the end of your life," she sobbed out. Mrs. Gould kept an unbroken silence till the carriage arrived. (*Nostromo*, First ed. 443)

Considering Mrs. Gould's acknowledgement of her connection with Dr. Monygham in the first edition, her silence now contains added significance. Giselle's statement drives home the cold reality of her domestic debacle. The girl may mistakenly suppose that Mrs. Gould, wealthy and powerful, is adored by her husband, but Mrs. Gould knows this to be untrue. Simultaneously, knowing Monygham's feelings for her, Mrs. Gould cannot deny that she will "live adored," but morally her adorer is the wrong man with which to form that intimate human connection.

Conrad's drastic development of Mrs. Gould's character in *Nostromo*'s first edition suggests that he perceives her role to be central to the novel's symbolic significance and overall meaning. As a wife ignored by a materialistic husband, her unhappy domestic situation spills over into the masculine world of commerce, war, and politics, resulting in powerful ramifications for everyone involved in the Sulaco revolution. Given greater dignity, self-awareness, and effective agency in the first edition, Mrs. Gould's actions act as a fatal, but sympathetic transgression of gendered boundaries, a warning to males treating females as no more than passive domestic goddesses removed from the public sphere of action and intrigue.

Winnie's Sexual Power, Agency, and "Madness"

Written directly after *Nostromo*, *The Secret Agent* revisits the dangers of female retaliation against male cruelty and neglect, which drive women to commit acts considered to be foreign to social concepts of femininity.[4] Serialized in the American weekly magazine *Ridgway's* from October 6 to December 16, 1906, Methuen & Co published the first edition in 1907, which contains substantial revisions to the character Winnie Verloc's looks and behavior in the first edition. These demonstrate how men in her life fatally misinterpret her moral and companionate worth, as she is first taken for granted by an unperceptive, troubled husband, Adolf Verloc, and then perceived by her suitor Comrade Tom Ossipon to be a mad, entrapping black widow type, punished and doomed because she retaliates against her husband after he causes her mentally challenged brother's death and tries to utilize her sexual power to avoid paying for her crime. In radically altering Winnie Verloc's physical description in *The Secret Agent* from that of drudge to bombshell, Conrad does not intend to endow her with more agency, unlike Mrs. Gould, but rather to make her effect on the male characters more believable.

Christened "Minnie" in the serial, she is far from functioning as "the possibility of transcendent truth" to her politically involved husband, Adolf Verloc. She is described in the serial as "young yet, of rounded form, very tidy about the hair, as also steady-eyed like her husband" (*Ridgway's* 1.1: 12). Though her husband is attracted to her, her attention to her disabled brother Steeve impedes their relationship. Their growing disconnection disturbs Verloc, who as a secret agent of an anarchical group occupies a markedly different sphere from his domestically minded wife. Winnie depresses him with her calm ignorance of and indifference to the internal struggles waging within him, which is portrayed figuratively through an incident in their bedroom. As Verloc gazes out into the night while she attends to her brother downstairs, he starts when the reflection of Mr. Vladimir's face, his new superior who has urged him to commit a crime, is suddenly and imperfectly irradiated against the pane:

> Discomposed and speechless with the apprehension of more such visions, he beheld his wife re-enter the room and get into bed in a calm, business-like manner which made him feel hopelessly lonely in the world. Mrs. Verloc expressed her surprise at seeing him up yet. (*Ridgway's* 1.4: 51)

As Minnie rambles on, the sentence "Mr. Verloc made no comment" is repeated twice at intervals, and then in answer to Minnie's question whether she should put out the light, the narrative equates the useless candle with the ineffectuality of Verloc seeking consolation from his wife regarding his problems: "the dreary conviction that there was no sleep for him held Mr. Verloc mute and hopelessly inert in his fear of darkness. He made a great effort. 'Yes. Put it out,' he said at last in a hollow tone" (*Ridgway's* 1.4: 51).

In the first edition, dowdy Minnie is transformed into attentive, attractive "Winnie," whose decidedly feminine, but inaccessible form behind the counter at her husband's pornography store comically disconcerts the customers:

> Sometimes it was Mrs Verloc who would appear at the call of the cracked bell. Winnie Verloc was a young woman with a full bust, in a tight bodice, and with broad hips. Her hair was very tidy. Steady-eyed like her husband, she preserved an air of unfathomable indifference behind the rampart of the counter. (Conrad, *Secret Agent*, First ed. 5)

While these strangers note, but cannot enjoy her charms, her husband fails to take advantage of his wife's sensuality, ignoring her concern for him in an added paragraph after the candle scene. When Winnie returns from looking after her brother (renamed "Stevie" instead of "Steeve" in the first edition), she attempts to connect with her husband:

> . . . turning towards her recumbent husband, [Mrs. Verloc] raised herself on her elbow, and hung over him in her anxiety that he should believe Stevie to be a useful member of the family. That ardour of protecting compassion . . . tinged her sallow cheeks with a faint dusky blush, made her big eyes gleam under the dark lids. Mrs Verloc then looked younger; she looked as young as Winnie used to look . . . Mr Verloc's anxieties had prevented him from attaching any sense to what his wife was saying. It was as if her voice was talking on the other side of a very thick wall. It was her aspect that recalled him to himself. (Conrad, *Secret Agent*, First ed. 58)

Now instead of ignoring her husband and causing his feelings of isolation, Winnie reaches out, cheeks flushing and eyes glowing, physical changes that recall her virginal youth, but promise immediate marital access. If Mr. Verloc could only perceive her efforts to bridge the gap between them, they could connect both intellectually and sexually, but he somehow cannot manage it due to the vastly different subjects each prefers to discuss.

Besides influencing the perception of how Verloc's character interacts with Mrs. Verloc, whether she is attractive or not effects how the reader interprets her ill-fated romance with the "big and muscular" Comrade Ossipon, Verloc's fellow anarchist (Conrad, *Secret Agent*, First ed. 63). Her sexuality, a potentially positive force before murdering Verloc, is transfigured by the act into something loathsome and unspeakable through many extended moments in the final two chapters. In the serial, Comrade Ossipon is motivated by Minnie's wealth, not her sexual appeal. Believing Verloc died in the blast, instead of Winnie's brother, he immediately has designs on the rich widow: "[He] paused abruptly and muttered to himself, 'I wonder what that woman will do now,' and fell into thought" (*Ridgway's* 1.5: 22). The Professor, a cynical explosives expert who crafted Verloc's bomb, suddenly breaks in on his thought a short time afterwards by saying "with sedate scorn": "Fasten yourself upon the woman for all she's worth" (1.5: 23). Consequently waiting on the street near her shop, Ossipon is led by "hope, by that instinct which, like the call of a vocation, impelled him to the conquest of women possessed of a little cash" (1.11: 45). A mercenary rogue "used to such situations" as placing his arm around a woman in need of "support" (1.11: 45), his wooing appears brusque and insincere. His claim "I've been devoted to you from the time I first set eyes on your face. It was only your husband" (1.11: 45-6) and her response "Love! I've never loved him. Don't you understand, it was for the boy" (1.11: 47) seem both premature and inexplicable despite his greed and her desperation. Why Minnie believes him to be so madly in love with her appears mysterious and the rapid pace allows for no nuance. As soon as Ossipon sees Verloc's body, he plans his escape, taking her pocketbook with him once she has boarded the train.

Comrade Ossipon's initial interaction with Winnie in the first edition hardly improves the reader's opinion of his character, but his sin is less mercenary in nature—he seizes on a strange woman reeling about who may be sexually amenable for cash, or out of drunkenness, and discovers her to be Winnie. His first advance, "I've thought of you too often lately not to recognize you anywhere, at any time. I've always thought of you--ever since I first set eyes on you" appears more believable considering his clear sexual attraction to her, and they have a much longer conversation. Back at the house, Ossipon discovers Verloc's murdered corpse. Horrified, he attempts to flee but becomes trapped in the darkened room due to the proximity of a suspicious policeman. In a gruesome parody of the sexual act, Winnie physically prevents him from abandoning her:

> He ceased to struggle; she never let him go. Her hands had locked themselves with an inseparable twist of fingers on his robust back. While the footsteps approached, they breathed quickly, breast to breast, with hard, laboured breaths, as if theirs had been the attitude of a deadly struggle, while, in fact, it was the attitude of deadly fear. (Conrad, *Secret Agent*, First ed. 286)

Entangling herself around him as she does, Winnie has assumed temptress-like proportions: "He positively saw snakes now. He saw the woman twined round him like a snake, not to be shaken off. She was not deadly. She was death itself—the companion of life" (Conrad, *Secret Agent*, First ed. 291). Her panic, terror of the gallows, and physical groping of Ossipon as a lifeline vividly illustrate his rising distaste and fear of being trapped by what he perceives as criminal, lethal physicality instead of sexual availability, a trade Winnie offers him in "shamefaced accents" (289) in return for protection from the law.

From wondering before seeing the murdered corpse what marital horrors have led Winnie to hate her husband and seek another, Ossipon now concludes after seeing Verloc's body that her madness is hereditary. By murdering her husband, Winnie has become a killer, an identity incompatible with that of a respectable, desirable woman, much less a wife, and utterly unfathomable except in scientific terms: "He gazed scientifically. He gazed at her cheeks, at her nose, at her eyes, at her ears . . . Bad! . . . Fatal! Mrs Verloc's pale lips parting, slightly relaxed under his passionately attentive gaze, he gazed also at her teeth . . . Not a doubt remained . . . a murdering type" (Conrad, *Secret Agent*, First ed. 297). Misinterpreting his intense physical scrutiny as attraction to her body, Winnie fatally lets down her guard. Ossipon steals her pocketbook and abandons her on the train, a betrayal that apparently leads her to commit suicide. Meanwhile, Ossipon returns to his lodgings, staring wide-eyed at the ceiling, and then finally falls asleep "in the sunlight" without being aware of Winnie's fate (301). Once he reads about the death of a mysterious female suicide in the newspaper, however, Ossipon is plunged into emotional and mental turmoil: "He could face no woman. It was ruin. He could neither think, work, sleep, nor eat" (310). Such is the power of the failed male and female connection in this instance, that Ossipon's ability to empathize with what he fancies to have been her emotions before death causes him to experience growing insanity at the thought that he alone knows her story while the rest of the world considers her suicide: *"an impenetrable mystery . . . [an] act of madness or despair"* (307).[5]

In conclusion, critics of Conrad's so-called literary misogyny should consider his dedication to the believability, accessibility, and details of each novel, as evidenced by textual revisions from the serial to the first editions of both *Nostromo* and *The Secret Agent*. These more clearly and precisely detail the personhood, anguish, and retaliatory actions of Mrs. Gould and Winnie Verloc, who, though suppressed, actively resist their victimization. Conrad did not portray his female characters as existing within an ideally constructed social setting, but rather as grappling with legitimate, historically relevant problems resulting from masculine abuse and neglect. While once-active, prominent, and respected men like Nostromo, Decoud, and Charles Gould involve themselves in failed military, commercial, and political schemes and spectacularly fail the women in their lives, Mrs. Gould's successful connivance at the political theft of her husband's silver and refusal to discover its whereabouts afterwards hint at the dangers posed to the "masculine" authority structure by discontented, aggrieved wives who have been denied emotional, intellectual, and sexual companionship. Similarly, Winnie Verloc's act of quiet, murderous rage stands in agreeable contrast to her husband's largely unsuccessful bombing attempt, juxtaposing the radicals, keen on disrupting the very foundations of European civilization, with women, denied agency and taken for granted, who murder spouses and reject domesticity as a result. Conrad's edits reflect his keen perception of gender tensions in changing times and dramatic interest in depicting the actions and fates of such voiceless, if not powerless female characters.

Notes

1. Note that this essay investigates Conrad's attitudes towards females in a literary sense as a writer, not as a private individual.
2. Conrad's excessive description was often misunderstood. A 1907 review of *The Secret Agent* by British literary magazine *The Athenæm* singles out Conrad's plot digressions in both this novel and *Nostromo*; the reviewer seemingly misses the author's artistic motive in excessively foregrounding each novel's "lurid" climax: ". . . we yet find some legitimate ground for regret in the case of this book, and of, say, 'Nostromo' . . . "Now wait there, says the author, in effect, "and I will tell you about a whole lot of things that came before the catastrophe" (*The Athenæm* 368).
3. Though envisioning the novel's overall trajectory, the rapid writing pace demanded by the serial's deadlines often compelled Conrad to sacrifice art to utility.
4. In his 1920 "Author's Note" to *The Secret Agent*, Conrad refers to the novel as "Winnie Verloc's story" though the titular character is supposedly her secret agent anarchist husband (xv). By suddenly and uncharacteristically murdering Verloc in their marital home to regain her freedom, as she expresses it to herself, Winnie reveals herself to be a similar revolutionary in disguise, a "free woman" (First Ed., 251). However, it should be observed that Conrad's "Author's Note" was written seven years after *Chance's* publication in the *New York Herald's* "Women's Pages," a novel centered around its heroine, which attracted a strong female readership and consequently proved to be Conrad's greatest publication success during his lifetime (Simmons vii).

5. Unlike the remorseful Ossipon, the anarchist Professor feels no empathy for the weak and therefore suffers no remorse for either Stevie or Winnie's violent fates.

Works Cited

"The Athenæum (28 September 1907): 361-2." *Joseph Conrad—Contemporary Reviews.* Vol. 2: *Typhoon* to *Under Western Eyes.* Compiled John G. Peters. Eds. Allen H. Simmons, John G. Peters, & J.H. Stape. Cambridge, UK: Cambridge UP, 2012. Print.

Conrad, Joseph. "Author's Note." *The Secret Agent.* London: John Grant, 1925. Print.

—————. *The Collected Letters.* Vol. 1. Ed. Frederick R. Karl & Laurence Davies. Cambridge, UK: Cambridge UP, 1983. Print.

—————. *Nostromo: A Tale of the Seaboard.* Ed. T.P. O'Connor. *T.P.'s Weekly* 4 (Jan 29–Oct 7, 1904). Print.

—————. *Nostromo: A Tale of the Seaboard.* 1904. Ed. Véronique Pauly. New York: Penguin Books, 2007. Print.

—————. *The Secret Agent: a Simple Tale.* Ed. Erman J. Ridgway. *Ridgway's* (Oct 6–Dec 15, 1906). Print.

—————. *The Secret Agent.* London: Methuen & Co., 1907. Print.

Peters, John G. "Joseph Conrad's Heart of Darkness and the World of Western Women." *Studies in Short Fiction* 37.1 (2012): 87-112. *JSTOR.* Web. 1 Dec. 2015.

Schnieder, Lissa. *Conrad's Narratives of Difference: Not Exactly Tales for Boys.* New York: Routledge, 2013. Print.

Simmons, Allan H. & Susan Jones, eds. *Centennial Essays on Joseph Conrad's Chance.* Boston: Brill, 2015. Print.

Straus, Nina Pelikan. "The Exclusion of the Intended from Secret Sharing." *Joseph Conrad.* Ed. Andrew Michael Roberts. London: Routledge, 2014. Print.

Thompson, Gordon W. "Conrad's Women." *Nineteenth-Century Fiction* 32.4 (1978): 442-463. *JSTOR.* Web. 1 Dec. 2015.

Watts, Cedric. "*Nostromo* in *T.P.'s Weekly.*" *Yearbook of Conrad Studies* 3 (2007): 97-113. *JSTOR.* Web. 1 Dec. 2015.

The Conradian Legacy: Portrayal of "Half-made Societies" in Joseph Conrad's *Nostromo* and V. S. Naipaul's *Guerrillas*

Hatice Övgü Tüzün

> What is a conviction? A particular view of our personal advantage either practical or emotional. No one is a patriot for nothing.
> (Decoud in *Nostromo* 189).

In Joseph Conrad's Shadow

According to Edward Said, Joseph Conrad:

> ... is the precursor of Western views of the Third World which one finds in the work of novelists as different as Graham Greene, V.S. Naipaul, and Robert Stone, of theoreticians of imperialism like Hannah Arendt, and of travel writers, filmmakers, and polemicists whose specialty is to deliver the non European world either for analysis and judgment or of satisfying the exotic tastes of European and North American audiences. (xix)

Widely considered to be one of the most prolific and controversial contemporary writers, Vidiadhar Surajprasad Naipaul has occasionally remarked on the great regard he has for Conrad's authority as an interpreter of the so-called "half-made societies." For Naipaul, the term namely refers to economically and politically underdeveloped—often but not necessarily postcolonial—nations that are characterized by mimicry and borrowed culture. Throughout his lengthy career, Naipaul has also drawn on insights Conrad offers about people who live in various areas of the developing world with whom he feels a close affinity.

V. S. Naipaul's fiction has been marked by an enduring interest in examining the significance of cultural identity and politics, particularly in the postcolonial context. Born in Trinidad to East Indian parents, Naipaul grew up in a multicultural environment that allowed him to observe interactions between various culturally and ethnically circumscribed communities that were struggling in the throes of social and political turmoil. The trials and tribulations that have fundamentally shaped West Indian societies are memorably depicted in his first travelogue *The Middle Passage* (1962) as well as in political novels such as *The Mimic Men* (1967) and *Guerrillas* (1975) in which Naipaul critically examines the clash of cultural values and dynamics of underdevelopment in relation to the plight of the postcolonial subject who is desperately trying to find his place in the world.

The extent of Joseph Conrad's formative influence on Naipaul's work has been the subject of heated discussions and needs to be examined in more detail for a better understanding of Naipaul's subjective vision. In his essay entitled "Conrad's Darkness" (1974), V. S. Naipaul observes that:

> Conrad—sixty years before, in the time of a great peace—had been everywhere before me. Not as a man with a cause, but a man offering, as in *Nostromo*, a vision of the world's half-made societies as places which continuously made and unmade themselves, where there was no goal, and where always 'something inherent in the necessities of successful action . . . carried with it the moral degradation of the idea.' Dismal, but deeply felt: a kind of truth and half a consolation. (208)

As this quotation illustrates, Joseph Conrad's shadow looms largely on V. S. Naipaul's work and his vision of the world. Not only does Naipaul strongly identify with Conrad's political skepticism and detachment, he also finds in his predecessor's work a keen and profound understanding of "half-made societies"—his native Trinidad and ancestral homeland of India being two of them. Yet, I would argue that his reading of Conrad is partially flawed in that it is considerably distorted by his own motivations and personal agenda. Whereas Conrad sees the futility of political action as universal phenomena, Naipaul tends to see it as particularly endemic to the developing world. Moreover, he also fails to see that the "half-made societies" in question do not continuously make and unmake themselves in isolation from the rest of the world, and thus he neglects the fundamental role played by the calculations and interventions of imperialist powers in their undoing.

Several critics including Edward Said and Rob Nixon have noted Conrad's seminal influence on Naipaul's professional output and argued that Naipaul's "neo-Conradian" writings perpetuate the colonial discourse that infuses the works of his literary predecessor. Unlike these critics, who observe that Naipaul's vision of the developing world is largely predetermined by the Conradian legacy and the Victorian writing tradition, I would argue that Naipaul's rewriting of Conrad is more nuanced and involves major detours. In other words, although Conrad's life and work resonate with Naipaul on very deep levels, Naipaul articulates his own authentic authorial voice as he travels through space and time. Thus, he does not simply discover Conrad "already in place" in places like Africa or enact conventions of an intertextual tradition that is "dogged by circular, self-confirming tendencies," as Nixon suggests (92). Taking these preliminary observations as my starting point, my aim in this chapter is to trace elements of the Conradian legacy in Naipaul's political fiction through a comparative analysis of Joseph Conrad's *Nostromo* and V. S. Naipaul's *Guerrillas*.

Nostromo and the Politics of Futility

Widely regarded as one of Conrad's most challenging novels, *Nostromo* won considerable critical acclaim following its publication in 1904. Hailed by literary critic Robert Penn Warren as "one of the few mastering visions of our historical moment and our human lot" (32), the book continues to dazzle readers with its diverse set of characters and fascinating plot that fuses elements of romance and adventure with sociohistorical analysis. According to Spittles, reading *Nostromo* is a frustrating yet exciting experience, since "Conrad presents ideas in an elusive way, and in picking our way through them we broaden our own minds" (47). The novel has a confusing narrative structure that does not follow a chronological sequence and events are narrated from multiple points of view. The absence of a stable point of reference as well as the convoluted chronology converge with Conrad's thematic concerns, mainly the idea that history is not linear and progressive but rather circular and repetitive.

The setting of the novel is Costaguana, a fictional South American country that has been the site of constant political upheaval for generations after independence. Although Costaguana is an imaginary republic, the topographical, cultural, historical, and demographic details Conrad provides in its presentation endow it with such a staggering verisimilitude that the place seems as real as any real country on the map. The action of the novel covers events leading up to the secession of Sulaco from Costaguana and the subsequent foundation of the Occidental Republic. The tragic story of the gold-hunting "gringos" whose "souls cannot tear themselves away from their bodies mounting guard over the discovered treasure" (Conrad 5) in the first chapter sets the tone and acts as foreshadowing, since, ultimately, *Nostromo* is about the destruction wrought by the blind pursuit of material interests. No matter what his primary motivation may be, every single character in the book finds his life and action affected to some extent by the silver mine. As Panichas remarks:

> In each of Conrad's fictive characters in *Nostromo* we see an assailable human being, ultimately unable to change one's fate or that of the universe. If anything they give constant witness to the state of disequilibrium; their personal histories lack any real or distinguishing sense of spiritual meaning or ascent. Confusion and, in the end, nullity are the basic qualities of an existence brutally trapped between political tyranny and material greed. (134)

The novel begins at a time of peace after a long period of civil war and the ruthless rule of a dictator named Guzman Bento. Charles Gould, a Costaguanero of English origin and heir to the San Tome Silver Mine, decides to reopen the mine believing that the wealth produced by the mine will bring order and lasting peace to the conflict-ridden country. In doing so, he goes against the dying wish of his father who, having himself suffered immensely due to the heavy taxes imposed on him, urged his son to stay away from

Costaguana and the mine. A sentimental idealist, Gould does not heed his father's warning and instead clings to the belief that the mine can become an instrument of peace and progress. Early in the novel, he remarks that:

> What is wanted here is law, good faith, order, security. Any one can declaim about these things, but I pin my faith to material interests. Only let the material interests once get a firm footing, and they are bound to impose the conditions on which alone they can continue to exist. That's how your money-making is justified here in the face of lawlessness and disorder. It is justified because the security which it demands must be shared with an oppressed people. A better justice will come afterwards. That's your ray of hope. (Conrad 84)

Gould's idealistic (and seemingly altruistic) optimism appeals to his wife Emilia, since she, too, is enamored of the idea of making the world a better place. Yet she is, at the same time, realistic enough to see that in Costaguana, "the constant saving of the country" is but a "puerile and bloodthirsty game of murder played with terrible earnestness by depraved children" (Conrad 49). In order to realize his plans, Gould seeks financial backing from the American silver and steel tycoon Holroyd, a devout Christian as well as a successful businessman who sees God as an influential business partner. With the mine's success, Gould is transformed into "the King of Sulaco", a powerful actor who wields increasing influence in Costaguana politics. It is with this power granted to him by the commercial success of the mine and the backing of "blancos" that Gould becomes part of the plan to install Don Vincente Ribiera as president and thus secure the future of the mine.

The success of this plan is short-lived as Ribiera's rule incites a nativist revolt led by his very own minister of war, General Montero, who rallies popular support with his anti-imperialist rhetoric. While Montero and his brother seem to champion the cause of the downtrodden and the oppressed against aristocrats and representatives of foreign capitalists, they are portrayed as manipulative demagogues seeking their own self-interest. The imminent threat they pose to the existing status quo leads to further political maneuvering on the part of Gould and his allies in Sulaco. One of the most important characters whose involvement shapes the unfolding of events is Martin Decoud, an "idle boulevardier" (Conrad 152) who is infatuated with Antonia, the daughter of the sentimental nationalist Don José Avellanos. A clear-sighted skeptic to the core, Decoud entertains no illusions regarding the history of his native land:

> "Now the whole land is like a treasure-house, and all these people are breaking into it, whilst we are cutting each other's throats. The only thing that keeps them out is mutual jealousy. But they'll come to an agreement some day—and by the time we've settled our quarrels and become decent and honourable, there'll be nothing left for us. It has always been the same. We are a wonderful people, but it has always been our fate to be"—he did not say "robbed," but added, after a pause—"exploited!" (Conrad 174)

It is ironic that Decoud, like other important figures, such as Nostromo and Dr. Monygham, who play important roles in the action, is not motivated by political passion or idealism. Emphasizing the fact that he only has the supreme illusions of a lover and not a patriot, he offers an irremediably bleak and deterministic reading of history that the novel as a whole seems to reinforce. In Decoud's view, the Costaguaneros have always been acted upon rather than been active agents in charge of their destiny, and thus they will eternally be manipulated and exploited by greater powers. Rejecting the sentimental idealism of characters such as Gould or Don Jose Avellanos, he can only envision the repetition of the same historical patterns.

The disheartening indictments of Decoud regarding the nature and future of places like Costaguana are confirmed by yet another character: the peripheral yet critically important Holroyd, who stands out as a mouthpiece for American imperialism. In this oft-quoted and prophetic passage, he observes:

> Now, what is Costaguana? It is the bottomless pit of 10 percent: loans and other fool investments. European capital has been flung

into it with both hands for years. Not ours, though. We in this country know just about enough to keep indoors when it rains. We can sit and watch. Of course, some day we shall step in. We are bound to. (Conrad 76-77)

Although they play integral roles in the eventual founding of the Occidental Republic, Decoud, Nostromo, and Dr. Monygham are not motivated by the desire to genuinely contribute to the secession. Rather, they are driven by their own personal agenda. The fact that their unintentional cooperation eventually brings about the secession shows that chance rather than strategy plays a huge role in the making of history. Even though humans, consciously and unconsciously, play their part in the unfolding of events, there is no sense that whatever agency might be exercised on their part will make a big difference in the wider scheme of things. As Howe succinctly puts it:

> the civil war brings capitalism and capitalism will bring civil war, progress has come out of chaos but it is the kind of progress that is likely to end in chaos. Perhaps the central point of *Nostromo* is that imperialism does indeed bring order, but a false order, an order imposed, an order which destroys the rhythms of native life and gives rise to the fumes of nationalism. (106)

The novel's ending supports Howe's reading and reinforces the belief that enduring peace is not possible. Arguably, this is the central message of the novel and is brilliantly articulated by Dr. Monygham, another skeptic who finds solace in his love for Mrs. Gould:

> "There is no peace and no rest in the development of material interests. They have their law, and their justice. But it is founded on expediency, and is inhuman; it is without rectitude, without the continuity and the force that can be found only in a moral principle. Mrs. Gould, the time approaches when all that the Gould Concession stands for shall weigh as heavily upon the people as the barbarism, cruelty, and misrule of a few years back." (Conrad 511)

All in all, Costaguana is a representative third-world country that has been subject to social, cultural, political colonization, and economic imperialism. Given its prescience and intellectual breadth, *Nostromo* continues to remain relevant and can be read in relation to several other political novels that deal with the plights of developing nations.

Guerillas and the Dynamics of Underdevelopment

The Nobel laureate V. S. Naipaul is best known for his scathing portrayal of third-world societies' internal deficiencies, which he records with meticulous detail in his fiction and nonfiction. Although admired as a prolific writer of great tact and skill, Naipaul's controversial diagnosis of the postcolonial condition as doomed as well as his provocative enunciations on a wide variety of subjects ranging from Islamic fundamentalism to third world underdevelopment have won him numerous detractors over the years. Naipaul is often cited as a prominent contemporary novelist, yet he has also written several travelogues on the Americas, India, Africa, India, and what he calls "converted Muslim societies." It is important to note that his works of fiction and nonfiction are intimately related, since he often draws on subjects he had already written about in his nonfiction when writing his novels.

In this regard, the pessimistic tone of *Guerrillas* can be traced back to *The Middle Passage* (1962), a travel narrative in which Naipaul records his observations on Trinidad, British Guiana, Surinam, Martinique, and Jamaica. Early in the book, he remarks: "How can the history of this West Indian futility be written? . . . The history of the islands can never be satisfactorily told. Brutality is not the only difficulty. History is built around achievement and creation; and nothing was created in the West Indies" (Naipaul, *Guerrillas* 29). It is, indeed, on the basis of this historical outlook that *Guerrillas* stands as a chronicle of West Indian futility. In many ways, the fictional island Naipaul depicts is reminiscent of Costaguana, which was described in *Nostromo* as a country characterized by its "story of oppression, inefficiency, fatuous methods, treachery, and savage brutality" (Conrad 109). However, whereas Conrad's Costaguana is a fictional creation primarily shaped by research, the unnamed island in *Guerrillas* is eerily reminiscent of Naipaul's native Trinidad.

The story Naipaul tells in the novel is also drawn from actual historical events and people. Widely known as Michael X, or Michael Abdul Malik, the notorious left-wing radical Michael de Freitas was executed in Trinidad on May 16, 1975 for his involvement in the killing of Joseph Skerritt, a local, and the visiting Englishwoman Gale Ann Benson. The case, reported by Naipaul for the London *Sunday Times* in 1972, became the basis of this political novel as well as a long essay, "Michael X and the Black Power Killings in Trinidad," published in *The Return of Eva Perón*. By the time of his arrest, Michael X had become a kind of political celebrity with a literary bent and associated with outstanding figures of his time, including Malcolm X, John Lennon, and Leonard Cohen. Lionized by his liberal supporters, he became the British representative of Black Power movement but was eventually forced to leave England due his violent behavior.

Michael X's counterpart in the novel is Jimmy Ahmed, a would-be revolutionary leader who is, in fact, a deeply conflicted and insecure character riddled by both self-hatred and delusions of grandeur. Like Malik, Jimmy was once celebrated by English liberals as a radical activist but was later deported from the country due to allegations of rape and indecent assault. His agricultural commune, the ironically named Thrushcross Range, is subsidized by Sablich's (an old colonial trading company), yet the authorities have come to suspect that it harbors guerrillas. Jimmy reports to Roche, a politically exiled white South African who is currently working as a representative of Sablich's. Lacking a sense of deep commitment to anything, Roche now feels quite adrift and is simply described as "a doer of good works with results that never showed, someone who went among the poor on behalf of his firm and try to organize boys' clubs and sporting events, gave this cup here and offered a gift of cricket equipment there" (Naipaul, *Guerillas* 47).

Roche's girlfriend Jane, on the other hand, is a kind of 'revolutionary' tourist who is drawn to the Caribbean and to the likes of Jimmy Ahmed, believing that "the future of the world was being shaped in places like this, by people like these." Deeply unsatisfied with her life in England, Jane turns to men for self-validation and specifically looks for men who would be doers. We are told that she "lived in the midst of change, repetitive and sterile; it did not disguise the fact of the greater impermanence. But she was privileged: she told herself one day. Security was the basis of her privilege" (Naipaul, *Guerillas* 50-51). Having mistakenly assumed that Roche was a man of action, Jane is now deeply disappointed with his passivity and eventually turns to Jimmy Ahmed for sexual excitement. Yet, her false sense of security and mistaken assumption that she can "play with fire" with impunity eventually leads to her death at the hands of Jimmy Ahmed and her male lover, Bryant.

Jane's "vision of decay piled on decay, putrefaction on putrefaction" (Naipaul, *Guerillas* 71) that seems to characterize the country as a whole, is introduced in the following opening paragraph of the novel:

> The sea smelled of swamp; it barely rippled, had glitter rather than colour; and the heat seemed trapped below the pink haze of bauxite dust from the bauxite loading station. After the market, where refrigerated trailers were unloading; after the rubbish dump burning in the remnant of mangrove swamp, with black carrion corbeaux squatting hunched on fence-posts or hopping about on the ground; after the built-up hillsides; after the new housing estates, rows of unpainted boxes of concrete and corrugated iron already returning to the shanty towns that had been knocked down for this redevelopment; after the naked children playing in the red dust of the straight new avenues, the clothes hanging like rags from backyard lines; after this, the land cleared a little. (Naipaul, *Guerillas* 1)

Images of decay and desolation that pervade this paragraph evoke a general atmosphere of gloom that dominates the novel. The island's bauxite plays a similar role to the silver of the San Tome mine in *Nostromo*. We learn from Roche that the American bauxite company literally "owns the island"; although the island is no longer officially a colony, neither is it truly independent. Like *Nostromo*, *Guerrillas* is full of deceptive and self-deceiving characters who act out their personal dramas against a backdrop of constant political turmoil. The self-contradictions and deficiencies of characters are similarly revealed through a constantly shifting point of view. The famous epigraph of the novel comes from Jimmy Ahmed, who observes: "When everybody wants to fight there's nothing to fight for. Everybody wants to fight his own little war, everybody is a guerilla [sic]." This being the case, the possibility of meaningful collective action that can bring about a better society does not seem to exist. As Zahlan suggests, when "there's nothing to fight for, any hope of effectively transforming the social order is displaced by a prospect of upheaval devoid of ideology and devoid of purpose" (103). There is, admittedly, constant chatter about guerrillas on the streets, on television and the radio, yet there is no real presence of an organized revolutionary group with a coherent political agenda that goes beyond empty slogans. Thus, the name of the novel is heavily ironic and the book as a whole renounces redemptive possibilities of popular violence.

In the absence of social and political stability, the island is portrayed as a place where "everyone lived in a state of suppressed hysteria" and "where ambitions and jealousies no longer had to do with motor-cars or houses or fine things, but with security—money shipped abroad, residence visas for Canada and Australia and the United States" (Naipaul, *Guerillas* 94-95). It is, moreover, poignantly obvious that identities in this country are fundamentally shaped and maimed by the colonial experience and influence. The traumatic and lingering effects of the colonial past are very much apparent in the literary fantasies of Jimmy Ahmed, the brutal rape and murder of Jane, and in the absence of an independent economic and political infrastructure.

Whereas the native people are represented as mute and shadowy figures in *Nostromo*, it is the interaction between the natives and foreign expats that take the center stage in *Guerrillas*. In fact, Naipaul's focus throughout the book is on the deluded Western liberals who flirt with third world radicalism, rather than on larger historical patterns as was the case in Conrad's *Nostromo*. In "The Killings in Trinidad," Naipaul describes Jimmy's real life counterpart Malik as "a fake among fake" (14), playing his part in "a sentimental hoax" (73). Although Jimmy is certainly portrayed as a pathetic "fake," just like Malik in the novel, he remains an object of pity as well as scorn. Naipaul's real wrath, it seems, is reserved for "people who keep up with the revolution as with the theatre", revolutionaries who visit centers of revolution with return tickets.

As one critic suggests, characters in *Guerrillas* "desire an apocalypse; they look to the end of the world for meaning. But the meaning lies in the beginning. Naipaul, on the other hand, is able to read this meaning, and to locate his fictional characters in a master narrative. Naipaul thus asserts his authority over the reader of the novel as well. He wants the reader to read only as he intends, and he is careful that we see how limited are all the characters and how skewed their vision" (Kortenaar 331). It is this narrowness of vision coupled with an absence of self-awareness on the part of all those who are involved that nullifies the possibility of any real or meaningful political action and direction in *Guerrillas*. Devoid of any substantial agency or even vitality, characters in the book seem to be mere puppets that unwittingly act out the scripts assigned to them. By exposing the self-serving delusions and misconceptions of would-be revolutionaries and their Western liberal supporters in this setting, Naipaul asserts his vision of the third world as trapped in a cycle of violence and destruction. Towards the end of the novel, when rioting erupts in the poor quarters of the city, it is an American military intervention that quells the riots to safeguard American "material interests."

In brief, *Guerrillas* offers an unsettlingly bleak vision of yet another underdeveloped postcolonial state that seems to match Decoud's description of Costaguana in *Nostromo*:

> Imagine an atmosphere of opera-bouffe in which all the comic business of stage statesmen, brigands, etc., etc., all their farcical stealing, intriguing, and stabbing is done in dead earnest. It is screamingly funny, the blood flows all the time, and the actors believe themselves to be influencing the fate of the universe (Naipaul, *Guerrillas* 152).

Neither Conrad nor Naipaul would endorse the seemingly lighthearted sarcasm of Decoud, who perhaps resorts to dark humor as a coping mechanism. However, as the prevalent air of doom and gloom in both *Nostromo* and *Guerrillas* illustrates, both writers cast a highly critical eye on the political life of representative postcolonial states and do not seem to envision a way out of this vicious cycle.

The Conradian Legacy

Despite Naipaul's consistent efforts to promote an image of himself as a truthful chronicler of third-world decrepitude, his authority has often been challenged, especially by postcolonial critics who saw in his work confirmation and extension of Western discourses on the third world. As mentioned before, some critics have further suggested that Naipaul's desire to be accepted by mainstream Western literary circles and his subsequent appropriation of Western literary traditions and modes of representation account for the lopsidedness of vision and the excessively bleak portrayal of developing nations in books such as *Guerrillas*. While it is important to recognize the significance of various influences, including literary, which act on Naipaul, it would be reductive to claim that his work is solely shaped by these factors. Neither would it be fair to assert that Naipaul simply writes to confirm Western prejudices or blindly follows the trajectory of his literary predecessors.

Although Naipaul himself once remarked that Conrad had no influence on him and denied the possibility that there is a direct link between his Conrad essay and his subsequent exploration of similar themes and places ("The Irascible Prophet"), I believe this is far from being the case. In my view, Naipaul "found" in Conrad a kindred spirit, a perpetual exile like himself, who matched his experience and sensibilities on different levels. The struggle and fragility of their early lives and the subsequent challenges they faced—Conrad as a Polish émigré, Naipaul as a colonial—in the metropolitan center, can also be cited as other common points of reference.

Like Conrad, Naipaul has been haunted by the moral dilemmas that lie at the heart of the human condition. Moreover, he shares with

Conrad a profound and sustained interest in the nature of political behavior, the politics of (neo) colonialism and the personal tragedies of men caught up by forces beyond their control. As my discussion of *Nostromo* and *Guerrillas* illustrates, they are also similarly pessimistic regarding the possibilities of colonial independence. It is possible to suggest that their portrayal of "half-made societies" in these works is strongly influenced by their avowed political skepticism. Deeply suspicious of political causes and believing that ideology effectively usurps the autonomous identity of the individual, both writers cultivated a stance of political detachment throughout their lives.

Of primary importance for both Conrad and Naipaul is the desire to attain a clear vision of the world. In Conrad, this passionately sought "clarity of vision" remains, ultimately, an elusive ideal as he comes to settle for the haziness at the heart of human condition and human conduct. In Naipaul, by contrast, one observes an obsessive concern to grapple with, make sense of, and ultimately transcend the encompassing darkness that, in Conrad, exists as an insurmountable force. In the words of Pankaj Mishra:

> No writer has mediated more consistently on such ironies of history than Naipaul himself, but with a vitality that seems the opposite of Conrad's calm, slightly self-satisfied melancholy. Naipaul appears to be constantly clarifying and deepening the knowledge or experience that seems hardened in Conrad. Taken together, his books not only describe but also enact how he, starting out in one of Conrad's "dark and remote places," moved slowly and fitfully towards a "clear vision of the world." There is no point of rest in this journey, which now seems an ironic reversal of Conradian journey to the heart of darkness. (xv)

In conclusion, it is probably Naipaul's partial pessimism regarding mainly the developing world rather than Conrad's universal pessimism that embraces humanity as a whole, which accounts for the principle difference in their respective outlooks. Whereas Conrad's darkness indiscriminately envelops all nations and individuals, Naipaul finds darkness in particular places and in particular societies. Thus, for Naipaul, darkness can be overcome. In fact, it has more or less been overcome in parts of the world where ideals of the Enlightenment have been consolidated and where material progress has been achieved. Consequently, the conviction in the possibility of a clear and infallible vision is what distances him from Conrad and inevitably leads him to take sides, leading, perhaps, to a clearer, yet also deeply flawed understanding of how the world is organized.

Works Cited

Conrad, Joseph. *Nostromo: A Tale of the Seaboard*. Oxford: Oxford UP, 1984. Print.

Donadio, Rachel. "The Irascible Prophet: V.S. Naipaul at Home." *Sunday Book Review*. The New York Times Company, 7 Aug. 2005 Web. 30 Sept. 2016.

Howe, Irving. *Politics and the Novel*. New York: First Meridian Printing, 1987. Print.

Naipaul, V. S. *The Middle Passage: Impressions of Five Colonial Societies*. London: Picador, 2001. Print.

_____. "Conrad's Darkness." *The Return of Eva Peron with the Killings in Trinidad*. London: Penguin, 1981. 199-218. Print.

_____. *Guerrillas*. London: Picador, 2002. Print.

_____. *Literary Occasions*. London: Picador, 2003. Print.

Nixon, Rob. *London Calling: V.S. Naipaul Postcolonial Mandarin*. New York: Oxford UP, 1992. Print.

Kortenaar, Neil ten. "Writers and Readers, the Written and the Read: V. S. Naipaul and *Guerrillas*." *Contemporary Literature* 31.3 (Autumn 1990): 324-334. Print.

Panichas, George A. "The Powers of Moral Darkness in Joseph Conrad's *Nostromo*." *Modern Age* (Spring 2002): 129-146. Print.

Said, Edward. *Culture and Imperialism*. London: Vintage, 1997. Print.

Spittles, Brian. *How to Study a Joseph Conrad Novel*. London: Macmillan Press, 1990. Print.

Warren, Robert Penn. *Selected Essays by Robert Penn Warren*. London: Eyre & Spottiswoode, 1951. Print.

Reading *Lord Jim* in the Twenty-First Century: The Context, the Immigrant, and the Lord

Fouzia Reza and Vikarun Nessa

Land and Sea

> ... you have to understand/ that no one puts their children in a boat/ unless the water is safer than the land.
>
> (Warsan Shire)

Clad in a red T-shirt and blue jeans, the drown body of Aylan Kurdi, a Syrian boy, washed ashore after a failed journey through the "perilous" route from Turkey to Greece's Aegean Islands in 2015. Photos of his lifeless corpse captivated the world and crystalized media attention on the refugee crisis. The viewer might look at this image and wonder, "What 'Lords' of world politics played the part in his death?" The current refugee crisis and the overall status of immigration offers an opportunity to reread Joseph Conrad's novel *Lord Jim,* in order to show refugee status in contemporary world politics is also not immune to stereotyped tropes. The visual of a dead Muslim young boy was captivating enough to take over global media. Yet meanwhile, hundreds of men and women have died, unphotographed, trying to flee their war-engulfed homeland. Immigration status of first-world citizens in the third world replicates invented literary fantasy. This chapter explores *Lord Jim* by juxtaposing Conrad's novel with small glimpses of everyday current events. It examines, for example, an American female social worker's random photograph with a desi rickshaw puller, publically shared by US Embassy-Dhaka's Facebook page and then reported as an interracial marriage by the web-based local media. Social media and Conrad's fiction have unseen overlaps. When an Asian Muslim immigrant in the first world gets escorted out from a US presidential candidate's speech as she stands in silent protest in an allegedly stereotypical remark regarding her religion, Conrad's *Lord Jim* has a relevant connection. If terrorism from fringe fundamentalist groups is one of the presumed main issues the world is facing today, at least according to politicians, then its other is the politics surrounding Muslim immigrants and the refugees. Here Conrad's creation of the Patna ship travelers reemerges in today's global socio-economy of opening and closing borders.

The relevance of *Lord Jim* to the present world makes for a stirring read. This chapter aims to map out the global, contemporary context of Joseph Conrad's text by reading *Lord Jim* alongside media reports and public reactions to world news. This chapter aims to create reliability between Conrad's world and our own.

Joseph Conrad dreamed of becoming sailor. This is quite an uncommon profession for a Polish national, as Poland is a landlocked country. In *Lord Jim*, the character Jim can be seen as a representation of Conrad's own desire to become a seaman. And it is through Jim that Conrad showcases the unpredictability of the sea and notions of displacement. The reader sees at different times throughout the novel that the sea commands Jim do things that he thinks he "seemed to" have done (70). A century later, "the sea" still remains a symbol of unpredictability. This is particularly prevalent in regard to the recent immigration situation and its role in the global media. Émigrés arrive lacking knowledge and certainty in their futures. Moreover, for immigrants in a twenty-first century context, "the land" itself embodies unpredictability due to the always-changing political situations on all shores. Immigrants and refugees venture to the sea, in a blind plunge, clinging to a fleeting promise of finding land.

Warsan Shire's poem "Home," quoted at the beginning of this chapter, acutely describes the dilemma faced by immigrants when they need to choose between land and sea. For Conrad, sea-roaming as an immigrant began in fantasy. His life, like his writings, became an Odyssian travel towards the unknown, which function to legitimize his "hero ideal." One is reminded of Lord Tennyson's poem "Ulyssess," particularly the stanza where the eponymous Greek hero, in exploring the world, shows the resolute desire "to strive, to seek, to find, and not to yield." However, for immigrants in today's rocky political and social climates, "to strive" is to relocate themselves in an idealized but often never realized "safer" place. For these migrants, travel into the unknown takes on both literal and metaphorical shifting status. One finds they must "marry" the uncertainty to live and accept the reality of being subaltern in the world's socioeconomic power game.

The sea as a symbol of unpredictability is what makes *Lord Jim* relevant in today's discourse of immigrant literature. Like the 800 Muslim pilgrims of *Patna*, Aylan Kurdi floating in the Aegean Sea became a key discussion point within the moral underpinnings of the West. Yet, this discussion often eschews the factors that triggered the crisis, while ignoring the nations who were most involved in creating the situation in the first place.

Semantic Snares
>Who are immigrants?
>you broke the ocean in half
>to be here
>only to meet nothing that wants you.
>   (Nayyirah Waheed)

The post-2015 world has seen a drastic shift in the term "immigrant." The word is marked by dislocation, embodying a pluralistic distinction of different types. The term has, necessarily, become stigmatized. It conjures up an array of images to the reader, supplemented by media blitz of visual iconography. "Immigrant" suggests photos of darker skinned people floating at sea in a dinghy under a red Aegean sun, or people arriving at airports with makeshift packs filled with homemade food, or parents with children on their lap sitting behind barbed wire awaiting decisions by port authorities. Immigrants reside in "era of space" not a condition of people. The term has come to signify a class.

Apart from the physical loss of space, immigrants also face the threat of losing family members, their rights, and their faith. Immigrants become a class who suffer from the loss of a sense of belonging while in migration. They can no longer return home without having been altered and transformed by their journeys. Their migration creates a series of confusions. As they reach new "lands," they often lose their language, identity, national connections, and hence their very footing in the world.

Unlike migrants from developed Western nations, immigrants never seem to be able to become what are known as "expats." Expats create exchanges. Expats are the superior being extending their series of belongingness, adding an Eiffel Tower or other works of art to the landscapes of their newly adopted homes. They create hybridized ethnic cuisines and multinational urban spaces. These experiences augment the expats' mental capital of space. Immigrants search for this capital, but often fail to cross over, making the transformation from "foreigner" to "expat." While immigrants want to belong, expats conversely try to extend their space of belonging. Expats, in the world of today's political discourse, are the white Westerners exploring, adventuring, and communicating across the globe. Immigrants are the non-white, black, or brown-skinned pilgrims learning to fit in, cope with, and work within established systems. In an article published in *The Guardian*, Mawuna Remarque Koutonin, the editor of SiliconAfrica.com, argued that "expat" is a term reserved exclusively for Western white people going to work abroad. "Africans are immigrants," wrote Koutonin. "Arabs are immigrants. Asians are immigrants. However, Europeans are expats because they can't be at the same level as other ethnicities. They are superior. Immigrant is a term set aside for 'inferior races'" ("Why Are White People Expats").

When describing Conrad's character Jim, one cannot use the contemporary meaning of the term "immigrant." Rather, the reader sees him as an expat. He does not suffer from the crisis associated with seeking a sense of belonging. On the contrary, he becomes Tuan Jim, or Lord Jim in Patusan, owning and claiming the space that would, for immigrants of today's world, only exist in the pages of a fictional novel. Jim's condition is defined by his position within the white community. He is deemed as superior from his very first encounter. In one scene, Jim is captured in Patusan and imprisoned in a cage. Importantly, Conrad uses this scene to subtlety suggest Jim as a master of his own fate. Conrad does not have him "rescued" but rather gives him the agency of an expat by allowing him to escape from the cage through his own actions and, importantly, without the assistance from any other characters. To escape his imprisonment, Jim jumps down from the cage. He takes the plunge into the metaphorical sea that immigrants are literally forced to cross. And yet Jim skips the sea and lands safely on the land. This "jump" can be read as a symbol of a descending "white god." Because of this status, he is readily accepted as "Tuan" the lord of the natives of Patusan. Even though he is lord in Patusan, he escapes from his own land as he carries the stigma of a sailor who not only abandons his ship but also prayed for 800 Muslim pilgrims to die so that his "spotless white" image would not be marred. He escapes from his own lands in moral peril, unable to live up to his ideal European image. Yet Jim has not lost his homeland and instead has migrated in the self-imposed exile of moral luxury. He is an expat, taking a route that is closed off for immigrants.

In the "white god" status-holder, Lord Jim escapes from his own moral and emotional peril created within his white psyche by moving locales. In the real world, the darker-skinned immigrants flee actual physical and the mental torture and violence, often created by the very Western powers they attempt to settle in. The United States and its allies invaded and attacked Iraq, Afghanistan, Syria, and Libya because there needed to be a culprit within their "Western burden," analogous to the "white man's burden" of Conrad's time. Imperialism has been replaced with a global war on terror, where problems are to be solved by declaring wars. In the wake of these international conflicts, hundreds of thousands of civilians are forced to escape, and then become estranged, from their own lands. The current political situation in the Middle East continues to increase the number of immigrants fated to look for work, a land, a "safe" space to call home.

Unlike Lord Jim, immigrants in today's world cannot simply go to a Western Patusan and obtain god-like status. The term "barbarism" in Conrad's world has been replaced with the contemporary term "extremist." In the case of today's immigrants, their racial and religious identities have been stigmatized with erroneous links to terrorism. Like the 800 Muslim pilgrims in *Lord Jim*, this Othering can be compared with the entire Muslim immigrant community in the post-9/11 world. Following the September 11, 2001 terrorist attacks of The World Trade Center, a heightened suspicion of non-Americans, predominantly Muslims, in the United States and in the other Western countries intensified. When Conrad depicts all 800 pilgrims of Patna ship drowning, he importantly has all of them sleeping at the same time. Asleep, the passengers are wrapped in the veil of ignorance, existing without any knowledge of their current status and impending demise. Readers may question how it is possible all 800 of them were asleep at once, as, statistically, at least some would be awake at any given time. Having them all sleeping allows Conrad to focus on their ignorance and total dependency on the white crew of the ship who commanded the upper deck. Considering the physical form of the ship, they existed in a system of dependence. Unlike Jim, who could later free himself from the cage, the ship's lifeboats were unavailable to these passengers. It is noteworthy that in the group of 800, Conrad writes that not a single soul stirred. Rather than individuals with their own agency, these pilgrims are a uniformed mass. Their description in *Lord Jim* shows them more as a number, like cargo, than a group of living human beings. In a modern interpretation, these passengers can be read under the notion of being unconverted travelers in need of saving; like the Arab communities fleeing from Middle East. Their situation seems to be ahistorical, existing always in flux, in a transition of being in the sea rather on land. Their very existence becomes dispensable and interchangeable with other "numbers."

In a recent book on migrants, Thomas Nail writes, "Today, most people fall somewhere on [a] migratory spectrum between the two poles of 'inconvenience' and 'incapacitation.'" Nail goes on to state, "what all migrants on this spectrum share, at some point, is the experience that their movement results in a certain degree of expulsion from their territorial, political, juridical, or economic status"(2). However, this is not the case for Jim, who does not fit Nail's spectrum or even his definition of "migrant." Jim's migration to the island of Patusan cannot be termed as "inconvenient." Rather Patusan provides him a site to exercise his heroic ideals. Jim's migration to Patusan is for his ideology, for his desire to become a hero and validate his superior notions of self. For Jim, migration is not a necessity. The reader should see his relocation as enabling Jim to achieve his moral vision, not through the "expulsion" detailed by Nail, but in his heroic validation and recognition as Tuan Jim.

Migrations and Humans and Donald Trump

The United States' global reach grew on the economy founded and developed by immigration. Yet the country often finds it hard to accommodate its mixed diversity. Recently, during the 2016 presidential election campaign, Republican candidates capitalized on fears that American Muslims and Mexican Americans have on the established diversity of the nation in order to capitalize on immigration reform for their own political advancement. In the final chapters of *Lord Jim*, Conrad attempts to show how difficult it is in Jim's world to accommodate mixed ethnicities. Written 116 years ago, the novel still shows how mixed ethnicities have conflicted with normative values and Western society's acceptance of racial diversity. Jewel, whose real name is intentionally never given, is triply marginalized within the narrative. She is a woman, a hybrid child of a Western-Eastern fascination game, in an unreciprocated and unequal "relationship with" Gazer who doesn't really care about her. The heroic death Jim embraces at the novel's conclusion does not take into consideration Jewel, his partner. She becomes irrelevant in Jim's mental narrative of hero ideals and instead becomes a "pastime." Even her name "Jewel" can be interpreted as being only precious in words—a found treasure, with value only based on perceived beauty. She is an idea and, as such, can be dismissed and become irrelevant in Jim's mental discourse, like the 800 Muslim pilgrims repackaged as cargo. In the current American elections cycle, mixed ethnicities are, like Jim's "Jewel," becoming campaign talking points, where the people themselves have been replaced by the idea they occupy. For Republican presidential nominee Donald Trump, these mixed ethnicities have also become a pastime, as they did for Jim. They are an item he needs only when he wants to use it.

The process of "becoming" an American citizen is itself a journey, similar to the physical process of coming to the United States. Within the state system, the immigrant can drown in a sea of bureaucratic paperwork. Migrants reaching the shores are questioned about their profession, their financial situation, and martial and family statuses. Once documented, and even after becoming an American citizen, unlike language, personal history, and other forms of identity, a migrant's ethnicity is always carried externally. The 2016 presidential election heightens rhetorical, religious, and racial blurring. Not all ethnically Middle Eastern Americans are Muslims. And not all Muslims practice their religion. Certainly very few devoted Muslims are terrorists. Rose Hamid, a Lebanese woman clad in a headscarf, stood up in protest when Trump attempted to blur the lines between Muslims and terrorists. His comments linked all Syrian refugees to the militant group ISIS, in one of his typical divisive statements, such as when he claimed all people of Mexican heritage were rapists. Hamid was escorted out of a presidential debate in a way that reminds the viewer of Conrad's portrayal of Jewel. She is thought of as being unable to decide for herself. She has lost her agency. She is denied a voice and instead has become a pastime. When Hamid was escorted out of the auditorium, no one in the crowd opposed her treatment. The voice of the masses involved jeers and boos. This incident goes against the sentiments etched into the pedestal of the Statue of the Liberty. The lines written there were once about welcoming immigrants. They were taken from Jewish poet Emma Lazarus's 1883 poem, "The New Colossus":

> Give me your tired, your poor,
> Your huddled masses yearning to breathe free,
> The wretched refuse of your teeming shore.
> Send these, the homeless, tempest-tost to me,
> I lift my lamp beside the golden door!

Popular Culture, Media, and the Exotic
> Cool me down
> I'm feeling so exotic
> Yeah right now

> I'm hotter than the Tropics
> Take me there...
> Desi girl
> I'm feeling so exotic.
>   (Priyanka Chopra)

Priyanka Chopra's song featuring the Cuban American rapper Pitbull is an excellent example of how the phenomenon of the Other, a termed coined by Edward Said, is still as "exotic" today as it was hundred years ago, despite the advent of global technologies that have interconnected the world. The girl in the above song is "exotic" because she is "desi," a term connoting people from India, Pakistan, or Bangladesh. Fear and fascination plays into this relationship. Popular media still struggles in its presentation of the East within the Western lens. The British musical group Coldplay staged their song "Hymn to the Weekend" in India, as if the country were still the jewel of the British Empire—an island of Patusan—specifically because of its Othered exotic landscape. *Lord Jim* similarly began as a novel of geo-physical exploration. In 1899–1900 *Blackwood's Magazine* published Conrad's novel in serial form. Surrounding Conrad's pages were a preoccupation with other publishing narratives pertaining to "conquests in exotic lands" (Conrad vi). While *Lord Jim* moves the exploration of landscapes into a navigation of Jim's moral identity, the phenomenon of the "exotic" is nevertheless what grounds Jim as a lord-like character. Jewel can never be the equal of the white male hero, as Jim's agency creates a self-centered nature. "You always leave us," admonishes Jewel to Jim, "for your own ends" (xvii).

A century removed from Conrad's context, being equal to a white man or even white woman still occupies the Western discourse and media. For example, a series of interesting events followed the publication of one photo on the US Embassy-Dhaka's Facebook page, triggering a false news report in local media. The photo depicts a US Fulbright exchange researcher in traditional Bangladeshi clothing sitting next to a desi rickshaw puller. Local news reports picked up the image and circulated it as a post-wedding photo. The story went viral on social media, which in part, reveals the stigma still attached to interracial marriage and clash divisions in a globalized world.

Interestingly, with so many rumors circulated in local news, tabloid press, and now new web-based agencies, the authorities of this page felt "responsible" to clear up the "misleading" story. A statement was released, stating: "The false story, which claims that the two persons in the photograph have married, is misleading and untrue." A second photo was printed where both individuals were smiling together, only now they were circled in red and intersected with a diagonal line, the international symbol for an action that is forbidden. In attempting to retract a factual mistake between two individuals, the press suggested that the interracial marriage itself was prohibited act. As one commenter wrote, "First of all, its [*sic*] not wise to put red mark on photo. Its [*sic*] their photo and they r smiling . . . respect their honest intention." Commenters went on to thank the page, one even said: "It seemed false and fabricated right from the beginning. I personally have never believed this story. It seemed too good to be true. Anyways, thanks U.S. embassy for the clarification." Yet a space for divergent opinions does exist, if only subtly. In one comment, a reader wrote "The first false news was more beautiful than the second true one."

It is noteworthy that local media created hype by using the Western presence in the photo. While a white person's visit to the country created a fantasy that could go on towards creating fabricated news of marriage, immigrants with dark complexion, irrespective of where they were born or where they had been living for several generations, cannot dispel the imposed viewpoint of a barbaric nature that is today termed terrorism. Media imagery in the form of ISIS or other Islamic militant groups has only added to the plight that Muslim immigrants face in a post-9/11 world. As a result, immigrants face racial profiling during the time they require assistance the most. Instead, their transition from sea to shore goes unaided, with perilous results. Rose Hamid, the Lebanese woman escorted out of the Trump rally, commented that "People don't have a chance to see anything other than the Muslims they see on TV." She added, "This demonstrates how when you start dehumanizing the other it can turn people into very hateful, ugly people. . . . It needs to be known." It is a lack of knowledge that creates the figure of the Other, and this is often done intentionally. Similarly, if Jewel had been born in the West, she would not be "a tiny white speck, that seemed to catch all the light left in a darkened world" like Jim, rather, she would be the "darkness," unwelcomed and by its mystery a subject of terror (Conrad xvi).

The Western Dream and Reality
In *Lord Jim*, Conrad uses the metaphor of "jumping," which underscores a similar romantic notion that immigrants today carry when they are migrating to a Western country. While Jim was training to become a sailor, he fails to jump when he is instructed to do so. Jim consoles himself in a romantic way that, in the "real" world, he will perform better. Similar things happen with immigrants. They think they will perform better once they are out of the uncertain homeland and current perilous situation. They end up failing to live up to their romantic ideals, which no longer exist in the land of inflated promise. When Jim manages to jump for the second time, he actually abandons a seemingly sinking ship with 800 sleeping Muslims in it. When presented with his "real" scenario to jump, Jim's failure is much bigger and weighted with moral failure than his failure to jump during training exercises.

Conrad does not give the reader Jim's last name when he resides in the West. However, with only a token silver ring, he manages to gain the trust of the local chief Doramin and, with his "superior" knowledge, solves an age-old feud between two tribes with little effort. He then becomes Lord, his title of nobility subsuming his first name. He manages to do so because his skin color creates a sense of superiority that pervades the lives of Eastern browns. Bestowed with an honorary title, "Jim" then becomes the character's surname, his Christian name replacing family attachment as Jim creates his own heritage as a lord outside of Europe. Lord Jim has become the archetypal expat.

Capturing and Silencing
The sudden influx of immigration is being documented at every moment, to the point that there are literally too many visuals and

articles for the viewer to consume. The information, aided by social media, is organized predominantly through a Western filter. In fact, the viewers pay much less attention to the stories of other, more localized sources. The created hype becomes credible when one only looks through the lens of the West. This manifests itself in the Foucauldian idea of a knowledge-power nexus, which has evolved into an information-power nexus. The photo of Aylan Kurdi created a sensation when it was presented to audiences through the Western media. But, with its privileged position, can Western media portray the whole picture? How can subaltern sources be used to complement the narrative and give a fuller and more complete picture? T. S. Eliot wrote "History has many cunning passages, contrived/corridors" (23). A similar problem in the narration can also be found in Conrad's writings. Marlow is like the Ancient Mariner of Samuel Taylor Coleridge's poem, "The Rime of Ancient Mariner," in which the protagonist needs to retell his story to validate an act of killing. He is Ulysses, whose actions are only remembered if they are recited by the muses. While Marlow is narrating the story of Jim, he is aided by the journal Jim has left behind. Both sources present biased perspectives. Marlow is Jim's friend, and the journal is the written recollections Jim chose to save. In short, missing in *Lord Jim*, like in the media portrayal of the "migrant crisis," are the local sources and multiple perspectives of all characters, which add veracity to the account. Readers only get to know the point of view of Marlow and Jim as the entire Patusan chapter has been narrated from their vantage point. Like the non-Western media, the voices of the Patusan natives have been marginalized and silenced.

In the binary of Western whites and their Other, the subaltern brown, early colonialism accommodated Jim's self-imposed ideals as "the ideal Western superior." A century later, Western supremacy is still the supposed ideal, and the trope of the "white savior" has yet to be fully dismantled and decentered. While in Jim's case the intervention was done and welcomed directly under nation-state-imposed imperialism, today this intervention manifests within a cultural phenomenon. When non-Western countries desire intervention, they seek it through agents of local government in a way that preserves sovereignty. This assumption of having a local government gives the neo-colonialized nations an impression of power. In *Lord Jim*, when Jim arrives at Patusan, he finds himself in the middle of different local parties, Doramin on one side, and Sherrif Ali and Rajah Allang on the other. Once he allies with the group of Doramin, they immediately feel backed by Western power. In today's world, the local authorities might not be in direct political alliance, but they may ally culturally and thus feel empowered through that collaboration.

Conclusion

The image of Aylan Kurdi, a photo if presented out of context might appear that the lifeless boy is seemingly sleeping on the seashore, poses a crucial question to "civilized" human societies. What was this boy doing there? He was a nonparticipant in the political turmoil that created the humanitarian crisis, yet he ended up dying because of it. The question triggers uneasiness to civilized minds. In the twenty-first century, these kinds of images are not supposed to exist. The same uneasiness is seen in *Lord Jim* when Gentleman Brown questions Jim about what he was doing in Patusan. There could be two reasons for Jim's uneasiness. He realizes how right Brown was that he did not belong to Patusan. Or perhaps Jim realizes that he can never go back to his pre-Patna situation when his moral shape and character was as "spotlessly . . . white" as his attire (3). Patusan is the last place where Jim can become a hero, a Lord.

In today's context, no one is immune from the uneasiness created by the image of a dead child, floating from sea to shore. The globalized connection of the world is suppose to prevent Patusan escapes, where the viewer can leave their past mistakes behind and reinvent their narratives as heroic figures. The symbolic nature of Aylan Kurdi makes one question the civilization in which we live in and also the essential humanity that connects us all of us. In this case, unfortunately, an image does not have the lifespan of a frame, and like Jim's diary or *Lord Jim* itself, we turn the page and escape into something new.

Works Cited

Alam. "'Home' by Warsan Shire." *SeekersHub*. SeekersHub Global, 2 Sept. 2015. Web. 01 May 2016. <http://seekershub.org/blog/2015/09/home-warsan-shire/>.

Chopra, Priyanka. "Exotic (feat. Pitbull)." *AZLyrics*. AZLyrics.com, 2016. Web. 25 May 2016. <http://www.azlyrics.com/lyrics/priyankachopra/exotic.html>.

Conrad, Joseph. *Lord Jim*. London: Wordsworth Classics, 1993. Print.

Diamond, Jeremy. "Silently Protesting Muslim Woman Ejected from Trump Rally." *CNN*. Cable News Network, 11 Jan. 2016. Web. 14 May 2016. <http://edition.cnn.com/2016/01/08/politics/donald-trump-muslim-woman-protesting-ejected/>.

Eliot, T.S. *Selected Poems*. Book World: New Delhi. Print.

Frost, Robert. "The Death of the Hired Man." *Poetry Foundation*. Poetry Foundation, n.d. Web. 15 Mar. 2016. <http://www.poetryfoundation.org/poems-and-poets/poems/detail/44261>.

Hardt, Michael & Antonio Negri. *Empire*. Cambridge, MA: Harvard UP. 2001. Print.

Koutonin, Mawuna Remarque. "Why Are White People Expats When the Rest of Us Are Immigrants?" *The Guardian*. The Guardian News and Media Limited, 13 Mar. 2015. Web. 15 Mar. 2016. <http://www.theguardian.com/global-development-professionals-network/2015/mar/13/white-people-expats-immigrants-migration>.

Lane, Oliver J. J. "Government Funded Website Teaches Migrants How To Have Sex... In 13 Different Languages." *Breitbart*. Breitbart, 11 Mar. 2016. Web. 15 Mar. 2016. <http://www.breitbart.com/london/2016/03/11/government-funded-website-teaches-migrants-how-to-have-sex/#ixzz42rTk0xKX&f>.

Laurence, Davies & Karl. R. Frederick, ed. *The Collected Letters of Joseph Conrad*. Cambridge, UK: Cambridge UP, 1983. Print.

Nail, Thomas. *The Figure of the Migrant*. Stanford, CA: Stanford UP. 2015. Print.

"U.S. Embassy-Dhaka." *Facebook*. Facebook, Inc., 20 Dec. 2015. Web. 10 Jan. 2016. <https://www.facebook.com/bangladesh.usembassy/photos/a.114158334806.98967.103157219806/10153508800194807/?type=3&theater>.

Waheed, Nayyirah. "Immigrant." *nayyirah.waheed*. Instagram, n.d. Web. 10 Feb. 2016. <https://www.instagram.com/p/BBVK6skBCdd/>.

Joseph Conrad's Sense of Individuation in *Almayer's Folly*

Fitrilya Anjarsari

Almayer's Folly is Joseph Conrad's first novel, published in April 1895. It is the first of a trilogy written by Conrad that takes place in Malaya Archipelago. This chapter classifies *Almayer's Folly* as belonging to the literary genre of "travel writing," due to the text being based on Conrad's personal experience while travelling to the Malaya Archipelago. Conrad's writing style in this novel is quite interesting. As a first-time author, Conrad courageously, if subtlety, challenged British imperialism. Yet, a deeper reading of *Almayer's Folly* reveals Conrad's confusion when he saw two different cultures encountering a colonized country. According to him, these encounters were more cultural shock than missions of civilization. Conrad thus created what this chapter terms the "unheroic styling" of a white-skinned main character in his novel.

The trilogy written by Conrad is unique because the first book, *Almayer's Folly*, encapsulates the ending of the entire trilogy. The text talks about Kaspar Almayer, a Dutch trader who has an ambition to become rich and revered. In order to pursue his dream, Almayer then agrees to marry the daughter of Lingard, the richest sailor, irrespective of the fact that she is half-caste. However, his marriage is not a happy one, even after his Malayan wife has a daughter named Nina. Nina grows up confused about her double identity and mixed heritage. Later in the novel, Almayer meets a Malay man named Dain Maroola, who falls in love with Almayer's daughter. Nina's mother does not want her daughter to marry a white man, like she did with Almayer, because she believes they cannot be trusted. Through Dain, Nina's mother sees the opportunity for Nina to maintain her Malayan identity. She arranges for Nina to meet Dain without her husband's knowledge. Meanwhile, Dain purposefully creates conflict between Almayer and Lakamba the Rajah Laut (Sea King) by claiming to have found a gold mine and that a Dutch ship has stolen the gold. After that, Dain also plans another lie in order to take Nina away.

This story is highly praised by many because Conrad chooses Malaya as the setting of his literary work, which, at the time, was unprecedented for European authors. Moreover, his writing style is quite clever. Conrad is praised for his originality in using so called "exotic" writing. For example, Conrad does not translate words like *kampong*, *sarong*, or *punkah* into something familiar for Anglophone readers. Yet, there are also detractors who severely criticize this work. They argue that what Conrad writes does not depict the "real" Malaya. The debate over *Almayer's Folly* is analyzed in this chapter in order to focus on Conrad's view of individuation within his writings and his creation of "unheroic styling."

Almayer's Folly and Conrad's Early Career

Like other travel writers living in the colonial era, Conrad wrote about his own journeys to colonized countries. During this period, the power of colonizers toward their colonized countries influenced the writing style of travel authors. While the founding of the "new world" involved global trading and the monopolization of the colonized countries' political and economic sectors, colonialism was nevertheless organized around one presumed mission: the spread of civilization. Civilization aimed to educate people in colonized countries, who were deemed savages, in order to create civilized subjects. Travel writing was an important tool to persuade global audiences that colonialism could be a way to improve the livelihoods of the people in the colonized countries. Through travel writings, the mission of civilization was reported back to Europe and to the whole world. Thus it functioned to perpetuate a reinforcing loop, where further explorers were drawn to the colonized countries to continue the mission of civilization. Therefore, travel writings were written with the intended purpose of showing how uncivilized people in colonized countries were compared to those living in Europe. Furthermore, travel texts showed how Europeans, with the heroic mission, would improve life in colonized countries.

Travel writing itself focuses on how the "I" describes "the other" they meet during their journey (Thompson 122). The position of the author in a blending of two cultures—that is, the encounter between author's culture and the new culture—can easily be seen by examining their writing style. Travel writings are subjective, and there will always be debate over the author's objectivity. For instance, one needs detailed data from alternative visual and written texts (such as survey, census data, and photographs) in order to support the objective information in travel writing to suppress the possibility for travel writers' subjectivity.

Readers of travel writing enjoy not only scientific accounts but also works of fiction, such as novels. Along with the change in readers' interest, travel writing in the form of novels, short stories, and even poems became popular alongside the colonial project. The question about the objectivity of a travel writing in the form of literary work expands. Paul Fussel notes this when he states that there are certain requirements for a travel writing written as a publishable literary work. First, the journey taken by the author should be personally experienced. Second, more than narrating the experiences they have, the author should consult secondary sources of data in scientific books about the places they visit (Fussel 12).

As an author of travel writing, Conrad, during his career, was said to have a double vision that sided with British imperialism. It is an important point to see how he aligned with British colonial endeavors because he himself was a Polish-born British national. Conrad's double vision was that while he wrote novels of white protagonists, they mostly concluded with the imperial agent who had failed to become a hero in the colonized settings (Hampson 16).

One of the more phenomenal features regarding Conrad's first work, *Almayer's Folly*, was Conrad's status as an unknown writer at the time. With this publication, Conrad suddenly became one of new writers who challenged the older well-known travel manuscripts with his unique writing style. Conrad's writing style differed dramatically from that of his predecessors. Through *Almayer's Folly*, Conrad gave a touch of unheroic prose that had never been in any other travel writings before that time. Conrad put white people on the same level as any other Malayan people and illustrated the confusion and cultural shock caused by the encounter of two different cultures. The confusion faced by white people—like Almayer—in encountering and adapting to the local people made him unheroic. In his writings, Conrad eliminated the standard trope of white people as messianic bringers of civilization into the colonized world. According to Conrad, the mission of bringing benevolent changes through "civilization" was an impossible task, perhaps unneeded and certainly undesired from the perspective of the colonized. This was what he wanted to point out in his writings by using the unheroic style (White 116).

Conrad's style in reporting the Others did not follow the grand narratives of that time. These standard texts marked the Other as savage and uneducated, while white people were seen as the enlightened bringers of civilization to improve colonized countries. Basset argued that people in Asia already had culture, and the coming of white people, with European culture, into their land only raised confusion (113). Conrad seems to agree that the confusion was faced not only by the local people but also the white colonizers. Beyond the issue, Conrad also criticized the ambition of white people to take over these colonized countries and return to the metropole as heroic victor (Wellager 40).

Conrad's "unheroic style" brought him critiques and mockery; however, there were also many readers who admired his style and courage. Furthermore, Conrad felt that his publisher did not appreciate *Almayer's Folly* when it was first published. In his letter to his aunt in 1894, Conrad told her that for *Almayer's Folly* he was paid only twenty pounds (Karl 178). His low salary was due to his novel writing style, which had never been used to discuss colonialism and, thus, did not guarantee profitability. The publisher decided to pay Conrad a very low amount because they worried that *Almayer's Folly* would be poorly received and anticipated low sales. This payment amount, however, underscores Conrad's pioneering approach to travel writing as truly being the first of its kind.

Fact and Fiction: Critics on *Almayer's Folly*

Joseph Conrad began his career as a travel writer well by choosing to write about Malaya. Most travel writers had ignored Malaya at that time, choosing instead to write about Africa. Conrad's writing gave Malaya a focus on human life, unlike a story featured in *The Nation*, which said that Borneo (Malaya) was a fine field for the study of monkeys, but not for men.[1] Fisher Unwin also gave his pre-publication publicity of *Almayer's Folly* in *The Daily News* on April 25, 1895. In it, Unwin stated that no novelist had yet annexed the island of Borneo—in itself almost a continent. But Mr. Joseph Conrad, a new writer, was about to make attempt in a novel entitled *Almayer's Folly*.[2] This surprising press caused Conrad to be called the "Kipling" of the Malay Archipelago by *The Spectator*.[3]

The various responses to *Almayer's Folly* also attracted the attention of numerous critics. One critique, from D. J. M. Tate said that Conrad was not the first to write fiction about Borneo. Tate shows in that on November 29, 1845 the *Illustrated London News* published a dramatic story about James Brooke fighting pirates in Celebes and the Borneo Sea (91). Although it was proven that Conrad was not the first one to write about the Malaya Archipelago as a work of fiction, his work succeeded in drawing both public attention and inspiring many scholars to conduct research on and in the Malaya Archipelago. Conrad's writing made readers curious about Malaya Archipelago, especially Borneo. The attention to *Almayer's Folly* and the Malaya Archipelago, however, also created many other critical approaches to Conrad's work.

While research about Malaya gained popularity, the truth about the story of Borneo people in *Almayer's Folly* was questioned. Scholars who researched the Malay people right after *Almayer's Folly* was published began to compare their conclusions with the story that Conrad wrote. This was articulated by a well-known critique of *Almayer's Folly* entitled *Mr. Joseph Conrad at Home and Abroad*, written by Hugh Clifford in the *Singapore Free Press* in September 1898:

> With all that the English critics said in praise of Mr. Conrad's system, of his power of description, of his knowledge of the aspects of the land in which he set his characters moving, everyone who has the gift of appreciation must agree cordially. It is when the critics leave their own province, and begin to discuss the truth of Mr. Conrad's personages that we dwellers in Malayan lands find reason to differ from them…a complete ignorance of Malays and their habit and customs. Mr. Conrad's Malay are only creatures or Mr. Conrad, very vividly described, very powerfully drawn, but not Malays. (Hampson 5)

Clifford said that what Conrad had written was fictional and only existed in his mind. Clifford himself had conducted field research on Malay people in his two books: *In Court and Kampong* (1897) and *Studies in Brown Humanity* (1898). In those books, Clifford claimed to accurately represent how Malay really was (according to him), and in this way, Clifford's writings challenged Conrad's narrative.

Another critique came from Lloyd Fernando in *Conrad's Eastern Expatriates*. He noted that Conrad did not have an intimate knowledge of Malaysian life:

> He certainly had no intimate Malay friends, and his acquaintanceship with other Malaysians does not appear to have extended significantly beyond shipping clerks, waiters in colonial-style hotels, and other persons whom a visitor or seaman will encounter of necessity during his travels…the Eastern world of Conrad's fiction falls within the expatriate round of hotels, other expatriate acquaintances shore gossip, books by other expatriates, some of them distinguished in colonial history, and a skillful seaman's knowledge of certain harbors, bays, rivers, creeks and shores. Nevertheless, what he lacked in intimate knowledge he made up for by way of a prodigiously sensitive understanding. (Fernando 53-54)

Fernando's critique was similar to Clifford's. Both doubted the veracity of *Almayer's Folly* in its explanation and depictions of Malay people and their culture. This shows that there were always conflicts about the facts within travel writings, even in works of fiction. Although Conrad wrote *Almayer's Folly* based on his experience while in Malay, he did not include all aspects and points of view that he observed when creating his fictional narrative.

Issues about accurate depictions will always appear in the genre of travel writing, even when the author himself is not engaged in scientific or academic writing. The power of a fictional account is that the reader will attempt to discern between the facts and fiction in travel writing. Readers will always demand that narratives and experiences be based on facts, even if they are written in literary form. Travel writing offers facts in an engaging narration, not scientific prose, creating accounts that are consumed on a much wider scale by the general public and create stories that allow the reader to feel they are experiencing the travel along with the author.

Travel writings make the readers interested in knowing or even visiting the place that the author has mentioned. Related to the issue of fact and fiction in travel writing, the audience can then compare what they have found on their own journey to what appears in the travel writing. However, if they did not have a chance to visit the place directly, they could still augment the journey with their own library research to corroborate the facts they have read in travel writings. These approaches have been called the scientific legalization of travel writing in the form of literary work (Adams 56).

Observing the facts in travel writing cannot easily done by consulting only one source. The way that will bring the readers closer to the facts of fictional travel writing is by looking at the author's biography. Clifford's critique, mentioned above, thus ignores the facts that he and Conrad undertook a journey to Malaya in a different way, interacted with different Malay people with different stories, and read different scientific books about the Malay. Conrad's experience was no more or less authentic than Clifford's, and the writing purpose differed, even if they were writing for similar audiences. Fernando's critique that Conrad did not have an intimate relationship with the Malay, since he wrote it from the point of view of a sailor is also erroneous. Fernando failed to account for the fact that Conrad was himself a sailor; thus, he could not write the story with any other point of view than his own perspective.

Conrad's Sense of Individuation

The construction of facts about Malay people in *Almayer's Folly* cannot be separated from all the things about Malay that relate to Conrad—the books he had read, the people he interacted with—the totality of his experiences while in Malay. The critiques of *Almayer's Folly* have never touched the deeper point of Conrad's nature as a subject. It means that, as a subject, Conrad natural inclination for a nomadic lifestyle and own personal history will always be present in something he creates. "Nomadic" here refers to more than Conrad's own geographical movement during his life. It also means that the subject is connected to a lot of experiences that he cannot separate from his writings, irrespective of the topic. The work of shifting and combining all the things he has experienced happen within subject's psyche, and Conrad's own sense of individuation unconsciously manifest in the text. In a novel, a work of fiction, what happens in the writer's psyche will affect him in creating the narrative style he chooses; and those processes will be called as sense of individuation.

Following the concept of schizoanalysis from Deleuze and Guattari, the subject can be seen as being schizophrenic. Deleuze and Guattari have a different view about schizophrenia than the clinical psychological definition. What they mean by "schizophrenic" is that the subject does not only consume one signifying chain of identity. Thus the identity of subject is constructed as polyvocal (Deleuze & Guattari 49). The theory of schizoanalysis should be applied to literary work, particularly the genre of travel writing, which always has pros and cons regarding fact and fiction within the produced work. By understanding that the travel writer is a subject that relates to many objects and has productive desires to be randomly shifted and combined with other objects to create his work, the debate over facts within fiction is no longer needed. The process of how the travel writer creates his work must also be seen as developing from the writer's psyche.

The subject's identity—as stated above, is created through the psyche, or to be precise, it is created through the subject's unconscious, which can be explained in three syntheses. Those three syntheses of the psyche are connective, disjunctive and conjunctive.

The first synthesis is connective; through this synthesis, the subject will be connected to a lot of objects he has interacted with. As explained in *Anti-oedipus* (1983) the connection between subject and object happens like organ-machine plugged into an energy-source machine (Deleuze & Guattari 1).

In the disjunctive synthesis, this synthesis is also the process of recording in the psyche. Deleuze and Guattari state that a subject has a system to record all the connectivity he has with numerous objects. The recording will be about the pleasure from all the connections with objects in the first synthesis. The system that organizes the subject's psyche in recording all the pleasures also functions as a drive for the subject to decide in which pleasure they must turn. This is called "body-without-organs" (Deleuze & Guattari 9). The subject has the freedom to control which connections he wants the most when filtering everything simultaneously. From the process of recording, the subject does not only record the pleasure of every connection but also responses to each of the connections. Finally, conjunctive synthesis shows how the two syntheses mentioned above lead into the polyvocal signifying chain of identity in the subject. While the two syntheses will leave the pattern of how subject connects and shifts from one object through another, the last synthesis will be the combination of it or the result.

Those three syntheses should be applied to see the process of how Joseph Conrad, as a subject, created *Almayer's Folly*. The first thing to be seen in Conrad's psychological syntheses is the junction of all objects he encountered in the Malaya Archipelago. A careful study of Conrad's biography would reveal many of the Malayan objects and experiences with which he is connected. Conrad started his journey to the Malaya Archipelago in 1883. He had signed on as a second mate on the *Palestine*, which was bound for Bangkok with a cargo of coal in September 1881. However, after extensive delays, the *Palestine* finally reached Bangka Strait, off Sumatra, in March 1883. Here the coal spontaneously combusted and the crew had to abandon ship. They took to the lifeboats and rowed to Bangka Island. The officers and crew were taken to Singapore on March 21 for a Marine Court of Inquiry, while Conrad stayed in Singapore until mid-April before returning to London (Hampson 6).

His journey to the Malay Archipelago in 1883 was not his only one. Conrad returned again in February 1887. In Amsterdam, he signed on as first mate of the *Highland Forest*, which was bound for Java. Apparently, because of the back injury caused by falling, he signed off in Semarang on July 1 and went to the European hospital in Singapore in August of the same year (Hampson 8). After a brief period in Singapore, Conrad signed on once more as a mate on the *Vidar* (Resink 307). Aboard the *Vidar*, Conrad was able to explore Malaya even better, since this ship had a routine schedule and traveled around the Malaya Archipelago, mostly to Celebes and Borneo. The *Vidar*'s route is well recorded by Jerry Allen:

> Leaving Singapore, she (*Vidar*) sailed through Carimata Strait, called at Bandjermasin on the south coast of Borneo, cruised up PuloLaut Strait, stopping at the coaling station of Kota Baru on the Island of PuloLaut, crossed Macassar Strait to Donggala on Celebes, recrossed the strait to Samarinda in the Kutai or Coti district Borneo rounded point Mangkalihat as she moved along Borneo's east coast to the Berau River, steamed slowly up that unpredictable stream to the settlement of Berau . . . came down the river passed TandjungBatu on the Bornean Coast as she headed north to her last outward call, the Bulungan River and its upstream settlement of Bulungan or TandjungSelor. The return to Singapore was over the same route. (190)

On the *Vidar*, Conrad made four trips and signed off in January 1888. After signing off, Conrad lodged at the sailors' home in Singapore. The places where Conrad had stopped in Malay are, indeed, well connected to his psyche and had a significant impact while writing *Almayer's Folly*.

The important connection is not only between Conrad and the places he had been in Malay but also the books about Malay that he had read. Travel writing was an established genre before Conrad began his career. *The New Cambridge Bibliography of English Literature* states that by the start of the twentieth century, travel writing had already been a prominent genre for over two centuries. Andrea White sees the genre's origins in Richard Hakluyt's *The Principal Navigations, Voyages, Traffiques and Discoveries of the English Nation*, first published in 1598. Travel writing that talked about newly discovered land by English adventurers created an increasingly interested readership at home, while encouraging continued exploration, colonization, and the development of trade. Growing alongside the colonial project, publishers began competing with each other to publish the travel writings from all explorers. The genre of travel writing was booming for a long time before Conrad ever went to sea. By the time Conrad wanted to travel to see the "new world," he had already encountered much of it through the travel writing he had read.

Conrad had read the travel writing about the colonized countries in Asia, Africa, and Australia. For the travel writing about Malaya Archipelago, Conrad read the accounts of Sir Rajah James Brooke of Sarawak and Alfred Wallace. Brooke was a famous explorer, who left England for Borneo in 1838 simply because he wanted to "add knowledge, increase trade and spread Christianity" (White 37). Brooke was granted the title "Rajah" while he was in Sarawak due to the bravery he showed in fighting the pirates. These travel writings were framed as colonial tools for empire building, using the heroic trope. Henry Keppel in *Expedition* (1846) wrote more about Brooke: "to carry to the Malay, so long the terror of the European merchant vessel, the blessings of civilization, to suppress piracy, and extirpate the slave trade, became his humane and generous objects."[4] The news about Brooke's fight against piracy had been the headline and a favorite story back in England at that time, and thus Conrad would have been quite familiar with Brooke's adventure and its heroic framing.

Alfred Wallace's book entitled *Malay Archipelago* was said to be Conrad's favorite book. As Richard Curle writes:

> There were certain books which Conrad read over and over again. Of all such books, I fancy that Wallace's *Malay Archipelago* was his favorite bedside companion . . . of Wallace, above all, he never ceased to speak in terms of enthusiasm. (109)

Wallace and Brooke had similar points of view in seeing Malay people—both of them thought that Malay still needed English help to civilize their people. Thus Wallace and Brooke were full supporters and harbingers of the civilization mission. However, Wallace and Brooke did disagree. Wallace was worried that the civilization the English brought to Malay would only be a failure. Wallace felt the civilization mission might corrupt the Dyak (Borneo native people):

> Wallace goes beyond Cook's momentary envy of 'the happy native' to wonder if in fact England could not benefit morally from the Malays, English society being plagued at the moment by crime and disease. In a moving conclusion to his book, he in fact questions the progress and moral development of civilized societies. Perhaps such societies as the Dyaks have something to teach us about respecting the rights of others and living together with few inequalities. (White 28)

Wallace supported the spread of European civilization but then grew to question the development of those missions in colonized countries. He thought if England's expansion would have an effect on Dyak society, then the reverse could also happen—the Dyak could also influence England. In his conclusion, Wallace suggested that they might live in one place but let it be two cultures coexisting, without the need to further civilize the Dyak or make one side better than the other.

Beside his readings, as Conrad was moving along Malatya on the *Vidar*, he met the single most important person in writing *Almayer's Folly*. Conrad knew a man named Charles Olmeijer, as he wrote in his *Personal Record:*

> I had seen him for the first time some four years before from the bridge of a steamer moored to a rickety little wharf forty miles up, more or less a Bornean river... He stepped upon the jetty, he was clad simply in flapping pyjamas of Cretonne patterns (enormous flowers with yellow petal on a disagreeable blue ground) and a thin cotton singlet with short sleeves . . . I had heard him on Singapore, I had heard him on board. . . . I had heard of him in a place called PuloLaut . . . I had heard of him in Dongala, in the Island of Celebes, when the Rajah of that little-known sea-port . . . came on board in a friendly

way with only two attendants, and drank bottle after bottle of soda water on the after-skylight with my good friend and commander. (74-75)

Olmeijer was a famous person at that time, and a lot of Malay people spoke about him. Thus Conrad would have heard rumors about Olmeijer even before he had met him.

Olmeijer was the prototype of the character Almayer in *Almayer's Folly*, both in the real and the fictional worlds; he was William Lingard's representative at the trading post in Borneo. As Norman Sherry in *Conrad's Eastern World* explains:

> Olmeijer had for seventeen years been the representative of William Lingard, a famous trader and adventurer with special interests on the eastern coast of Borneo, who had set up the trading post there. In 1862, Lingard had been rewarded the title 'Rajah Laut' (Sea King) for his assistance to the Sultan of Gunung Tabor . . . this was a strategy designed to evade the terms of a Dutch contract which banned foreigners from settling in the Sultan's territory without permission from Batavia, but, in Batavia, Dutch East Indies officials became apprenticeships that Lingard might follow Brooke's example and establish himself as an independent ruler. However, Lingard's monopoly of trade in Berau was broken and in the 1880s, his trade diminished; his last ship; The Rajah Laut, was put up for sale in 1884; he had returned to England in 1883 and he died there in 1888. (175-180)

The story of Lingard had a big impact in all of Conrad's novels about Malaya, especially *Almayer's Folly*. Conrad never met Lingard directly, but since he was a well-known person who had the title "Rajah Laut" (Sea King), without even meeting Lingard personally, it was not hard for Conrad to obtain information about him.

Conrad not only connected all those objects mentioned above, he also connected them to his own experience working as a sailor in the Malaya Archipelago. As a traveling sailor, he had connections to lot of people in Malay beyond, Olmeijer. Conrad encountered traders in the traditional market. He encountered everyday life in bars and on shore leave. He tasted the local foods and beverages of the Malay, saw how the Malay dressed, and observed some of their customs. His individual, common, and everyday experiences would not be recorded in Conrad's biography. Yet those little moments shaped Conrad's creation of *Almayer's Folly,* both intentionally and unconsciously.

Looking at the disjunctive synthesis, where Conrad as a subject controlled all of the connections between objects using his "body-without-organs," it is clear that in creating *Almayer's Folly*, Conrad would not only be affected by one connection in the previous syntheses, but every connection. From each connection, Conrad would synthetize parts of his experience with other connections. All of the shifts he had made can be seen in his novel *Almayer's Folly*, but to be aware of this shifting the researcher must also know the historical background, such as what objects Conrad had connected in Malaya. During his journey in Malaya, Conrad never travelled to Bali. However, he wrote the character Dain Maroola as originating from Bali. Conrad would have needed information about the local customs in Bali in order to build Dain's characterization, since he was central to the story. Hampson states that the information about Bali and Timor that Conrad used came from Wallace's book:

> Conrad used the *Malay Archipelago,* in particular, for backgrounds with which he was unfamiliar. He had never visited Bali or Timor, all the information which Dain Maroola of *Almayer's Folly* gave Nina Almayer about his country on Bali could have been gleaned from Wallace. (73)

This shows that, in writing *Almayer's Folly*, Conrad was not only inspired by his journey into Malaya but also by what he had read. Therefore, all the connections between subject and objects will always stay; as all of Conrad's connections in Malaya were recorded well in his "body-without-organs."

All of Conrad's biographers note that Conrad was an admirer of Sir Rajah James Brooke. Conrad even dedicated his novel *Lord Jim* to Brooke. Brooke was the first European who had been given the title as "Rajah" (King) in Sarawak. He was granted the title "Rajah" from his brave acts in protecting Sultanate of Brunei.[5] His love for the Malaya Archipelago is shown in the heroic identity fighting piracy gave Brooke. When documenting nature in Malaya, Brooke described the climate and rivers in Malaya as: "unlike the white man's grave, Borneo's climate is healthy, her rivers are navigable and then the soil of her plains is moist and rich" (14). When Conrad, who experienced the Malayan climate directly, chose to write about climate in Borneo, he uses unheroic imagery: "The tree swung slowly round, amid the *hiss* and foam of the water and soon getting free obstruction began to move down stream again, rolling slowly over, raising upwards a long, denuded branch, like a hand lifted in mute appeal to heaven against the river's *brutal and unnecessary violence*" (5, emphasis added). In comparing these two passages, it underscores that even with Conrad's admiration for Brooke, the two did not agree on their depictions of the beauty of a Malay nature. In part, this is explained by their different personal experiences. Conrad emphasized the hardest parts of nature in Malaya, while Brooke record the beautiful aspects in contrast to "the white man's grave" in order to accentuate the pristine beauty he had protected from piracy and corruption.

There is a lot of shifting that can be seen in *Almayer's Folly*, which Conrad recorded through his connectivity with all the objects encountered during his stay in Malaya Archipelago. The most remarkable shifting is that when he used his connections with Charles Olmeijer—hearing all the stories about him and meeting him directly—with the issue of civilization that was questioned by Alfred Wallace in *Malay Archipelago*. Through the meeting with Olmeijer, Conrad expressed Europe in colonized countries, as Olmeijer was the one who was left as Lingard's representative in an almost bankrupt trading post. Conrad was thinking about what Wallace wrote, that one question about the negative impact of the civilization mission was what it did to white men. This was shown in how Conrad wrote in the beginning of *Almayer's Folly* about Almayer's big dream of fortune:

> He absorbed himself in his dream of wealth and power away from the coast where he had dwelt for so many years, forgetting the bitterness

of toil and strife in the vision of a great and splendid rewards. They would live in Europe, he and his daughter. They would be rich and respected. (Conrad, *Almayer's* 1)

The final expression of conjunctive synthesis shows the combination of the shifting a subject has made within the disjunctive in order to find meaning. Conrad himself shifted from one object to another without being bound to one single connection. Through these syntheses, it can be seen that Conrad's sense of individuation is polyvocal. He shared the beliefs with explorers like Brooke and Wallace, who supported the colonial mission, but he also did not want to write something that he thought would damage the Malaya Archipelago nor encourage further explorers to seek prestige and wealth by hiding behind the banner of "civilization." Thus Conrad created Almayer as a polyvocal image of European corruption, while still conforming to the travel writing narrative that would sell books. Conrad's "unheroic styling" can thus be concluded to be a manifestation of his unconscious anti-imperial beliefs trapped within his desire to adopt British colonial justification, just as he adopted British citizenship.

Notes

1. Unsigned Review, *Nation* LXI (17 Oct. 1895): 278.
2. *Almayer's Folly* was published by Fisher Unwin on April 29, 1895.
3. Unsigned Review, *Spectator* (19 Oct. 1895): 530.
4. Keppel, Henry, *Expedition to Borneo of H.M.S Dido For The Supression of Piracy: With Extracts From The Journal of James Brooke, Esq, of Sarawak*. 2 vols. London: Chapman and Hall, 1846.
5. Singh, D.S Ranjit. *Brunei 1839–1983*. Singapore: Oxford UP, 1984.

Works Cited

Adams, Percy. *Travel Literature and The Evolution of The Novel*. Lexington: UP of Kentucky, 1983. Print.

Allen, Jerry. *The Sea Years of Joseph Conrad*. London: Methuen. 1967. Print.

Bassett, Daniel K. "British Commercial and Strategic Interest in The Malay Peninsula during The Late Eighteenth Century." *Malayan and Indonesian Studies.* Ed. J. Bastin and R. Roolving. Oxford: Clarendon, 1964. Print.

Brooke, James. *Letter from Borneo with Notices of The County and Its Inhabitants.* London: L & G Seeley, 1842. Print.

Conrad, Joseph. 1895. *Almayer's Folly.* New York: Doubleday & Page, 1924. Print.

_____. *A Personal Record.* New York: Doubleday & Page, 1912. Print.

Curle, Richard. *The Last Twelve Years of Joseph Conrad.* New York: Russell & Russell, 1968. Print.

Deleuze, Gilles & Fellix Guattari. *Anti-Oedipus.* Trans. Robert Huxley, Mark Seem, & Helen R. Lane. Minneapolis: U of Minnesota P, 1983. Print.

Fernando, Lloyd. "Conrad's Eastern Expatriates" *Joseph Conrad: Critical Assessment.* Ed. Keith Carabine. Robertsbridge, East Sussex: Helm Information, 1991. Print.

Fussel, Paul. *Abroad: British Literary Travelling Between The Wars.* Oxford: Oxford UP, 1980. Print.

Hampson, Robert. *Joseph Conrad: Betrayal and Identity.* London: Palgrave Macmillan, 1993. Print.

_____. *Cross-Cultural Encounters in Joseph Conrad's Malay Fiction.* London: Palgrave Macmillan, 2001. Print.

Holland, Eugene W. *Deleuze and Guattari's Anti-Oedipus.* London: Routledge, 1999. Print.

Karl, Frederick R & Laurence Davis, eds. *The Collected Letters of Joseph Conrad 1861–1897.* Cambridge, UK: Cambridge UP, 1983. Print.

Resink, Gertrude J. *The Eastern Archipelago under Joseph Conrad's Western Eyes, Indonesia's History between the Myth.* The Hague: W. Van Hoeve, 1968. Print.

Sherry, Norman. *Conrad's Eastern World.* Cambridge, UK: Cambridge UP, 1966. Print.

Tate, D J M. *Rajah Brooke's Borneo.* Hong Kong: John Nicholson, 1988. Print.

Thompson, Carl. *Travel Writing.* New York: Routledge. 2011. Print.

Wellager, Mark A. *Conrad and the Fiction of Skepticism.* Stanford, CA: Stanford UP, 1990.

White, Andrea. *Joseph Conrad and The Adventure Tradition: Constructing and Deconstructing the Imperial Subject.* Cambridge, UK: Cambridge UP, 1993.

Joseph Conrad on the *Titanic*: A Pioneering Spirit of Safety and Life at Sea

Stefania Elena Carnemolla

> There is nothing more heroic in being drowned very much against your will, off a holed, helpless big tank in which you bought your passage, than in quietly dying of colic caused by the imperfect salmon in the tin you bought from your grocer.
> (Joseph Conrad, *Some Aspects of the Admirable Inquiry* 595)

In 1912, twelve years before his death, Joseph Conrad witnessed one of the most infamous tragedies in maritime history. On the moonlit night of April 14, sailing at twenty-two knots through the North Atlantic Ocean, the huge leviathan of steel struck an iceberg and sunk in the frozen waters, drowning affluent passengers, sailors, engineers, ship officers, and immigrants. The sinking of the *Titanic* broke the myth of modern seafaring safety technology.

The saga of the *Titanic* is well beyond the scope of this chapter and indeed this book. Nevertheless, a brief history is necessary in order to set the backdrop in which Conrad would have been familiar and to stress the overall global connections the *Titanic* occupied. It all began one summer evening in 1907 at Downshire House in Belgrave Square. The London home was that of Lord William James Pirrie and his wife. Lord Pirrie, an Irish shipbuilder and businessman, was the chairman of Harland & Wolff, a shipbuilding company based in Belfast, and one of the three directors of the White Star Line, a British shipping company that had been founded in 1845 to operate a fleet of clippers from Great Britain to Australia. After the company's 1867 bankruptcy, Thomas Ismay purchased it.

When, in 1899, Mr. Ismay died, his son, J. Bruce Ismay, became the head of the company. In 1902, the White Star Line was absorbed by the International Mercantile Marine Company, a trust created by the American private merchant bank J. P. Morgan & Co. as a combination of six steamship companies—White

Star Line, American Line, Red Star Line, Leyland Line, Atlantic Transport Line, and Dominion Line—with eight Americans and five Englishmen as board directors. J. Bruce Ismay, who was already chairman and managing director of the White Star Line, joined together with Lord Pirrie as one of the firm's directors.

On that 1907 summer evening back in Lord and Lady Pirrie's London home, J. Bruce Ismay and his wife had been invited for dinner to discuss business. The two men—seated around a table glittering with silver cutlery, fine china, and crystal glasses in a display resembling the future stately dining areas of the *Titanic*—dreamed of modern, luxury ocean liners with comfortably appointed cabins and state-of-the-art navigation equipment. The ghost of Cunard Line, the rival company, with its new ships *Mauretania* and *Lusitania*, lingered in the parlor air. How, the two men wondered, to gain supremacy of ocean travel if not through huge tonnage, exaggerated width, cruising speed of twenty-two to twenty-four knots, while creating glitz and luxury to satisfy rich passengers? At that London dinner, with the shipping companies' war looming the background, the dream of *Titanic* was born. *Titanic*, *Olympic*, and *Gigantic* (then *Britannic*): three ships as a symbol of supremacy of modern technology and naval architecture.

The construction of the *Titanic* commenced under the survey of the British Board of Trade, starting in 1909 at Harland & Wolff shipyard. She was registered as a steamship at the port of Liverpool, official number 131,428, for the sea-lane between Southampton and New York. The ship weighted 46,328 tons cross and 21,831 net register tons.

A leviathan of steel and false safety, what the ship lacked in lifeboats, she compensated for with a Parisian café outside the first-class restaurant, with open-air dining surrounded by troops of stewards and waiters. A transplant of a pavement Parisian café in the middle of the Atlantic Ocean, where first-class passengers enjoyed its triumph of *hors-d'oeuvres*, including oysters, consommé Olga, cream of barley, poached salmon in mousseline sauce, cucumber, filets mignons Lili, sauté of chicken à Lyonnaise, vegetable marrow farci, lamb in mint sauce, roast duckling in apple sauce, sirloin of beef with Château potatoes, green peas, creamed carrots, boiled rice, parmentier and boiled new potatoes, punch romaine, roast squab & cress, cold asparagus in vinaigrette, paté de foie gras, celery, Waldorf pudding, peaches in Chartreuse jelly, chocolate & vanilla éclairs, and French ice-cream.

Such a ship required a media campaign. *The Shipbuilder*, a quarterly magazine devoted to the shipbuilding, marine engineering, and allied industries was one of those which contributed to the marketing campaign, as when, in 1912, it praised *Titanic*'s Café Parisien as "an entirely new feature on board ship"—a café, which had "the appearance of a charming sun-lit verandah, tastefully decorated in French trellis-work with ivy and other creeping plants" provided with "small groups of chairs surrounding convenient tables" ("The 'Real' Café Parisien"). Yet, for the *Titanic*'s media hype, she sank on her maiden voyage with the ingredients for filets mignons Lili and sauté of chicken à Lyonnaise still filling her kitchen: a coffin of steel with more dishes than lifeboats.

She had left Southampton, England, on April 10, 1912, calling at Cherbourg, France, and at Queenstown on the south coast of County Cork, Ireland, from which she sailed on April 11, following the outward southern track toward New York. But on the night of April 14, the infamous luxury ocean liner struck an iceberg and sank in the icy North Atlantic waters.

Hearing of the sinking, Joseph Conrad spent days swimming through daily newspapers, creating piles of papers that lay together on the floor of his room, their cubic headlines murmuring about that leviathan of steel. Never before had such a maritime disaster contributed to the business of press as the *Titanic*. Beyond the details of the sinking itself, authors speculated on the minutiae of those final moments. Newspaper articles documented what the passengers ate that final evening, or what the ship's orchestra played on the deck while the ship was discharging its latest rumble before being swallowed by the sea. Conrad did not.

"I am not a sentimentalist; therefore it is not a great consolation to me to see all these people brevetted as 'heroes' by the penny and halfpenny Press," Conrad said in a statement just as powerful as any in his novels. "It is no consolation at all. In extremity, in the worst extremity, the majority of people, even of common people, will behave decently." The final actions of the crew and passengers would have been well known to Conrad, himself a shipwreck survivor. "It's a fact of which only the journalists don't seem aware. Hence their enthusiasm, I suppose," mused Conrad. "But I," he continued,

> who am not a sentimentalist, think it would have been finer if the band of the Titanic had been quietly saved, instead of being drowned while playing—whatever tune they were playing, the poor devils. I would rather they had been saved to support their families than to see their families supported by the magnificent generosity of the subscribers. (Conrad, "Some Aspects" 595)

For Conrad, journalism surrounding the *Titanic* had moved from factual reporting to sensationalist coverage. "I am not consoled by the false, written-up, Drury Lane aspects of that event, which is neither drama, nor melodrama, nor tragedy, but the exposure of arrogant folly." Conrad saw the reporting of final heroic actions as masking the true details of great tragedy: "There is nothing more heroic in being drowned very much against your will, off a holed, helpless, big tank in which you bought your passage, than in quietly dying of colic caused by the imperfect salmon in the tin you bought from your grocer" (Conrad, "Some Aspects" 595).

While daily newspapers and magazines around the world had already announced the sinking of the unsinkable ship, *The London Budget* published "On the Titanic," and in it, Conrad's first statement on the shipwreck. In this article, Conrad recommended scrapping large luxury liners in favor of smaller vessels traveling in pairs. For Conrad, ships like the *Titanic* sacrificed too much in safety to create great speed and size. Conrad's article on the *Titanic* as published in *The London Budget* was quoted in an essay titled "England's Indignation and Grief over *Titanic*" in the May 4, 1912 issue of *The Literary Digest* as a statement by "Joseph Conrad, the veteran author and master in the merchant service." Conrad reflected:

[T]he impact of a liner of 45,000 tons in contact with a submerged iceberg is bound to prove fatal. This would be less likely if the vessel were only of 20,000 tons displacement. Safety is sacrificed to speed building of mammoth ships. It is a question of size, not of the number of life-boats. The trouble is there were too many people aboard the ship. It is absurd to say that a ship such as the Titanic is unsinkable. Such large boats necessarily endanger the lives of more passengers in proportion to smaller vessels. The large boats are able to hold more passengers and crew in proportion to the smaller. ("England's Indignation" 925)

Conrad saw the solution to split the tonnage into two ships, purely out of safety concerns. "I think the increase in ocean travel and the enormous number of persons who cross the ocean every year warrants the scheme of dispatching transatlantic liners across the ocean in pairs," wrote Conrad. Using modern communication technologies, Conrad believed that the two ships should never be more than about "forty miles apart" from one another, where the ships could be "constantly . . . within easy call of each other . . . [and] in constant touch by wireless, and should anything of a perilous nature arise." With his focus on the safety of the crew and passengers, Conrad's main critique was against the ship financiers and big business, aspects of the global economy that Conrad was well acquainted with through his own career in the merchant fleets. "The big ship is a mistake," Conrad believed, "except from a commercial viewpoint. I have sailed in ships for years and know what strain and responsibility is thrown on the commander of an Atlantic liner." Conrad then related a conversation between ship captains in almost in the same way his literary character Charles Marlow might to the reader of own of Conrad's novels:

> Captain Flaherty, of the Red Star Line, told me once that, in the dead of night, while he stood on the bridge of his ship, he sighted a bark in close proximity to his vessel. He reversed engines, but was unable to avert disaster. The ship crashed into the bark, which crumbled like matchwood. The captain told me that this experience so harrowed his mind (he had 1,100 sleeping passengers on board), that when he arrived in port, which happened to be New York, he resigned his post.

> The lives of travelers across the ocean are certainly endangered at this time of year by steering a course so near drifting icebergs. But in the Titanic's case it occurs to me that had she been fifteen feet shorter she might have cleared the berg. ("England's Indignation" 925)

Conrad's essay reveals some concepts—safety, speed, ship size—illustrated in a technical way, while still injecting Conrad's typical maritime writing style with moralism and sarcasm. Conrad built upon the notion of that the "impact of a liner of 45,000 tons in contact with a submerged iceberg," which had been proven to be "fatal" was due to "safety" being sacrificed in order to "speed build . . . mammoth ships" ("England's Indignation" 925) in a subsequent work published in *Some Reflections, Seamanlike and Otherwise*. Here Conrad attacked the luxurious nature of passenger ships created by the White Star Line and its competitors, as engineering feats thought up by upper-class businessmen, not experienced sailors. In a damning condemnation of aristocratic overindulgence and global capitalism, Conrad wrote:

> You build a 45,000 tons hotel of thin steel plates to secure the patronage of, say, a couple of thousand rich people (for if it had been for the emigrant trade alone, there would have been no such exaggeration of mere size), you decorate it in the style of the Pharaohs . . . to please the aforesaid fatuous handful of individuals, who have more money than they know what to do with, and to the applause of two continents, you launch that mass with 2,000 people on board at 21 knots across the sea—a perfect exhibition of the modern blind trust in mere material and appliances. ("Some Reflections" 308)

For Conrad, the sinking of the *Titanic* represented "the blind trust in material and appliances," which then received "a terrible shock" in terms of financial speculation. Conrad viewed the reaction surrounding the sinking a mere "general consternation. . . . You stand there astonished and hurt in your profoundest sensibilities. But what else under the circumstances could you expect?" Again, looking at the technical aspects of *Titanic*, Conrad echoed his statement that smaller ships are preferable, saying he "could much sooner believe in an unsinkable ship of 3,000 tons than in one of 40,000 tons." Conrad simply saw "bigger" as being the opposite of "better." Conrad looked at the steel hull and reasoned, "you can't increase the thickness of scantling and plates indefinitely. And the mere weight of this bigness is an added disadvantage." Conrad saw his call to scale down the size of ocean liners linked to an overhaul of the luxurious frivolities that had overtaken shipbuilding. Like his retelling of Captain Flaherty's nearly disastrous final sail under the Red Star Line, Conrad concluded that if the *Titanic* "had been a couple of hundred feet shorter, she would have probably gone clear of the danger. But then, perhaps, she could not have had a swimming bath and a French café" ("Some Reflections" 308).

In all of Conrad's writings on *Titanic*, his conclusions follow a circular pattern, with variants going around a central concept; the luxurious nature of first-class passage is detrimental to safety and against the nature of a seafaring life. Conrad described the *Titanic* not as a "ship" but rather "triumph of modern naval architecture," calling the vessel "a tank 800 feet long, fitted as an hotel, with corridors, bed-rooms, halls" contained inside a steel structure as "strong" as a "Huntley and Palmer biscuit-tin" ("Some Aspects" 584). Conrad viewed the "bigness" of these liners as a "mere exaggeration" of a ship in its normal state ("Some Aspects" 585). Yet Conrad's greatest critique regarding the *Titanic* centered on the businessmen pushing high-seas luxury: "The men responsible for these big ships have been moved by considerations of profit to be made by the questionable means of pandering to an absurd and vulgar demand for banal luxury—the seaside hotel luxury" ("Some Aspects" 585). Conrad then characterizes the demand for this luxury as being forced by shipping magnates onto the general public. He writes:

> [I]t is inconceivable to think that there are people who can't spend five days of their life without a suite of apartments, cafés, bands, and such-like refined delights. I suspect that the public is not so very guilty in this matter. These things were pushed on to it in the usual course of trade competition. If to-morrow you were to take all these luxuries away, the public would still travel. (Conrad, "Some Aspects" 585)

It is not surprising that after *Titanic*'s sinking, Conrad criticized new naval engineering. Years before Lord Pirrie and J. Bruce Ismay's dream of steel luxury leviathans, the progress of the industrial revolution had instilled a faith of science and technology in the general populace. In a near-Luddite stance, Conrad penned a 1905 article for *Harper's Weekly* on the safety of wooden and smaller ships. Once more, Conrad drew on his own personal seafaring experience. "The sailing-ship, when I knew her in the days of her perfection, was a sensible creature," wrote Conrad. "When I say her days of perfection, I mean perfection of build, gear, seaworthy qualities, and ease of handling, not the perfection of speed." Conrad's anti-luxury ocean liner stance once more focused on what he viewed as the obsession of making speedy ships of massive tonnage. Conrad believed that the "quality [or ships] reached its highest excellence in the discovery of hollow lines and departed with the change of building material." For Conrad, "none of the iron ships of yesterday ever attained the marvels of speed which the seamanship of men famous in their time had obtained from their wooden, copper-sheeted predecessors." Conrad wrote, perhaps satirically, that "everything had been done to make the iron ship perfect." Yet Conrad longed for the days of small wooden ships, which "no wit of man had [yet] managed to devise an efficient coating composition to keep her bottom clean with the smooth cleanness of yellow metal sheeting" on a wooden vessel. Conrad saw longevity in the older technology, writing, "after a spell of a few weeks at sea, an iron ship begins to lag as if she had grown tired too soon. It is only her bottom that is getting foul." Here Conrad showcased that modern technology paled in comparison to the skills of a seasoned seaman. "A certain mysteriousness hangs around the quality of speed as it was displayed by the old sailing-ships commanded by competent seamen," mused Conrad. "In those days the speed was still a matter for the seaman's care; therefore, apart from the laws, rules, and regulations for the good preservation of his cargo, he was careful of his loading, of what is technically called the trim of his ship" (Conrad, "The Weight" [*Harper's*] 880).

As universally observed within Conrad's reflections on the sinking of the *Titanic*, with its massive loss of life and sensationalist news coverage on the "unsinkable ship" and human arrogance as main cause of the disaster, Conrad had the opportunity to display, within a new milieu, his historical opinion on seafaring and naval engineering. Conrad opposed the building wisdom of the past to the limits of the present, where the desire for quick passages suddenly seemed far more important than seafarers' judgment. Old wooden ships against modern steel juggernauts juxtaposed the past against the present of the new marine industry, with Conrad as a symbol of a lost epoch and yet as a prophetic voice of the importance of safety of life at sea.

Arguably the most famous sinking of the twentieth century, the *Titanic* makes for an interesting case study on Conrad's opinions surrounding capitalism, technology, and the aesthetics of luxury's influence on naval transit. Conrad, however, also expressed a differing opinion on a second sinking just six months after the *Titanic*. In "The Lesson of Collision" published in *The Illustrated London News*, Conrad examined the collision between the Norwegian collier *Storstad* and the *Empress of Ireland*, a Canadian Pacific Steamship Company ocean liner, which occurred on Saint Lawrence River, Canada, on May 29, 1914. Conrad wrote, "the loss of the Empress of Ireland awakens feelings somewhat different from those the sinking of the *Titanic* had called up on two continents. The grief for the lost and the sympathy for the survivors and the bereaved are the same; but there is not, and there cannot be, the same undercurrent of indignation." Here Conrad compared the large, but less stately *Empress of Ireland* with the *Titanic* by showing that the former was created without the hubris and overindulgent luxury that befell the latter. "The good ship that is gone," wrote Conrad,

> had not been ushered in with the beat of the big drum as the chief wonder of the world of waters. The company who owned her had no agents, authorised or unauthorised, giving boastful interviews about her unsinkability (mostly in the States, I must say) to newspaper reporters ready to swallow any sort of trade statement if only sensational enough for their readers—readers as ignorant as themselves of the realities of things outside the commonest experience of the man in the street" ("The Lesson of Collision" 944).

Conrad's comparative method of maritime disasters can also be found in an *English Review* essay, where the story of *Douro*, a Royal Mail Steam Pocket Company iron screw steamer wrecked in spring 1882 after colliding with the Spanish steamer *Yrurac Bat* in the Bay of Biscay on her way back to Southampton. Comparing the incident with the *Titanic*, Conrad noted that during the sinking, lifeboats were immediately "lowered, all the passengers put into them, and the lot shoved off" ("Some Reflections" 314). Conrad attributed the safe rescue of all crew and passengers to the fact that the *Douro*,

> was a ship commanded, manned, equipped—not a sort of marine Ritz, proclaimed unsinkable and sent adrift with its casual population upon the sea, without enough boats, without enough seamen (but with a Parisian café and four hundred of poor devils of waiters) to meet dangers which, let the engineers say what they like, lurk always amongst the waves, sent with a blind trust in mere material, light-heartedly, to a most miserable, most fatuous disaster. (Conrad, "Some Reflections" 315)

The circular pattern of Conrad's critiques against new naval construction and the safety measures that had been sacrificed to luxury for the benefit of affluent passengers is lampooned by Conrad in the mordacious imagining of an examination room of the future. "Enter to the grizzled examiner a young man of modest aspect: 'Are you well up in modern seamanship?' asks the circus barker of a character. 'I hope so, sir,' replies the young man" ("Some Reflections" 309). Conrad then sets the stage with a ship of hilarious exaggeration:

> "You are at night on the bridge in charge of a 150,000 tons ship, with a motor track, organ-loft, &c., &c., with a full cargo of passengers, a full crew of 1,500 café waiters, two sailors and a boy, three collapsible boats as per Board of Trade regulations, and going at your three-quarter speed of, say, about forty knots. You perceive suddenly right ahead, and close to, something that looks like a large ice-floe. What would you do?" (Conrad, "Some Reflections" 309)

The young man, created as a voice of reason, claims he would:

"Put the helm amidships."
"Very well," states the barker, but "Why?"
"In order to hit end on" replies the young man.
"On what grounds should you endeavour to hit end on?" (Conrad, "Some Reflections" 309)

Here, the young man embodies Conrad's feared disconnect between able-bodied sailors and company appointed business interest. "Because," answers the young man, "we are taught by our builders and masters that the heavier the smash, the smaller the damage, and because the requirements of material should be attended to" (Conrad, "Some Reflections" 309).

Once more, Conrad also attacks the opulence of the *Titanic*. He imagines future Transatlantic voyages operating under the maxim:

> [Passengers] shall go bounding across from iceberg to iceberg at 25 knots with precision and safety, and a 'cheerful, bumpy sound'. . . It shall be a teeth-loosening, exhilarating experience. The decorations will be Louis-Quinze, of course, and the café shall remain open all night. But what about the priceless Sèvres porcelain and the Venetian glass provided for the service of Transatlantic passengers? Well, I am afraid all that will have to be replaced by silver goblets and plates. Nasty, common, cheap silver. But those who will go to sea must be prepared to put up with a certain amount of hardship. ("Some Aspects" 589-590)

These essays are masterpieces of sarcasm and humor, which, on one side, are typically Conradian, while, on the other, reflect that the loss of the *Titanic* was considered beyond simple mourning and memorialization. Conrad's satire was recognized by some newspapers of the time, such as *The Cairns Post*, which published excerpts from "Some Reflections on the Loss of the Titanic." Ironically, it was the sensational coverage of the *Titanic* disaster that created a broader audience for Conrad's writings on the merits of old wooden sailing ships. Excerpts of his essays were published in *The Paterson Daily Press*, *The Gainesville Daily Sun*, and *The Spartanburg Weekly Herald*, while his first reflections on *Titanic* in *The English Review* were excerpted by *The Daily Express*, *The Chicago Examiner*, *The Poverty Bay Herald*, and *The Cairns Post*.

For Conrad, this was a different press, not the tabloid journalism that had "wrapped around" such a "most unnecessary disaster" like a "romantic garment" ("Some Aspects" 595). Behind Conrad's façade of satire, there existed a raw wound in the former sailor's psyche regarding the *Titanic* loss of "how much the merchant service, ships and men" had meant to Conrad ("Some Reflections" 312).

Conrad's reflections were the result of a pioneering spirit criticizing the new naval engineering, which he considered too ambitious and an affront to established maritime law. His writings about naval disasters anticipated the international community's decision to create uniformity to the standard of safety at sea. Fittingly, it was in the United Kingdom, Conrad's adopted homeland, where a conference convened to lay down universal rules for the safety of shipping. The result was the establishment of the International Convention for Safety of Life at Sea (SOLAS), whose first draft, adopted at the London conference on January 20, 1914, was delayed from entering into force due to the First World War. After the adoption of 1929, 1948, 1960, 1974 versions, it finally entered into legal force in 1980, long after Conrad's death 1924.

Today, SOLAS is the most important of all international treaties regarding the safety of merchant ships. It fulfills Conrad's dream, creating an international basis, which has saved the lives of incalculable sailors and passengers. Since the London conference, representatives of thirteen countries have introduced new international requirements on the safety of all merchant ships, including provision on watertight and fire-resistant bulkheads, life-saving appliances, and fire prevention and firefighting appliances on passenger ships. Further requirements mandate radiotelegraph equipment for ships carrying more than fifty people and the establishment of a North Atlantic ice patrol, an echo of Conrad's call to sail ships in pairs, with constant radio contact.

Conrad's contribution to maritime safety can still be felt today. His writings on the *Titanic* influenced IMO Secretary-General Koji

Sekimizu's speech on the 2012 World Maritime Day, held on the hundred-year anniversary of the *Titanic*'s sinking. The speech also used a comparative approach, reflecting on how much had improved since the *Titanic*'s sinking in 1912 and how important IMO's commitment, as the United Nations maritime agency, was (and is) to preventing the recurrence of disasters on such a scale in the future:

> Many ships have sunk—too many—but few have had the lasting impact of the Titanic, a ship which, at the time, was the most technically advanced vessel afloat and which seemed almost invulnerable. And yet, as history has recorded, she was transformed in a few short hours from the world's most celebrated ship into a name forever associated with tragedy. The sinking of the Titanic prompted the major shipping nations of the world, at that time, to take decisive action to address maritime safety. . . . Today, 100 years since the Titanic, IMO has developed—and maintains—a comprehensive regulatory framework for shipping and its remit has expanded to include not only safety, but also environmental protection, legal matters, technical co-operation, maritime security and the efficiency of shipping. It could fairly be said that the Titanic disaster of 1912 was the catalyst that eventually led shipping into a new era of maritime safety. (Sekimizu)

The creation of these new and evolving safety mechanisms and agencies are reminiscent of Conrad's poetic truism: that there is "nothing . . . heroic in being drowned" in a "a tank 800 feet long, fitted as an hotel, with corridors, bed-rooms, halls" as "strong [as a] . . . biscuit-tin" ("Some Aspects" 595).

Works Cited

Conrad, Joseph. "Certain Aspects of the Admirable Inquiry into the Loss of the Titanic, 1912." *Notes on Life and Letters*. Garden City, NY: Doubleday, Page & Company, 1921. 229-248. Print.

_____. "England's Indignation and Grief over the 'Titanic'." *The Literary Digest*. 44. Ed. Edward Jewitt Wheeler, Isaac Kaufman Funk, & William Seaver Woods: 925. Print.

_____. "The Lesson of the Collision." *The Illustrated London News* (June 6, 1914): 944. Print.

_____. "On the Titanic." *The London Budget* (April 20–21, 1912): n.p. Print.

_____. "Some Aspects of the Admirable Inquiry." *The English Review* (July 1912): 581-595. Print.

_____. "Some Reflections, Seamanlike and Otherwise, on the Loss of the Titanic." *The English Review* (May 1912): 304-315. Print.

_____. "Some Reflections on the Loss of the Titanic, 1912." *Notes on Life and Letters*. Garden City, NY: Doubleday, Page & Company, 1921. 213-228. Print.

_____. "The Weight of Her Burden." *Harper's Weekly* (June 17, 1905): 880-881. Print.

_____. "The Weight of the Burden." *The Mirror of the Sea*. New York and London: Harper & Brothers Publishers, 1906. 77-78. Print.

"Danger of Big Ships: Mr Joseph Conrad on the Lesson of the Titanic". *The Daily Express* (May 2, 1912): 7. Print.

"Danger of Big Ships: Mr Joseph Conrad on the Lesson of the Titanic." *The Poverty Bay Herald* (June 15, 1912): Supplement, 1. Print.

"The Lost Titanic: Small Ships are Better. J. Conrad's Stinging Satire." *The Cairns Post* (June 18, 1912): 6. Print.

"Manageableness at Sea." *The Chicago Examiner* (June 7, 1912): editorial page.

"The Old Sailing Ships: Why the Wooden Ones Were Better Than Those Built of Iron". *The Paterson Daily Press* (July 14, 1905): 17. Print.

"The Old Sailing Ships: Why the Wooden Ones Were Better Than Those Built of Iron." *The Gainesville Daily Sun* (August 13, 1905): 7. Print.

"The Old Sailing Ships: Why the Wooden Ones Were Better Than Those Built of Iron." *The Spartanburg Weekly Herald* (November 28, 1905): 7. Print.

"The 'Real' Café Parisien." *Café Parisien*. Café Parisien, 2006. Web. 27 May 2013. <http://cafeparisien.com/history.php>.

Sekimizu, Koji. "World Maritime Day: opening remarks." *IMO News*. International Maritime Organization. Web. 17 Oct. 2012. <http://www.imo.org/en/MediaCentre/SecretaryGeneral/SpeechesByTheSecretaryGeneral/Pages/World-Maritime-Day-Parallel-Event1023-8802.aspx>.

Modeling Modernity
Phillip A. Lobo

At the turn of the century—1904 to be precise—Joseph Conrad published a work unlike anything he had previously written. *Nostromo: A Tale of the Seaboard* was remarkable not because it was set in South America—Conrad's stories are frequently located in what were, at the time, exotic, colonial locales, such as the Congo or Malay—but because this setting was created from whole cloth. In writing *Nostromo*, Conrad invented the country of Costaguana, an entire fictive republic rendered in unprecedented detail. Whereas his earlier works had offered glimpses of corners of the world unfamiliar to readers, this was the first that was so carefully and explicitly constructed. Indeed, it is one of the earliest examples of what might be understood as 'world-building' in literature. Moreover, it establishes a newly developing mode of representation, one which remains an influence on the production not just of novels, but of newer media forms, including—as we shall see—video games.

From Mythology to Modernity

What is world-building? It should not be confused with myth-making. Myths about world creation are pre-modern inventions. They serve ancient functions, providing explanations for the constitutions of powers in the world, by reinforcing age-old values and traditional practices: the repetitions of ritual that form ancient theater, the oral histories passed on generation after generation. It is an archaic form of representation, appropriate to an archaic age and, in many ways, pre-historical. World-building, on the other hand, is a distinctly modern practice, and it answers modern demands, expressed in a modern (historical) temporality. It is a new practice, one that reflects a shift in the larger world, and one concurrent with the maturation of the novel, and thus of literary realism. It is a shift towards a globalized world, governed by standardized, historical time, antithetical to the timeless quality of mythic narrative.

Conrad dramatizes this shift within the first chapter of *Nostromo*, with our first glimpse of Costaguana, a glimpse centered around the locale's movement from a mythic past of isolation to a historical present of globalization:

> In the time of Spanish rule, and for many years afterwards, the town of Sulaco [a city in Costaguana]—the luxuriant beauty of the orange gardens bear witness to its *antiquity*—had never been commercially anything more important than a coasting port with a fairly large *local trade in ox-hides and indigo*. The clumsy, *deep-sea galleons* of the conquerors, that, needing a brisk gale to move at all, would lie becalmed, where your *modern ship*, built on clipper lines, forges ahead by the mere flapping of her sails, had been barred out of Sulaco by the prevailing calms of its vast gulf. Some harbors of the earth are made difficult of access by the treachery of sunken rocks and the tempests of their shores. Sulaco had found an *inviolable sanctuary* from the *temptations of a trading world* in the solemn hush of the deep Gulfo Placido as if within an enormous semicircular and *unroofed temple* open to the ocean, with its walls of *lofty mountains* hung with the mourning draperies of cloud. (Conrad, *Nostromo* 3, emphasis mine)

The emphasis in this passage is on the tranquility and essential timelessness of the scene; Sulaco is both Arcadian and Edenic— ancient, isolated, and paradisiacal—with a traditional agricultural and pastoral economy. Sheltered from the invasive influence of larger trade forces, Sulaco would seem to exist in a kind of mythic golden age.

This is not to say that Costaguana is presented as bereft of sin, but rather subject to the simple, premodern morality of the fable. Hence the story—appearing early in the novel—of the 'two wandering sailors' and their 'good-for-nothing mozo' guide who steal a mule and seek hidden treasure in the treacherous reaches of the Azuera peninsula. This expedition ends as morality tales so often do:

> . . . the two gringos, spectral and alive, are believed to be dwelling to this day among the rocks, under the fatal spell of their success.

Their souls cannot tear themselves away from their bodies *mounting guard over the discovered treasure*. The are now rich and thirsty - a strange theory of *tenacious gringo ghosts* suffering in their starved and parched flesh. . . . These, then, are the *legendary inhabitants of Azuera, guarding its forbidden wealth*; and the shadow on the sky on one side, with the round patch of blue haze blurring the bright skirt of the horizon on the other, mark the two outermost points of the bend which bears the name of Gulfo Placido, because never a strong wind had been known to blow upon its waters. (Conrad, *Nostromo* 4-5, emphasis mine)

At first, it seems that this brief tale serves to prefigure the events of the novel, and this is essentially, if simplistically, true. The lure of precious metal hidden within the San Tome mountain becomes the bane of nearly every character in *Nostromo*. Both foreign invaders and compromised locals suffer the consequences of their greed, a greed that seems to be the foremost engine of evil in the story of *Nostromo*.

If, however, the fable were capable of doing all that work in and of itself, why not simply expand *its* narrative? Why go to the trouble of unfurling Costaguana in all its manifold detail, a detail so intricate that it is commonly seen as Conrad's—to quote his contemporary John Galsworthy—"most sheer peace of creation"? (Najder 243). No small feat, if we believe the author. In *A Personal Record*, Conrad wrote of Costaguana: "There was not a single brick, stone or grain of sand of its soil I had not placed in position with my own hands" (170).

This rather Joycean conceit—brick by brick, as it were—is a sign of *Nostromo*'s distinct modernity. The fable of the gringos is insufficient to account for all that modernity's arrival will do to change Costaguana; they do not prefigure, but rather predate. In fact, another, closer look at the above passage reveals that these 'legendary guardians' are associated not with the invasion of English steamboats, but rather with the preserving calm of the Gulfo Placido itself. They are not so much the result of the violation of the forbidden, but the very condition of that forbidden-ness.

Critical comparisons between Costaguana and Conrad's other invented spaces must, therefore, take into account that—while his African and Malaysian spaces represent the unmapped, mythic 'hearts of darkness'—Costaguana is experienced as mythical only in the past of the story. In this way, it represents not an escape from the claustrophobia of an all-too-ordered modernity into a mythical 'outside,' but rather the final triumph of modernity and an endemic claustrophobia that comes about due to advances in transportation and telecommunication. For this was the new reality: by the turn of the century, mapping techniques and modern engineering were literally reshaping the land, changing and contracting the space such that mythic representations no longer function (Acheraïou 173; Ho 2).

It is also worth noting that this most 'well mapped' of Conrad's worlds is the one that itself cannot be found on any map. Though Conrad was hailed as a 'realist' as early as 1914—specifically for the richness of *Nostromo*'s detail—this sense of Costaguana's 'realness' must be considered alongside the fact of its total synthesis. For we must beg the question: how 'real' could such a representation possibly be, when it is so thoroughly artificial?

Moreover, for all that the book serves as a colonial critique, is it not still a literary analog to colonialism? What are the ethics of representing a foreign nation and a foreign culture that is wholly fictional, yet lays claim to 'realism'? Is *Nostromo* complicit in making South America, by way of fiction, yet another playground for the political fantasies of the developed world? Critics could well argue that the novel serves only to generalize and naturalize the political woes of Latin America, to paint with a broad brush and thus 'tropicalize' them. Can we uphold the value of Costaguana in spite of its fictiveness and generalizations?

Ironically, the setting's 'realism'—Costaguana's capacity to represent reality—is *dependent* on that very generality. As critic Zdzisław Najder affirms, the history and politics of Costaguana are "synthetic," composed by Conrad from a mix of customs and features, all drawn from various regional sources. However, rather than deeming this result pastiche, Najder considers this synthetic approach a precondition for Costaguana to *be* "representative." How so? Because such an act of synthesis is necessary in order to produce a "convincing whole" with representational validity unto itself (Najder 233-4).

In order for Costaguana to act as more than *merely* an allegory for an individual country—say, Columbia, Venezuela, or Panama—it must be free of facile, one-to-one comparisons. To be more than a mythic space, however, it must also reflect the "material conditions" of its geopolitical milieu while retaining a "material specificity" that grants it the autonomy necessary to serve as a laboratory space, a space in which Conrad can do more than represent colonial politics, but in a sense 'run' them, as one runs an experiment, or a simulation (Ramirez 108). In this way, the necessary self-containment of the whole allows Conrad to treat Costaguana as both "an experimental crucible" and a "laboratory-like situation where factors of secondary importance are eliminated" (Najder 237).

Thus by maintaining an internal self-validity through a fundamental independence from external reference, the constructed world gains the authority to present itself as more substantial, in and of itself, than an allegorical narrative. Moreover, this very substance allows the constructed world to serve as a critically useful space. It provides a basis for investigating Costaguana on its own terms, while additionally serving as a foundation for numerous comparisons with external events without retreating into narratology, which too often traps us in the vice grip of the plot's inevitability. Costaguana is, in effect, the possible setting for many stories, without resorting to one single story's authority. It manages to be both groundless and wholly grounded. It is real—or, rather, is able to lay claim to reality—not in spite of its imagined status, but because of it.

As previously discussed, this form of representation was necessitated by the failure of mythic narrative to cope with the problems of modernity. What the steamboats bring with them is that very thing that made spaces such a Patusan necessary in the first place: the claustrophobia-inducing arrival of modernity, with its telecommunications, transportation technology, and cartography. This changes the way in which Sulaco—and Costaguana as a whole—must be represented; in fact it must be represented as just that: a whole. This 'whole' is heterogenous and torn apart by internal divisions, many of these symptoms of a premodern colonialism, but even these divisions are framed by the way in which modern technology quite literally reshapes the landscape.

The clearest example in the novel is that of the National Central Railway, the keystone in the plan to hasten Costaguana's modernization. This railway project involves the technological conquest of old geographical limitations, and it is not without a historical referent: the Panama Canal. A thoroughly modern realization of the long-held dream of a Northwest Passage, the Canal is an ideal example of the way in which technology (with the pressure of global capital behind it) ploughs through natural barriers, simultaneously realizing the goals of colonial exploration while hastening the end of that exploration.

Conrad is acutely aware of how this transformation of the landscape presents a challenge to traditional modes of representation. A prime example comes from a description of one of Costaguana's hidden natural treasures (to borrow from the parlance of tourist brochures), a fragment of idyll radically transformed by the necessities of industrialization:

> The waterfall existed no longer. The tree-ferns that had luxuriated in its spray had died around the dried up pool, and the high ravine was only a big trench half filled up with the refuse of excavations and tailings. The torrent, dammed up above, sent its water rushing along the open flumes of scooped tree trunks along the open flumes of scooped tree trunks striding on trestle-legs to the turbines working the stamps on the lower plateau—the mesa grande of the San Tome mountains. (Conrad, *Nostromo* 75)

The prose here is highly suggestive. The natural feature of the 'high ravine' is transformed into the infinitely more practical and infinitely less aesthetic 'big trench,' and the chance falling of the stream is redirected into purposeful use by means of repurposed tree trunks, as good a metaphor for the conversion of nature into labor as one could ask for. Even the trestle legs these flumes stand on create a descriptive match to the telegraph cables and the railway tracks that are similarly redrawing and recreating the landscape of Costaguana.

In the face of this total transformation, the role of representation becomes problematized:

> Only the memory of the waterfall, with it amazing fernery, like a hanging garden above the rocks of the gorge, was preserved in Mrs. Gould's water-colour sketch; she had made it hastily one day from a cleared patch in the bushes, sitting in the shade of a roof of straw erected for her on three rough poles under Don Pepe's direction.
>
> Mrs. Gould had seen it all from the beginning: the clearing of the wilderness, the making of the road, the cutting of new paths up the cliff face of San Tome. (Conrad, *Nostromo* 75)

This aesthetic preservation is a practice tied to nostalgia, an understandable sentiment that nevertheless undercuts the usefulness of Mrs. Gould's attempt. Her witnessing does nothing to change events; quite the opposite in fact, since her artistic practice (landscape painting) and even her very presence (as wife to the Englishman of Sulaco) are already indicators of those very events, and the object of her attempt is moored firmly in a mythic past that is, once more, figured in prelapsarian terms—a 'hanging garden,' a 'paradise of snakes.'

Mrs. Gould's difficulty can be seen as a reflection on Conrad's own. J. M. Robertson contends that Conrad might be "a painter or a man of science," a conflation he justifies by linking the two practices—science and (representative) painting—through what he calls Conrad's "universal response to all visible phenomena" (Jefferson 443). That Conrad chooses the novel—the modern literary form *par excellance*—serves to help reconcile the divide through this commonality, the bridge between his two sides of vision. Independently each technique is inadequate to deal with Costaguana's situation; painting captures only lost images, while science (by way of technology) is deeply implicated in the very changes it would be used to describe. His answer is a fusion of the two, to represent neither the impalpable nor the palpable, the 'real invisible forces' or the 'real material facts,' but rather to use the novel form to demonstrate their essential imbrication and, in so doing, provide a convincing model of Costaguana.

Here we've hit upon just the word. As Rupert Croft-Cooke so eloquently states: "... *Nostromo* rises like a great building, every pilaster in place, as though constructed from a highly finished model" (Conrad xi). *Nostromo* the novel *is* built from a model: that of Costaguana itself.

Simulation and Discontent

There could be no better time to properly introduce *Tropico* (PopTop 2001) an administrative simulation not unlike *SimCity*, in which the player takes on the role of president and dictator of a small, fictional Caribbean island. Tasked with managing the nationalized economy and political system of a nation of fewer than a hundred citizens (at first), the player makes numerous decisions as they pursue a variety of goals, including the technological and economic development of their island. As such, the centerpiece of the game is the island itself, and its complex economic and political simulation.

To head off confusions over terminology, and to better demonstrate the link between the notions of 'model' and 'simulation,' it is worthwhile to mention that PopTop's initial success as a developer came from its revitalization of the *Railroad Tycoon* franchise. *Railroad Tycoon II* represents eighteenth through twentieth century economic and transportation development as motivated by its simulation of the stock exchange, procedurally demonstrating how market pressure acts to reshape terrain, just as they do in Costaguana. It also illustrates how the very idea of modeling is motivated by modern transportation advancements; it is telling that one of the most ubiquitous and detail-obsessed types of model-hobbyism is that of the model train. Previous to the advent of these systematized transportation methods, the ability to even imagine the world in such a way would have been difficult. After their advent, it became impossible to simulate the world in a representative way without some recourse to modeling.

This shift in representation is also concurrent with the emergence of the 'God's eye view,' a radically new perspectival possibility enabled by another advancement in modern transportation technology. Only from an airplane, or from the lofty perch of a zeppelin, would it be possible to view the landscape in all its transformed totality—like a model, a miniature in exact scale. From this perspective it is also possible to plot future changes to the landscape, or to enact change directly with a strafing of machine gun fire or the dropping of a bomb.

Such a perspective is the only one through which *Tropico* is played; the game's camera hovers over the island, zooming in and out, shifting perspective, and rendering the island as a highly detailed map. This map can be further overlaid by informational filters, meant to assist in the development (or exploitation) of the island and its resources. Communications critic Shoshana Magnet identifies this system of map overlays—which use this aerial perspective to provide information on the demographic, economic and social constitution of the island—as one of the many symptoms of what she considers *Tropico*'s naturalization of imperialist assumptions. "Maps are one of the means," she claims, "by which *Tropico* mystifies and makes explicit its connection to colonization. . . . In simply revealing good locations for planting cash crops, *Tropico* presents the preference for profit as cartographic fact. The map becomes a means to represent the values of the game 'in the guise of scientific disinterestedness'" (Magnet 152). This 'scientific disinterest,' guise or not, is very much in keeping with the principles of modeling.

One trouble with Magnet's reading is that her central complaint - that "[t]here is no graphical representation of [*Tropico*'s] map that indicates overall human well-being and suffering" (Magnet 153)—is patently false. There are in fact many, many such views—views that represent healthcare and housing quality, job and dietary satisfaction, personal liberty and happiness—and these views are crucial to any player interested in playing successfully. While *Tropico* certainly allows and perhaps even invites an attitude of development towards its setting's terrain, for a player to ignore the welfare of the citizens is to invite ousting, either by electoral means, coup d'état, or armed revolution.

Admitting that *Tropico* can and does possess the means to represent human suffering even from the totalizing gaze of the airplane or the model-maker, however, does not mean that this view is any less historically or technologically determined. Rather, since history and technology have *already* inflected the landscape in such a way, such a gaze is necessary if only to represent those systems which *produce* suffering. Simply put, these systems are already effectively enacted upon spaces infiltrated by modern global commerce—the mountains have given way and the Gulfo Placido is even now disturbed by steamer turbines—but their significance and function remain, if not invisible, then to some great extent concealed. It is made visible only when one is able to adopt this totalizing perspective. *Nostromo* is a historical documentation of just this dawning representative necessity: the personal romance of Jim, the political disillusionment of Razumov, even the murky journey of Marlow cannot properly speak to the changes undergone by Costaguana and all its possible referents.

It would be fair to say that this totalizing view is instrumental and must be understood in those terms. In the case of *Tropico* the map overlay serves precisely to assist the player in their modernization of the island nation, a process that the game makes necessary to some greater or lesser extent. Simply put, the human condition is hardly paradisiacal in either Tropico or Costaguana prior to the arrival of modern technology. When the player takes up their presidency there is no proper housing on Tropico, no healthcare, no variety in diet, no educational facilities, and no prospect of addressing any of these problems unless the island develops something like a modern social economy. Similarly, in Costaguana, the only reason the San Tome mine is closed is that, lacking the necessary technology, it can no longer be made profitable for anyone, foreign or national, no matter how ruthlessly its workers may or may not be exploited. However ambivalent Conrad may feel, however ambivalent we may find ourselves feeling, a confrontation with the forces of modernity can no more be avoided than can the mythical past be maintained or restored.

Both *Nostromo* and *Tropico* address this ambivalence directly, without retreating into nostalgia; they recognize that even the most fiercely Manichean of colonial struggles can ill afford to leave technology solely in the hands of exploiters. In *Nostromo*, as Ramirez puts it, "[t]he technologies of empire" can just as easily be "turned against British enterprise" by revolutionaries whose ostensible goal is to place the tools of modernization, and its benefits, in the hands of the colonized, "aim[ing] to nationalize foreign and oligarchic properties" (Ramirez 112). In *Tropico*, which posits this nationalization *a priori*, technology can be used either to augment the liberty of the populace or to further an agenda of exploitation. A radio station, for example, comes with the various broadcast options selected by the player upon construction, subject to change at any time during or after. One of these options—"All Presidente, All Day"—reserves the radio waves for broadcast of government propaganda and can help sway public opinion towards supporting the player's regime regardless of island conditions. Just as easily, however, the player can select "Radio Free Tropico," which increases the liberty of all citizens within range, and encourages their commitment to the democratic process.

For each of these texts, the issue of modern technology and the totalizing view it both enacts and makes necessary, becomes a matter of deployment. Since this technological gaze and the developments it enables seem to have the capacity for both good and ill, the question becomes: how to use this view ethically? Is it going to be 'naturalizing' or critical? Magnet contends that *Tropico*'s view is essentially colonial and exploitative, but the text of the game itself resists such pigeon-holing; rather it seems to beg the question Magnet believes she has already answered: can this act of generalizing and totalizing be progressive, or is to doomed only to enact that which it is a product of? The question can just as easily be put to Conrad, and often is; Chinua Achebe, in his unflinching piece *An Image of Africa*, is at least as condemnatory of Conrad—

whom he convincingly argues is a "bloody racist"—as Magnet is of *Tropico* (9).

A Critical God's-Eye

The basis upon which critics have seen fit to forgive Conrad—or at least his literature—can shed light on how we might view *Tropico*. This possibility for redemption, we will find, deals with two subjects we've already been grappling with: representation and perspective. First, Costaguana's tropicalization seems to be legitimate insofar as it productively reflects the political and economic 'realities' of Latin America; that is to say, even where his narrative and opinions are 'wrong,' Conrad's model of Costaguana itself can be 'right'. This 'rightness' of representation, as we've established, cannot be claimed without some recourse or reference to a totalizing technological perspective. So the further onus then rests upon the perspective itself: is it critical of its own totality and power, or does it naturalize it?

Conrad is spoken for. Thomas Jeffers—who rightly alleges to Conrad a 'pluralistic criticism' of imperialism—notes the historical difference between Costaguana and his previous fictional locations. "Unlike Africa or the Malay Archipelago," Jeffers states, "[Costaguana] has been under European influence for nearly half a millennium, and therefore all questions of who's robbing or who's helping whom are exceedingly difficult to sort out." (Jeffers 91) In such a circumstance, Conrad's work would appear to try and use the totalizing perspective as a way to express this problematic plurality. Jeffers asserts that Conrad thinks "[w]e need to be on the ground, trying to see problems and opportunities from the point of view of each of the players" (Jeffers 91).

Nadjer points to Conrad's use of irony as central to this attempt. The function of irony in *Nostromo* is, according to him, "to undercut appearance—social, psychological, and moral," and, when properly and consistently applied, irony even "works as an optical device, which produces an effect of multi-dimensionality, of in-depth vision . . . it makes the reader see everything from many sides simultaneously" (Nadjer 234). This ironic view—one that already sounds like that of the mobile three-dimensional camera perspective used in many game interfaces, including *Tropico*'s—seems very similar to the totalizing gaze we have previously discussed. Yet it is politically progressive—or contains the potential for political progressiveness—insofar as it *is* critical.

So the litmus test for *Tropico* rests on what extent its perspective encourages critical engagement, as opposed to—as Magnet would have it—"encourag[ing] the player to lose themselves in the game and forget the implications of the gamescape they are constructing" (148). The power to control and reshape the island of Tropico is very real; it is, in fact, the basic premise and purpose of gameplay. However, does the game perform a feat of imperial world-building? Does it re-inscribe the colonial gaze such that the player, like that archetypal colonist Robinson Crusoe, "experiences the world as all before him, a spatial expanse he is free to grasp and take" (Ho 1)?

My answer is both a yes and a no. Yes, the game is committed to an experience of power over the landscape, a power that is granted expressly for the purpose of bringing modernity to the island of Tropico. Yes, the player takes the role of a dictator; while assembling the dossier that will define the qualities, traits, and personal history of their dictatorial avatar, the player can in fact choose to be "Installed by the CIA." They may also opt to be "Installed by the KGB." They may choose the option "Bought the Election," or "Fascist Rebellion." But the player can just as easily be "Elected as a Socialist," or even come to power in a "Velvet Revolution!" When Magnet explains how it is "easy to imagine your avatar 'presidente' in the role of [a] . . . U.S. Puppet government official coming in to fix the 'unruly' problems of the locals through oppressive governance and micromanagement" (Magnet 151), she neglects to mention that this need not be imagined, but is in fact an option included within the game, along with a variety of other options that confront the player from the outset.

Matthew Shields is far closer to the mark when he says that the designers of the game "create a world of economic and political cynicism they use to describe the benefits of modern Western-style social welfare" (Shields i). Far from fostering imperial impunity,

Shields suggests the total perspective of *Tropico* "creates a very humanizing world view in which political actors are not only held accountable for their decisions, but must acknowledge their own failings and strengths" (49). The option to intern or eliminate, exploit or oppress any of your citizenry is always available, but never as a necessity, and not without manifest consequence.

It is outside the scope of this chapter to level a critique of the Western social welfare state. However, taking that ideological background as implicit, we can still see how interaction with a system such as *Tropico*'s demands a series of decisions and considerations that preclude any easy or passive interpolation into ideological assumptions. While the game's humorous tone encourages a playful and unserious engagement—games, like novels, are always intended as entertainment—they also make each choice deliberate and grant each decision's effect an observable effect on the island and its inhabitants. The ideology a player enacts, be it capitalist, socialist, democratic, or fascist, is a matter of explicit nomination, rather than passive acceptance.

Above all else, I contend that world-building—in that it produces a model system for examination and application—is intrinsically a critical appraisal of a type that only grows more important as the global web of capitalism grows thicker and more tangled, more difficult to discern let alone meaningfully represent. Worlds, like words, cease to belong to the one that formed them the moment they are let loose. Costaguana is an object that can be abstracted from the text that produces it, one that can be appropriated and put to new uses, as more than one author has, in fact, done. Similarly, games also lend themselves to conversion and modification. Even Magnet points to patching and 'modding' as a possible method for countering continued colonial discourse. As Jennifer French correctly asserts, *Nostromo* ought to be "ambivalently embraced and interrogated—translated, falsified, and subjected to new processes of admixture and adaptation" (French 262). And the same goes for *Tropico*, and for any world structure robust enough to allow for a critical examination of its workings as it works. For even if the structures of colonization have settled into the very way we view the world, without convincing models of that world, how can we even start to describe it, let alone begin to invent a new one?

Works Cited

Achebe, Chinua. "An Image of Africa: Racism in Conrad's 'Heart of Darkness.'" *Research in African Literatures* 9.1 Special Issue on Literary Criticism (Spring 1978): 1-15. Print.

Acheraïou, Amar. "Going Beyond Limits: De-territorialization in Conrad's Novels." *Conradiana* 37.1-2 (2005): 173-84. Print.

Carpenter, Richard C. "The Geography of Costaguana, or Where 'Is' Sulaco?" *Journal of Modern Literature* 5.2 (1976): 321-26. Print.

Conrad, Joseph. *Nostromo: A Tale of the Seaboard*. Produced by Judy Boss and David Widger. Kindle EBook.

_____. *A Personal Record*. New York: Harper Brothers, 1912. Print.

Croft-Cooke, Rupert. Introduction. *Nostromo: A Tale of the Seaboard*. By Joseph Conrad. New York: Heritage, 1961. ix-xviii. Print.

French, Jennifer L. "Martin Decoud in the Afterlife: A Dialogue with Latin American Writers." *Conradiana* 40.2 (2008): 247-65. Print.

Ho, Janice. "The Spatial Imagination and Literary Form of Conrad's Colonial Fictions." *Journal of Modern Literature* 30.4 (2007): 1-19. Print.

Huneker, James. "The Genius of Joseph Conrad." *The North American Review* 200.705 (1914): 270-79. Print.

İçöz, Nursel. "Conrad and Ambiguity: Social Commitment and Ideology in *Heart of Darkness* and *Nostromo*." *Conradiana* 37.3 (2005): 245-58. Print.

Jeffers, Thomas L. "The Logic of Material Interests in Conrad's *Nostromo*." *Raritan* 23.2 (2003): 80-111. Print.

Magnet, S. "Playing at Colonization: Interpreting Imaginary Landscapes in the Video Game Tropico." *Journal of Communication Inquiry* 30.2 (2006): 142-62. Print.

Mallios, Peter Lancelot. "Introduction: Untimely *Nostromo*." *Conradiana* 40.3 (2009): 213-32. Print.

Najder, Zdzisław. "A Century of *Nostromo*." *Conradiana* 40.3 (2009): 233-46. Print.

Ramirez, Luz Elena. "The Rhetoric of Development in Joseph Conrad's *Nostromo*." *Texas Studies in Literature and Language* 42.2 (2000): 93-117. Print.

Robertson, J. M. "The Novels of Joseph Conrad." *The North American Review* 208.754 (1918): 439-53. Print.

Shields, Matthew J. "A Pentadic Analysis of Tropico: Dramatism and Digital Games." Thesis. Oregon State University, 2009. Web. 30 Sept. 2016. <http://ir.library.oregonstate.edu/xmlui/handle/1957/12001>.

Tropico v1.07 April 24, 2001. PopTop Software.

Tropico 4 v1.03 August 30, 2011. Kalypso Media.

The Writer Who Foresaw Slow Food: Joseph Conrad and the Morality of Eating

Francesco Buscemi

Why Conrad and Food

In exploring Joseph Conrad's general views, political ideas and sentimental feelings on food, the aim of this chapter is to analyze how the Polish British writer thought about what we eat and how his conception anticipated perspectives on food that are widespread and popular today, especially thanks to the work of the Slow Food movement. Conrad and Slow Food never met each other, as Conrad died in 1924 and Slow Food originated in the second part of the 1980s. Slow Food, a movement rooted in themes of localism, is considered to be a reaction to globalized system of food distribution and the 1980s success of the fast food industry. In analyzing Conrad's perspectives on food, this chapter finds that many of Slow Food's ideas were, in fact, already present in the work of the novelist and that the roots of the movement can be traced back to the beginning of the twentieth century.

Investigating Conrad and food together may seem strange, as in Conrad's opus cooking and eating are not apparently central. Donovan, in his 2003 essay "Magic Letters and Mental Degradation: Advertising in 'An Anarchist' and 'The Partner,'" and Hawthorn, in his 2007 book *Sexuality and the Erotic in the Fiction of Joseph Conrad*, have already explored the field, although from a symbolic perspective and with other aims in comparison to this chapter. In many cases and like many other novelists, Conrad used food in his writing to underline his perspective on the world, create more authentic characters and plausible scenes in his narration, or for numerous other purposes. This chapter adds, however, an overlooked exploration into the way Conrad uses food as a way to describe the "new globalization," occurring since the end of the nineteenth century, as a dominant theme in his narratives.

In his many novels and short stories, Conrad's characters often venture to remote locales and encounter differing cultures, where they affect and are affected by global novelties and contribute to creating a world that has become smaller and better known. Certainly, Conradian "journeys" are an instrument to critically represent Western people as less trustworthy and less pure than people from remote countries (Rawa). However, in his stories, traveling is always seen as a means for his characters to better know themselves and the Other. It is in this sense that food acquires great importance for this study, as it has always been a key element in any form of globalization. Where people travel, food travels. Food bears with it tradition and novelty, curiosity for or fears of the Other, openness and closure, nostalgia, pleasure, discovery, and many other emotions and sentiments (Levenstein; Gabaccia). Thus, in analyzing a writer so engaged with traveling as Conrad, food is a valuable lens into understanding the way he sees the world.

Slow Food: A Brief Account

Slow Food is an Italian food movement founded in 1986 by a group led by Carlo Petrini. They rallied together against the opening of a MacDonald's fast food restaurant in Rome's city center (Parasecoli, *Food Culture*; Petrini & Padovani, *Slow Food Revolution*). To the Slow Food activists, the presence of a fast food chain in the center of the Italian capital challenged both Italian food and Italian identity.

In his many works (Petrini & Padovani, *Slow Food Revolution*; Petrini, *Buono*; Petrini & Scaffidi, "Cenni di Storia"), Petrini tells the story of the movement, explains that food must be local, fair, and clean. In this way, he pays homage to the French gastronome Anthelme Brillat-Savarin (1755–1826) when he says that food is not only a matter of biology and chemistry, but that it also involves politics and the economy (Petrini, *Terra Madre* 72). In 2004, Slow Food also founded a university and became a global movement thanks to *Terra Madre*, an international exposition in which food producers from all over the world gather together in order to defend the authenticity of their products.

The movement fights to support local products and defends them from the "invasion" of foods imported from other countries, particularly the industrial food products, which are often considered to be of inferior quality, with obscured origins, as well as a threat to Italian identity. In fact, in his 2001 book, *Slow Food: Le Ragioni del Gusto*, Petrini argues that Italy has rural roots and that industrialized foods are totally extraneous to Italy's history and Italian lifestyles. For Petrini, rural societies are based on diversification and variety, while industrialization homogenizes taste and daily life. Leitch, interestingly, has analyzed the Slow Food crusade in favor of *Lardo di Colonnata*, a "typical" Italian sausage. In defending it from the industrial enemy, for Leitch, actually Slow Food supports the commodification of rural foods. After the Slow Food crusade, the price of *Lardo* rose, and this specific sausage became a product for high and middle classes, while many local people could no longer afford it.

The Slow Food movement is not without detractors and has been criticized for a broad range of reasons. Parasecoli reports criticisms about how the specific foods supported by the movement usually become more expensive and that Slow Food has been accused of "'culinary luddism,' whose goal would be to stop the industrialization process of food" ("Slow Food" 335). Others find that Slow Food is ethnocentric, as its "model is clearly rooted in a conception of Europe, and more specifically Italy, as a source of civilized practice" (MacDonald 95). Finally, some critiqued Slow Food's gendered perspective, arguing that it creates a passive role for women (Meneley; Spring Kurtz; Probyn).

Many of these critiques are certainly true, but it must be said that the Slow Food movement has understood and promoted the centrality of food in cultural, social, and political fields. It is thanks to this movement that today many people talk about food with a greater awareness than they did in the past. Much of this has involved extremism, but the importance of the movement in the improvement of food awareness cannot be called into question. This brief sketch of the Slow Food movement has highlighted Slow Food's merits and elucidated some of its underlying detractions, as both the benefits and disadvantages of Slow Food are critical to understand Conrad's views of food.

Joseph Conrad: Food as a Moral Agent

To understand Conrad's perception of food, it may be useful to start from the brief preface that he wrote in 1923 for *A Handbook of Cookery for a Small House*, a cookbook by his wife, Jessie Conrad. It is the only work in Conrad's literary career entirely dedicated to food. In just the first paragraph, we are able to see how important food and writing about food was for Conrad. He writes that cookbooks aim "to increase the happiness of mankind" (Jos. Conrad, "Cookery" 112). A couple of paragraphs below, we read a phrase that is key to understanding Conrad's approach to food: "Good cooking is a moral agent" (112). The use of the word "moral" is significant in this quote, as it is often the same adjective used by Slow Food proponents, as issues of morality often frame Slow Food's conception of food (MacDonald).

In the preface of his wife's cookbook, Conrad states that good cooking is "conscientious preparation" (Jos. Conrad, "Cookery" 112) of everyday food. The term "conscientious" is key to this preface, and Conrad repeats it throughout: "Conscientious cooking is an enemy to gluttony" (112); "Conscientious cooking . . . promotes the serenity of mind, the graciousness of thought, and . . . optimism" (112); and finally, Conrad extolls the creation of "the conscientious cook" (113).

Thus, food for Conrad links to morality, conscience and the wellbeing of our mind. For Conrad, eating is not only the basic activity which allows humans to survive, but is also an everyday choice. Every time we eat, we may decide what to eat morally or immorally, conscientiously or not. This choice affects our inner life. In fact, as is shown below, dividing food into good and bad categories also allows Conrad to enter his characters' mental spaces. Eating bad food is not only an unhealthy practice; it also pollutes the human mind.

Today, the idea that food affects our external and internal lives is quite common (Conner & Armitage; Steel), but at the beginning of the twentieth century this concept was much less widespread. While today our media continually focuses on food morality and responsibility, the antecedences are found in concepts such as food authenticity, consciousness and knowledge, contemporarily pushed by Slow Food and its food philosophy. But in 1907, people were mainly concerned with the vast variety of food as it arrived from many parts of the world, where the Second Industrial Revolution allowed for the rapid and affordable transportation of global goods (Thomas). Food was perceived much more in its connections to novelty and discovery, while only a few intellectuals saw eating as a moral activity.

Importantly, in the second part of the cookbook preface, Conrad's morality of food becomes a social issue. In fact, the writer argues that food is key to the survival of an entire civilization. He takes the North American Indians as an example, and argues that "the Noble Red Man was a mighty hunter but his wives had not mastered the art of conscientious cookery" (Jos. Conrad, "Cookery" 113). In further pushing the relationships between food and morality, Conrad links bad food to an erroneous and invented trait that he extends to all American Indian populations: "The gluttony of their indigestible feasts was a direct incentive to counsels of unreasonable violence" (113). For Conrad, the American Indians' unconsciousness of food led to "fraudulent medicine men—quacks—who haunted their existence with vain promises and false nostrums from cradle to grave" (113). This is the other side of the morality of food, immorality. While morality is based on conscientiousness, ignorance of food produces immorality and fraud.

As often happens in Conrad writings, the representations of the lives and the problems of remote peoples serve the purpose of unmasking Western deficiencies (Rawa). In fact, Conrad points out that in early nineteenth- and late twentieth-century Britain also had its fair share of "quacks." They were the vendors of patent medicines, fraudulent products sold under the promise of curing various serious diseases, products that at the turn of the century were advertised insistently and sold in abundance. Like his stereotyped imagery of American Indians, the idea is that ignorance of food leads to immorality. For Conrad, food must instead be something that is known well. To avoid the "quacks" of the past and of the present, we should know very well what we eat. The refuge is everyday food, as opposed to the more refined dishes of the feast. The difference, again, is conscience, as "the conscientious cook is the natural enemy of the quack without a conscience" (Conrad, "Cookery" 113).

In the years of industrialization, globalization and homogenization, while a multitude of new foods arrived from every corner of the world and aroused the palates of Western people broadening the horizons of the Anglo-Saxon eater (Tansey & Worsley), Conrad goes against the grain. In this preface, he praises his wife's idea of celebrating the English little houses, inhabited by ordinary people, who are, for him, "the arbiters of the nation's destiny" (Conrad, "Cookery" 113). Thus, besides being a social issue, food habits are also a political choice, connected to the future of Britain. We can see, perhaps, an allusion in Conrad's preface to the 1825 work of Brillat-Savarin, who writes, "the fate of nations hangs upon their choice of food" (*Physiology of Taste* 3).

Using the quotation from the gastronome Brillat-Savarin is not by chance. In fact, he has always been considered a relevant source of inspiration by the Slow Food founder Carlo Petrini. It is easy to see a link between Brillat-Savarin, Conrad, and Slow Food, at least in this aspect. For all three, in affecting everyday lives and social habits, food becomes one of the most relevant elements shaping national identity and nation building. Among the many elements that build the nation, food has its proper place. This "nationalist" character of food suggests the need for a deeper investigation into Conrad's approach to food in other countries.

Food Coming from Other Countries

Even though they are not written by Joseph Conrad, it is important to note that out of all the recipes recorded in Conrad's wife's book, only one contains curry. Moreover, as underlined in the introduction of the 2006 edition of the book, in describing the preparation of the dish, Jessie Conrad focuses more on the cooking of rice than on the preparation of curry. This is quite strange, as curry was, and remains, an extremely popular dish in Britain. Moreover, the lack of recipes for curries and non-British cuisine is all the more striking considering Joseph's curiosity for remote places and cultures.

Mike Davis has illuminatingly summarized Conrad's view of the Other: "If Kipling's verse exalted colonizing optimism and scientific racism, Conrad's troubling stories warned that Europe itself was being barbarized by its complicity in secret tropical holocausts. *La Belle Epoque*, in his view, was dangerously downriver of the Apocalypse" (140). Actually, it is difficult to trace this sense of guilt in the way in which Conrad represents food coming from abroad. Instead, what we can see again is a strong divide between good and bad food. The first comes from Europe, while the second is always centered abroad.

In Conrad's 1907 novel *The Secret Agent*, Italian food is represented negatively not because it is Italian, but rather because it is not Italian enough. When the Assistant Commissioner goes to an Italian restaurant, Conrad describes it as an example of "fraudulent cookery" (Conrad, *Secret Agent* 141), the same term he uses to define patent medicines and the food of the American Indians. Moreover, the atmosphere is referred to as "immoral," again as in the preface to his wife's recipes. Importantly, Conrad writes that in this atmosphere the Assistant Commissioner "seemed to lose some more of his identity" (141). Even the habitual customers of the restaurant are described as people without personality, as "the patrons of the place had lost in the frequentation of fraudulent cookery all their national and private characteristics" (141). They are as "denationalised as the[ir] dishes" (141-142).

In this brief scene, there are the same ideas of food, and even the same terminology, as in the preface mentioned above. Clearly, therefore, Conrad underlines here that food is fundamental in shaping personal and national identities. Authenticity is a necessity, and cheating on food is considered immoral. These are the same principles often highlighted by many Slow Food publications (Petrini, *Buono, Pulito e Giusto*; Petrini & Padovani, *Slow Food Revolution*; Petrini & Scaffidi, "Cenni di Storia"). The entire scene has much to do with Slow Food's discourse on authenticity, where only food that is authentically local may guarantee good quality and psychological wellness for the eater.

This exclusive, even obsessive attention to locality and authenticity is a major cause of criticism around the Slow Food movement. Many studies have focused on the dark side of this obsessive attention. If local food is good, what about the rest of what we eat? Food sociologist C. Clare Hinrichs asks: "Is food system localization a liberatory project—or instead a reactionary response?" (33). David Goodman, Melanie DuPuis, and Michael Goodman convincingly answer that it is a reactionary strategy, as "nativist sentiments," like any localist and nationalist discourse, end up in extolling one *patria* at the expenses of the other nations (12). The problem, they say, is that these strategies aim "to delineate standards of what is acceptable as 'alternative' food practice rather than to support democratic political processes" in food choices (Goodman et al. 12). Finally, Carole Counihan has linked the general "nationalist" mood stemmed from Italian food localism (and not from specific policies of the Slow Food movement) to the bans that some Italian local councils have established against ethnic food shops in many historical town centers. In a field in which localism is synonymous with high levels of quality, ethnic food automatically becomes symbol of Otherness and inferior quality.

We may find the same approach in Conrad's writings. We have already seen the bright side of this approach in the episode of the Italian restaurant in *The Secret Agent*, where authenticity is represented as a positive and necessary characteristic of good food. Conversely, in his 1902 novel *Heart of Darkness*, we can find an example of the dark side of food localism, that is, the negative representation of the Other's food. The cannibals who accompany Marlow on the steamer, in fact, eat rotten hippopotamus meat. This allows them not to eat the white men on the ship. However, the food they eat is somehow inconceivable for Marlow. Conrad writes: "You can't breathe dead hippo waking, sleeping, and eating, and at the same time keep your precarious grip on existence" (Conrad, *Heart* 71). The quality of food marks the difference between locals and Europeans, and the bad status of the food of the Africans broadens the gap between "us" and "them," irrespective of the good intentions of the Other, such as choosing to sustain themselves on rotten meat in order to spare the lives of Marlow and his fellow Europeans. As acutely noted by Bart Westerweel, here the stench underlines "the rift between the Earth Mother and the white intruders" (265). The distance is unbridgeable: rotten hippopotamus meat, in fact, "made the mystery of the wilderness stink in my nostrils. Phoo!" (Conrad 2001, 62). Thus, rotten hippo meat saves the lives of the whites but widens the distance between the two groups. It does not matter that, in the end, the representation of these men is positive. What counts is that what they eat marks them as "different." What strikes us is that the writer who often represented journeys, remote places, and people coming from other countries as positive elements in comparison to Western corruption, is unable to escape his Othering gaze, as is betrayed by Conrad's very different perspective when it comes to talking about food.

The journey into Conrad's writing about food clearly echoes what was said above about localist and nationalist views of food in the Slow Food movement. The excessive celebration of "our" food inevitably corresponds to a negative approach to the food of the Other. Additionally, the scene of the consumption of rotten hippopotamus by the carnivorous cannibals in *Heart of Darkness*, raises issues surrounding meat, to which we now turn.

Meat: A Modern Issue

Meat is a relevant element in a few of Conrad's works and, interestingly, some of Conrad's views of this specific type of food may be linked to the Slow Food philosophy. These Slow Food views are quite relevant in analyzing Conrad's *Heart of Darkness*, and Jeremy Hawthorn has already associated scenes of cannibalism and meat in general in Conrad's works to themes of sexuality. Rather than investigating meat symbolically, however, here I aim to develop a historical discourse which links Conrad to other authors.

In his 1906 novel *An Anarchist*, Conrad tells the story of the promotion of an unhealthy kind of meat produced by the company B.O.S. and dishonestly advertised as a healthy food. This sort of "patent food" anticipates Conrad's preface to his wife's recipes. Here, the responsibility for inauthentic food seems to be with capitalism and the worship of money that it preaches. Advertising is seen as the main instrument of dishonesty, promising non-existent benefits and proving "the wide prevalence of that form of mental degradation which is called gullibility" (Conrad, *Anarchist* 286). Moreover, Conrad considers the globalized landscape in which all of this occurs as incompatible with good food. For the narrator, in fact, "in various parts of the civilized and uncivilized word I have to swallow B.O.S. with more or less benefit to myself, though without great pleasure" (287). Indeed, the accusation against globalized food could be lifted directly out of the pages of a Slow Food article. Instead, it was written nearly eighty years before the foundation of the Slow Food movement.

The theme of meat as an item of food compromised by capitalism is not new. In this sense, *An Anarchist* echoes Upton Sinclair's *The Jungle*, published the very same year. Conrad, however, did not like this novel and referred to it as an example of "pretentious emptiness" ("To John Galsworthy" 4:127). Yet both works see the industrialization of meat as a form of immoral food capitalism and are ferociously critical of it. In a letter, Conrad describes the meat market of Chicago, the setting of Sinclair's *The Jungle*, as worse than "the bomb of Madrid" activated by an anarchist which killed twelve people ("To John Galsworthy" 3:333). The critical account of the modernization of food (already underlined in Donovan) is another element linking Conrad to the Slow Food movement. Petrini has stated many times that, in the past, people used to eat better than they do in the present, while "fear of the future" is an accusation that scholars critical of Slow Food have frequently attributed to the Italian organization.

Apart from this, however, is the fact that in Conrad's view of meat there is something more. This also emerges in analyzing Conrad's representation of vegetarianism. Falk, in the 1901 eponymous short story, rejects meat to purify himself after a cannibalistic experience. While in the dominant view "a white man should eat like a white man . . . ought to eat meat, must eat meat" (Conrad, *Falk* 37), Falk undertakes a process of purification in his abstention from meat. Importantly, this point is not only a matter of fiction. In one of his letters, Conrad admits to having become vegetarian himself to escape from a stressful period ("To John Galsworthy" 4:10). Interestingly, here Conrad's philosophy regarding a strictly plant based diet as a form of mental cleansing differs from Slow Food, which has never supported vegetarianism.

This distancing oneself from meat has a much deeper past than the time of Conrad's writings. In her illuminating *Meat, Modernity and the Rise of the Slaughterhouse*, Paula Lee investigates how modernity has shaped the slaughterhouse as we know it today. Modernity has taken slaughterhouses far from city centers and has turned them into non-places, opaque sites that we do not want to see. As a result of this meat production, within these buildings marks the shift from open and acknowledged places to removed spaces, a hidden link of an industrial process of food.

It is outside of the scope of this chapter to examine the relationships between modernity and meat. However, Conrad and Sinclair's *The Jungle*, as well as other artistic representations, such as Chaim Soutine's *Le Boeuf* and *Carcass of Beef* and Francis Bacon's *Figure with Meat*, demonstrate that first, modernity shaped not only the slaughterhouse but also meat in general and, second, that the twentieth century also brought with it a critical account of this item of food, which was frequently associated with death, suffering, and overall negative sentiments. This is an interesting theme for further research, but presently, we can say that with modernity in general and Conrad in particular, meat has become fodder for industry in the social world, while remaining problematic in artistic representations and in people's minds. Returning to Conrad, his view of food also has to do with broader economic trends and, again, this surprisingly anticipates subsequent food theories such as those of the Slow Food movement.

A Different Economic Model
To fully understand Conrad's idea of food and his anticipation of Slow Food's theories, we must look at the economic model that

was dominant during his lifetime. At the beginning of the twentieth century, mass production shaped a new kind of consumption. While in the past, being avant-garde was associated with consuming something that other people did not have, modernity persuaded people that the "trendiest" consumers are those who share successful goods. Having that specific object allowed the ordinary and lone person to become part of a larger community, formed by all the people that also bought that same object. Meanwhile very expensive and luxury products only targeted the rich (Gartman). The famous Ford Model T automobile, first produced in 1908, helps to explain this concept. It was not a luxurious car, but rather was a commercialized product of assembly line industry sold to the masses in the millions (Lee, *Consumer Culture Reborn*). By the 1910s, having a Model T was quite common in the United States. Yet, the automobile was also considered "trendy," due in part to the incessant advertising campaigns that Conrad professed to hate. What conferred social distinction during those times was not buying something unique, unknown or "local"; instead, people acquired relevance among others by participating in this process of industrialization and, therefore, by buying the same goods as their neighbors. Goods such as the same radio, the same car, and even, the same food.

The food industry, in fact, followed this exact trend. Rather than creating exclusive and expensive refined foods, the industry homogenized taste and satisfaction, mobilizing the powerful weapon of advertising. This new food economy constructed the notion of "eating what the others eat" as positively imperative. By doing so, each person became part of a larger community. While Conrad was writing his novels containing his "Slow Food" perspective of eating, Walt Anderson, an unknown cook of Swedish heritage, prepared meatballs for the Kansas restaurant where he worked (Hogan). One day, angry at the length of time meatballs took to cook, he squashed one of them on the grill. The meatball became flat and thus cooked in a very short time. To his surprise, the customers also appreciated the finished product. Anderson realized that the flat meatball could be a good business and, in 1916, opened his first restaurant. After a series of uneven events, he finally founded a White Castle restaurant in Wichita, Kansas, and subsequently a chain of the same name, along with his new financial partner Billy Ingram. By 1924, White Castle restaurants were scattered across Kansas, and by 1930, White Castles were spread across the United States. White Castle thus became the world's first form of industrialized fast food (Hogan).

This is exactly what Conrad is fighting in terms of food. As with Slow Food in the 1980s, Conrad is challenging a form of fast food in his time. In the end, this is the conclusive affinity we may find between Conrad and Slow Food. Besides the many commonalities shown in this chapter, they both had to fight against the concept of fast food. A common, significant destiny that binds Conrad and the Slow Food movement to each other in terms of their own philosophy and shared history.

Conclusion

This chapter has analyzed Conrad's views of food and has related them to many of Slow Food's underpinnings. What has emerged is that Conrad anticipated many aspects of the Slow Food philosophy. First, Conrad frequently defined eating as a moral activity that shaped personal, social, and national identities. In considering eating as a moral activity, the Polish British writer has clearly foreseen one of the most important of Slow Food's tenets.

The moral perspective led the novelist to divide food into good and the bad binaries. Global and industrialized foods have been classified as bad ones, and this is certainly another point in common with the Italian movement. Conrad also looked suspiciously at products coming from abroad, although in a more moderate way. Even though this has never explicitly been one of Slow Food's assumptions, many scholars have considered bans of ethnic food shops in Italy as descending from Slow Food's exaltation of Italian food. In fact, over-consideration of national products always casts imported items in a suspect and distrustful light. What is more, Conrad found the solution of these problems in local, non-industrialized and unadulterated foods. Again, in doing so, he anticipated the nucleus of Slow Food's general approach to food.

Finally, this chapter has demonstrated that both Conrad and Slow Food had the same enemy, even though the Slow Food movement is nearly a century removed from Conrad. This enemy was fast food: in its initial version in the case of Conrad at the beginning of the twentieth century and in the permanent, and even declining, presence of MacDonald's in the case of the Slow Food movement.

As said from the outset, this chapter's principal aim was to analyze Conrad's view of food and to link it to various Slow Food assumptions. However, this research has also produced a second aim: that is, identifying Slow Food's roots. In fact, many studies have examined what Slow Food has produced, in terms of social movements and political approaches to food, as well as localist revolts against globalization. Conversely, very few studies have investigated where Slow Food comes from. Apart from the already cited Brillat-Savarin, Slow Food's historical roots have never been investigated consistently. This analysis argues that Slow Food's ancestors may be identified in Conrad; Sinclair; and in that branch of modernism that fought the nascent industrialization of food, supported local foods, and looked suspiciously at food coming from other countries. Thus, Slow Food has professed roots dating back to the 1980s era of globalization. But as this chapter has shown, globalization was born with modernity, and the link between Conrad and the Slow Food movement confirms that Conrad, writing in the time of industrialization's upheavals, creates the starting point of Slow Food's critical view. As in any modern reflection, in Conrad, food has lost its innocence and has become a vehicle of cultural, social, and political insistences.

Finally, this conclusion also puts forward an explanation for the reason why Joseph Conrad had this approach to food. Thanks to his work as a seaman, and differently from many ordinary professions, Conrad saw food travel across the oceans and experienced eating on the ships (Najder 2007). Thus, he had a more complete view of the complex process of food globalization in its origins. Testifying to the precarious conditions in which food was loaded and unloaded, stored and eaten on the ships, transported, and commercialized all contributed to his specific "Slow Food" view and to his skepticism toward globalized food in general. To the eyes of an expert sailor, food traveling around the world conjured up issues of hygienic conditions. Therefore, the job that allowed Conrad to create exotic characters coming from remote parts of the world also narrowed the writer's vision of food, suggesting that home products, at least in terms of food, were better than the exotic goods.

Works Cited

"About This Artwork." *Art Institute Chicago*. Art Institute Chicago, 2016. Web 5 May 2016. <http://www.artic.edu/aic/collections/artwork/4884>.

Brillat-Savarin, Jean Anthelme. *The Physiology of Taste or Meditations on Transcendental Gastronomy*. 1825. New York: Dover, 2002. Print.

Conner, Mark & Christopher J. Armitage. *The Social Psychology of Food*. Buckingham: Open UP, 2002. Print.

Conrad, Jessie. *A Handbook of Cookery for a Small House*. 1923. London: Kegan Paul, 2006. Print.

Conrad, Joseph. *Falk: A Reminiscence*. 1901. Auckland: The Floating Press, 2010. Print.

_____. "To John Galsworthy." *The Collected Letters of Joseph Conrad, vol. 3, 1903-1907*. Eds. Frederick R. Karl and Laurence Davies. Cambridge University Press, 1988. 333.

_____. "An Anarchist." 1906. *The Dover Reader*. Mineola, NY: Dover, 2014. 286-304. Print.

_____. "Cookery: Preface to Jessie Conrad's *A Handbook of Cookery for a Small House* 1907." *The Cambridge Edition of the Works of Joseph Conrad: Last Essays*. 1907. Ed. Harold Ray Stevens & John Henry Stape. Cambridge, UK: Cambridge UP, 2010. 112-114.

_____. "To John Galsworthy." *The Collected Letters of Joseph Conrad*. Vol. 4, 1908–1911. Ed. Frederick R. Karl & Laurence Davies. Cambridge, UK: Cambridge UP, 1990. 127. Print.

_____. "To John Galsworthy." *The Collected Letters of Joseph Conrad*. Vol. 4, 1908–1911. Ed. Frederick R. Karl & Laurence Davies. Cambridge, UK: Cambridge University Press, 1990b. 8-12. Print.

———. *The Secret Agent*. 1907. Plymouth: Broadview Editions, 2009. Print.

———. *Heart of Darkness*. 1902. Firenze: Giunti, 2001. Print.

Counihan, Carole. "Cultural Heritage in Food Activism: Local and Global Tensions." *Edible Identities: Food as Cultural Heritage*. Ed. Ronda L. Brulotte & Michael A. Di Giovine. Burlington, VT: Ashgate, 2014. 219-229. Print.

Davis, Mike. *Late Victorian Holocausts: El Niño Famines and the Making of the Third World*. London: Verso, 2001. Print.

Donovan, Stephen. "Magic Letters and Mental Degradation: Advertising in 'An Anarchist' and 'The Partner.'" *The Conradian* 28 (2003): 72-95. Print.

Gabaccia, Donna. *We Are What We Eat: Ethnic Food and the Making of Americans*. Cambridge, MA: Harvard UP, 1998. Print.

Gartman, David. *Auto-opium: A Social History of American Automobile Design*. London: Routledge, 1994. Print.

Goldberg, Elyssa. "Meet 'Le Boeuf,' a Painting of Beef Estimated to Sell for over $20 Million." *Bon Appétit*. Condé Nast, 6 May 2015. Web. 5 May 2016. <http://www.bonappetit.com/entertaining-style/trends-news/article/soutine-le-boeuf>.

Goodman, David, E. Melanie DuPuis, & Michael K Goodman. *Alternative Food Networks: Knowledge, Practice, and Politics*. Abingdon: Routledge, 2012. Print.

Hawthorn, Jeremy. *Sexuality and the Erotic in the Fiction of Joseph Conrad*. London: Continuum, 2007. Print.

Hinrichs, C. Clare. "The Practice and Politics of Food System Localization." *Journal of Rural Studies* 19 (2003): 33-45.

Hogan, David J. *Selling 'em by the Sack: White Castle and the Creation of American Food*. New York: New York UP, 1997. Print.

"In Praise of . . . the Kebab." *The Guardian*. The Guardian News and Media Limited, 16 Nov. 2009. Web. 30 Sept. 2016. <http://www.theguardian.com/commentisfree/2009/nov/16/italy-foreign-food-shops-immigrant>.

Lee, Martyn J. *Consumer Culture Reborn: The Cultural Politics of Consumption*. London: Routledge, 1993. Print.

Lee, Paula Young. "Introduction: Housing Slaughter." *Meat, Modernity and the Rise of the Slaughterhouse.* Ed. Paula Young Lee. Durham, NH: U of New Hampshire P, 2008. 1-10. Print.

Leitch, Alison. "Slow Food and the Politics of Pork Fat: Italian Food and European Identity." *Ethnos* 68 (2003): 437-462. Print.

Levenstein, Harvey. "The American Response to Italian Food." *Food and Foodways* 1 (1985): 1-23. Print.

MacDonald, Kenneth Iain. "The Morality of Cheese: A Paradox of Defensive Localism in a Transnational Cultural Economy." *Geoforum* 44 (2013): 93-102. Print.

Meneley, Anne. "Extra Virgin Olive Oil and Slow Food." *Anthropologica* 46 (2004): 165-176. Print.

Najder, Zdzislaw. *Joseph Conrad: A Life.* New York: Camden House, 2007. Print.

Parasecoli, Fabio. *Food Culture in Italy.* Westport, CT: Greenwood Publishing, 2004. Print.

_____. "Slow Food." *The Business of Food: Encyclopedia of the Food and Drink Industries.* Ed. Gary Allen & Ken Albala. Westport, CT: Greenwood Publishing, 2007. 331-335. Print.

Petrini, Carlo. *Buono, Pulito e Giusto.* Torino: Einaudi, 2005. Print.

_____. *Slow Food: Le Ragioni del Gusto.* Bari: Laterza, 2001. Print.

_____. *Terra Madre: Come non Farci Mangiare dal Cibo.* Milano: Giunti e Bra/Slow Food Editore, 2009. Print.

Petrini, Carlo & G. Padovani. *Slow Food Revolution, da Arcigola a Terra Madre: Una Nuova Cultura del Cibo e della Vita.* Milano: Rizzoli, 2005. Print.

Petrini, Carlo & Cinzia Scaffidi. "Cenni di Storia della Cultura Gastronomica in Italia: Dalla Complessità al Riduzionismo e Ritorno." *La cultura Italiana: Cibo, Gioco, Festa, Moda.* Ed. Carlo Petrini e Ugo Volli. Vol. 6. Torino: Utet, 2009. 221-231. Print.

Probyn, Elspeth. "In the Interests of Taste and Place: Economies of Attachment." *The Global and the Intimate Feminism in our Time.* Ed. Geraldine Pratt & Victoria Rosner. New York: Columbia UP, 2012. 57-84. Print.

Rawa, Julia M. *The Imperial Quest and Modern Memory from Conrad to Greene.* New York: Routledge, 2005. Print.

Sinclair, Upton. *The Jungle*. 1906. Minneapolis, MN: Lerner Publishing Group, 2016. Print.

Spring Kurtz, Gwendolyn. "Of Cabbages and Kings: Reading Food Culture and Other Compositions." *From Hip-hop to Hyperlinks: Teaching about Culture in the Composition Classroom*. Ed. Joanna N. Paull. Newcastle: Cambridge Scholars, 2008. 96-111. Print.

Steel, Carolyn. *Hungry City: How Food Shapes our Lives*. London: Vintage, 2013. Print.

Tansey, Geoff & Tony Worsley. *The Food System: A Guide*. Abingdon: Earthscan, 1995. Print.

Thomas, Brinley."Food Supply in the United Kingdom during the Industrial Revolution." *The Economics of the Industrial Revolution*. Ed. Joel Mokyr. Totowa, NJ: Rowman and Littlefield, 1985. 137-150. Print.

Westerweel, Bart. "'An Immense Snake Uncoiled': H. Rider Haggard's Heart of Darkness and Imperial Gothic." *Exhibited by Candlelight: Sources and Developments in the Gothic Tradition*. Ed. Valeria Tinkler-Villani, Peter Davidson, & Jane Stevenson. Amsterdam: Rodopi, 1995. 255-270. Print.

Quantitative Elocutionary Methods: Joseph Conrad's Harmony and Juxtaposition in *Heart of Darkness*

Gerardo Del Guercio

Heart of Darkness begins with an unidentified narrator sailing the River Thames. The narrative of the novella then transitions into Marlow as speaker while also playing with the currents of time, as when, for instance, the narration morphs the contemporary Thames River into the Thames of the ancient Roman period. Marlow enters the story as the main protagonist with his retelling of a previous voyage. The Thames then becomes an African river, on which Marlow sails after receiving his assignment from a company in a European city, tasked with recovering an ivory merchant named Kurtz. Eventually, Marlow finds Kurtz, although Kurtz dies on his way back down the river. In the conclusion, Marlow details his visit to Kurtz' fiancée. All told, the novella concludes with a final paragraph from the unnamed narrator back on the Thames River. The shift between narrators reveals an association between linguistic framing devices and the repetition of terms. This chapter analyzes the linguistic traits of Joseph Conrad's *Heart of Darkness* by exploring the frequency and placement of key terminology in the novella itself, as well as its association to outlines within verbal communication.

An important attribute of Conrad's novella is that major locative markers go unnamed. Conrad based his story on his own travel to Brussels, where he ultimately voyaged to the Belgian Congo as well as up the Congo River. Yet the words "Belgium" or "Congo" never appear in the text. Equally significant is that the word Africa is mentioned only once; when Marlow is depicting the maps he looked at when he was a child. Marlow says:

> Now when I was a little chap I had a passion for maps. I would look for hours at South America, or *Africa*, or Australia, and lose myself in all the glories of exploration. At that time there were many blank

spaces on the earth, and when I saw one that looked particularly inviting on a map (but they all look that) I would put my finger on it and say, 'When I grow up I will go there.' The North Pole was one of these places, I remember. Well, I haven't been there yet, and shall not try now. The glamour's off. Other places were scattered about the hemispheres. I have been in some of them, and...well, we won't talk about that. But there was one yet—the biggest, the most blank, so to speak—that I had a hankering after. (Conrad 1763; emphasis added)

Here, Marlow disuses the colonization of areas like South America; Australia; and, in particular, Africa. Although Marlow never explicitly states where "the biggest, the most blank" of these areas is located, the reader is to infer that Marlow means Africa, specifically the large center swath of the continent controlled by Belgium (Conrad 1763). The Eurocentric perspective Marlow advocates is that Africa is a space where Europe should impose its power.

In the principal core of Conrad's narrative, Marlow boats up the "river." Notably, Marlow's personal reason for travelling remains unclear, although the voyage develops into a hunt for and fixation with locating a man named Kurtz—a rogue company agent responsible for robbing ivory from the nearby villagers. Kurtz has allegedly gone insane, is idolized as a god by the locals, has taken an African lover, and may have engaged in cannibalism.

Heart of Darkness Critiques

Joseph Conrad published *Heart of Darkness* in *Blackwood's Magazine* in a three-part serial installment that ran from February to April 1899 and later published his story in book form in 1902 with William Blackwood. Conrad began composing his story eight years after getting back from Africa, and he drew his narrative from his travelogue recorded while in Africa. Indeed, the novella is a short one that contains just over 40,000 words. It is canonized and easily available in print as well as electronic form. Many carefully edited editions exist that draw on present-day interpretations in addition to classical ones. One important edition of *Heart of Darkness* is the Robert Kimbrough, as well as Robert Armstrong Norton Critical

Editions, which include the autobiographical sources from Conrad's *Congo Diary*.

Certainly, *Heart of Darkness* is an invaluable twentieth-century text. It remains continuously referenced even 114 years after its publication. According to Chinua Achebe, Conrad's story is arguably "the most commonly prescribed novel in twentieth-century literature courses in English Departments of American universities" (260). Still, given the changes to American foreign policy that started at the turn of the twenty-first century, it seems that American audiences have not read *Heart of Darkness* carefully enough, nor have they learned much from the film adaptation *Apocalypse Now* and its central theme that war causes madness. Further critical research is always needed.

On the surface, *Heart of Darkness* does not appear to be an appropriate text on which to conduct a linguistic analysis. Ostensibly, the novella's canonical status makes it seem as though no new light can be shed on a text that has been researched at length for over a century now. Furthermore, *Heart of Darkness* appears to be an improper choice for linguistic analysis given that it is a political book about late Victorian ideas of empire, which has been scrutinized from numerous points-of-view. Nigerian novelist, poet, professor, and critic Chinua Achebe most famously assailed Conrad's novella for its racists and stereotypical interpretations of Africans, claims corroborated by several other critics who view Conrad's character Marlow as skeptical in his depictions of the negative sides of colonial abuse. In fact, Conrad depicts colonialism as a "sordid farce" (1767) as well as "senseless delusion" (1767). According to Conrad scholar Khalil Hassan Nofal, "[t]he novel is most symbolic and ambiguous. Conrad deliberately leaves out almost people [*sic*], places and times [*sic*] unknown as indicators of darkness" (452). Yet, within these critiques a space opens up, which shows that one can always interpret a text from a new vantage point and that a stylistic observation does not provide an authoritative reading.

Despite over a century of critical discourse, astonishingly very little exists on the novella's style. Few researchers have attempted to correlate style with statistics. It is the goal of this chapter to attempt to shed new light on *Heart of Darkness* by analyzing its style using a statistical analysis of word placement and repetition. As H. G. Widdowson has argued, literature utilizes language in fashions that cannot be proven for using linguistic theories (159). This chapter does not advocate that a strictly routine stylistic interpretation is possible. Indeed, while the linguist chooses which traits to study, the corpus linguist is limited to characteristics that the existing software can locate, and these traits still have to be given literary analysis. Nevertheless, Conrad clarified his thoughts through the idiom of the text. There must consequently be items in the text that the computer can locate, and, arguably, techniques of traditional interpretation can define textual traits that have eluded experts. Additionally, as John Sinclair articulately stated, there must be errors with existing linguistic theories given that they are unable to explicate the language of those texts, which are regarded as the best in the literary canon.

Since there already exist libraries of critical analysis on Conrad's *Heart of Darkness*, researchers certainly cannot approach the novella as inexperienced readers. By looking deeper at the written words, some of the text's primary leitmotifs and themes are brought to the surface. For example, the insincerity of the colonizers and breakdown as a metaphor of capriciousness of technological development are more than mere plot devices. Throughout the narrative, Marlow's ship is constantly breaking down along the river. The colonial stations he visits are beleaguered with "decaying machinery" (Conrad 22). It would appear that the African backdrop breaks down superior Western technology. This decay of metal aligns with the decay of mettle. Beyond the doomed Captain Fresleven, Kurtz centrally experiences a mental collapse, and by the novella's conclusion, it is clear the Marlow's own mental state has been forever altered by his experiences. These physical, technological, and mental collapses occur alongside breakdowns in communication, as characters speak various dialects and tongues; Marlow recounts a lie about Kurtz's final words to Kurtz' fiancée; and amid the recurrent content, words are the lemma for "silence," a term in various forms that occurs thirty-seven times throughout the novella ("silence" occurs twenty-six times; "silent" eight times; while "silenced," "silencing," and "silently" appear one time each). Other key themes of the book are conveyed by recurring differences—especially "light/dark," "self-control/anger," and "form/authenticity." There are recurrent allusions to "dreams" (48), "nightmares" (100), "trances" (56), "ghosts," "spectres," and "apparitions" (85, 87, 105, 110). Marlow has difficulty maintaining "contact with reality" (19, 54) and introspectively reflects on "what it all mean[s]" (33). Critics have stated that Conrad uses these contrasts sarcastically. For instance, is he proposing that the titular "heart of darkness" stands in for "darkest Africa," as the typecast has it, or instead to the wickedness of the white colonizers? The phrases "Through the Dark Continent" and "In Darkest Africa" are titles of two books famed explorer Henry Morton Stanley, books that were released only few years before *Heart of Darkness* and would have been very familiar to Conrad's audience. Moreover, *Heart of Darkness* is based on a series of challenging and fake dissimilarities: Europe and Africa; Victorian England, Roman Britannia, and the Belgian Congo; the River Thames and the Congo River; Marlow and Kurtz; Kurtz's black lover and his white fiancée; lies and genuineness (Reeves 301).

Antonyms and contrasts are major themes in Conrad's *Heart of Darkness*. Patterns of antonym are more invasive than the small number of differences noted above. The opening three pages, where the narrator is the anonymous speaker, have a predominantly large amount of lexical contrasts. Just a few examples from pages 5-7 include: "the *sea* and the *sky*"; "from *glowing white* . . . to a *dull red*"; "a short day that *comes* and *departs*"; "borne to *the rest of home* or to *the battles of the sea*"; "knights all, *titled* and *untitled*"; "the *ships* and the *men*"; "the *adventurers* and the *settlers*"; "*hunters for gold* or *pursuers of fame*"; "the *sword* and . . . the "torch". The incident spanning pages 4-6 in which Marlow stops over in the anonymous European city, a veiled signifier for Brussels, to organize his indenture has many antonymous couplings as well: "*whited* and *black*"; "*right* and *left*"; "*fat* and *slim*"; "*plain* and *all the colours of the rainbow*"; "*skinny* and *plumpness*"; "*younger* and *old"*; *"feverishly* and *placidity"*. The final episode on pages 106-10, during which Marlow meets with Kurtz's fiancée, mirrors the introduction by giving an additional rupture of antonymous pairs, all in close proximity: *"floor* and *ceiling"*; *"opened* and *closed"*; *"black* and *pale"*; *"young* and *mature"*; *"dark* and *pale"*; *"rich* and *pauper"*; *"glow* and *darkness"*; *"happy* and *unhappy"*; *"died* and *lived."*

Antonyms are a prescribed attribute of the text, although it is hard to state their precise literary consequence. Foremost, they can be understood in a different way in the case of the two speakers. The unnamed chronicler is offered as honestly in support of British imperialism. He looks at the River Thames and thinks: "What greatness had not floated on the ebb of that river!" (Conrad 7). His antonyms conceivably articulate completeness, conjuring up biblical notions of creation: "the sea and the sky" (7). Marlow, on the other hand, expresses a very dissimilar perspective of colonialism in his first words: "And this [the Thames] also has been one of the dark places of the earth" (7). Conceivably his antonyms put forward his mystification connecting authenticity and appearance, in that everything implies its opposite and nothing is itself. Antonyms are a quality of numerous texts: a number of corpus studies (Justeson & Katz 1991, Fellbaum 1995, Jones 2002) illustrate that antonymous lexical contrasts within sentences are much more recurrent than could be expected by likelihood, and are an imperative apparatus of textual unity.

A main subject of the tome is Marlow's undependable and twisted knowledge. He is an especially unreliable narrator. His voyage is an anticlimax: we never truly find out what has occurred, or what Kurtz has done, what "monstrous passions" (Conrad 95) and "vile desires" (105) he has pandered to. Marlow himself never quite comprehends what is happening: he protests that his experiences are dream-like, and Marlow records little of what Kurtz has directly told him, leaving the unnamed listener in text, and by extension the reader, in the dark. Importantly, Kurtz has discussed at length by the youthful Russian trader, but he, in turn, is incapable of informing Marlow on what Kurtz has specifically said. Kurtz dies speaking the words "The horror! The horror!," yet Conrad is intentionally ambiguous if these words relate to a final moment of recognition and moral enlightenment, or if Kurtz's madness has finally fully consumed him.

The unidentified speaker in the exterior frame of the novella's conclusion is purposefully factious, and comments that "we knew we were fated . . . to hear about one of Marlow's *inconclusive* experiences" (Conrad 10; emphasis added). Critics have taken dissimilar perspectives—most notably F. R. Leavis and E. M. Forster, who deliberated that Conrad essentially did not know what he intended to advocate. On the other hand, Ian Watt contends the novella is urbane early modernism, and that ossification and impressionism are important elements to the narrative. Moreover, Watt has argued that "mist or haze is a very persistent image in Conrad" (175) and words from this vocabulary corpus are recurrent in the novella.

The obscuring descriptions elucidated by Watt become quite prominent when statistical analysis is applied to Conrad's texts. In all, words relating concealment amount to almost one hundred and fifty—an average frequency of once per page. The term "blurred" appears twice; "dark/ly/ness" fifty-two times; "dusk" seven times; "fog" nine; "gloom/y" fourteen; "haze" twice; "mist/misty" seven times; "murk" twice; "shadow/s/y" in twenty-one instances; "shade" eight times; "shape/s/d" thirteen times; "smoke" ten times; and "vapour" once. "Shade" and "shadow" are used to connote a sense of ghostliness and the deceased—at times rather unambiguously, as when Marlow refers to Kurtz as "that Shadow—this wandering and tormented thing" (94), and "a tragic and familiar Shade" (110). Importantly, "Shades" conjure up an allusion to the classical Greek mythological deity Hades. To an early twentieth century reader, biblical allusions would also be obvious. In biblical terms, the expression "shadow of death" is common, occurring twenty times within the novella, and "shadow" collocates with "darkness" on eight occasions.

Interestingly, Marlow is frequently looking into a fog, uncertain of what lies ahead. Inexplicable things occur, such as when he encounters a man who hanged himself without an obvious motive (Conrad 21). Occurrences are described as "improbable, inexplicable, and altogether bewildering" (78). As he moves closer toward Kurtz, Marlow is faced with a succession of symbols that he is unable to understand or misconstrues: "a message on a board" (53); "a book with strange writing" (54); "a figure dressed as a harlequin" (75); and round carved balls on posts, which turn out to be human skulls (75). Notably, everything that Kurtz has done must stay silent, an affront the supposed European civilizing mission, yet later shared to the unnamed narrator by an aged Marlow.

Stylistic Optimism and Pessimism

In the 1960s, Roman Jakobson confidently projected "an objective scholarly analysis of verbal art" (10). In the 1970s, Michael Halliday anticipated an examination of "stylistically relevant" (57) linguistic regularities in a William Golding novel *The Inheritors*. Stanley Fish assaulted what he termed "Halliday's machine" (109) and blamed such events of being "circular" (57) and "arbitrary" (58). In the 1990s, Michael Toolan and others countered Fish by protected, even straightforward, quantitative statistics, like word-frequencies. Back in the 1960s, John Sinclair contested that a fictional text has connotation merely "as a sample of an enormously large body of text" (75). This scrutiny still anticipates thorough study, although it can, at present, be examined with the corpus methods Sinclair's more recent theories.

A difficulty for stylistics is a discerning concentration on statistics. Stanley Fish indicates a rational quandary in which he considers stylistics as wedged. Fish posits that stylistics is subjective, spherical, or exists in cooperation. Either we choose a minute number of linguistic characteristics that we understand how to explain while we ignore the rest, or we opt for features that we previously know are imperative, explain them, and then assert they are significant. Recognizing that an inclusive portrayal is impossible and given the impossibility of creating authoritative definitions to explicit prescribed qualities, no escape exists. It is an authentic rational fork, which we may call the "Fish Fork." Navigating the Fish Fork requires a holistic view by seeing stylistics in relation to the study of everything. Recognizing the official characteristics that all articulate, in one way or another, becomes a topic of indecision and misshapen facts, which Marlow makes overt in one of his remarks to his addressees: "Of course . . . you fellows see more than I could then" (Conrad 39).

A Few Simple Frequency Matters

Among other things, corpus linguists explain word regularity. Isolated words and their frequencies have stern boundaries. While a word-frequency catalogue is an important preliminary point, as there must be some link connecting everyday terminology and imperative subject matters, the overall relation remains opaque.

Admittedly, a catalogue of the most common content words in *Heart of Darkness* appears unpromising at first glance. The top words and their frequency in the novel are: "said" (131 occurrences); "like" (122 occurrences); "man" (111 occurrences); "Kurtz" (100 occurrences); "see" (92 occurrences); "know" (87 occurrences); "times" (77 occurrences); "seemed" (69 occurrences); "made" (65 occurrences); "river" (65 occurrences); "came" (63 occurrences); "little" (62 occurrences); "looked" (56 occurrences); "men" (51 occurrences); "Mr" (51 occurrences); and "long" (50 occurrences). Recurrent proper nouns and common nouns are likely to point to just the surface motifs of a manuscript, with "said" being the most common word in literature in general. However, the list does detain other lexical items of note. Around 100 occurrences of "like" are in indistinguishable vocabulary such as "x was like y," and around twenty-five occurrences of "looked" are in indistinguishable expressions, for example, "x looked like y" or "it looked as though."

Indeed, we must be cautious in interpreting such catalogues. Corporal terms, such as "eyes" and "head" are numerous in countless fictional texts and naturally common in *Heart of Darkness*. For example, "eye" in its singular form appears four times; while "eyes" forty-nine times, almost with the exact same frequency as "head," where eyes are located, which comes up forty-eight times; while "heads" in the plural are mentioned twelve times. Yet, with proper contextualization the significance of these terms becomes clear. These words appear in places in the text where they have a specific implication: Marlow is continuously being watched over by "eyes" in the jungle, and "heads" are severed and impaled on posts. Verbs are often a superior contender for stylistically applicable words, although yet again, the psychosomatic verbs and verbs of insight (such as "see," "know," and "looked") are usually frequently repeated in fictional texts. In addition, nonfiction texts are more often than not "about" a given theme, and this might be indicative of how truthfully the vocabulary is presented. In fictional texts, normal terminology will, at the very least, recognize frequent personas and subject but will not say overtly what the text is truly about. To clarify with an example, the river is a vital theme in *Heart of Darkness*, although the novella is not "about" a river.

We can also verify which lexical items are considerably more recurrent in *Heart of Darkness* than in reference corpora. If we evaluate *Heart of Darkness* with a reference corpus of varied English literature, then the top twenty or more content words, which are both numerous in *Heart of Darkness* and as well drastically more recurrent than in the reference corpus are: "Kurtz" (100 occurrences); "seemed" (69 occurrences); "river" (65 occurrences); "station" (48 occurrences); "great" (36 occurrences); "manager" (42 occurrences); "earth" (39 occurrences); "ivory" (31 occurrences); "pilgrims" (31 occurrences); "darkness" (25 occurrences); "forest" (23 occurrences); "bank" (25 occurrences); "wilderness" (22 occurrences); and "cried" (20 occurrences). In total, the reference corpus was 41,436 words.

We can use software to lemmatize the story and examine once again the most common verb theorems. The top ten are: "say," "see," "look," "know," "come," "make," "seem," "hear," "take," and "think." Additionally, the nouns in these lists appear only to offer the foundation for the most unsophisticated type of content synopsis. Nevertheless, notice that the verb "seem" is amid the main words in all of these lists, and a number of previous verbs in the lists correlate to information, insight and manifestation. Consequently, even very straightforward occurrence lists do recognize words that articulate chief topics of *Heart of Darkness*.

How Words Are Distributed and Test Formed

A rationale as to why tallying individual words is surely insufficient is that the attractive content words are unable be consistently disseminated throughout the transcript, but are constrained to be gathered at dissimilar places. The placement of these words is also important. Some terms do not first appear until deep into the story. For example "Kurtz" is not mentioned until roughly a quarter of the way through the novella. Word allocation thus expresses part of the ambiguity and mysteriousness of his character.

Other lexical items, like "Buddha," are merely in the opening and closing parts of Conrad's book. This method of word sharing is an indication of text organization. For instance, the story frames are marked properly with word and phrase repetition. The novella commences on the Thames, depicts a voyage up the River Congo, which is never named and thus escapes lexical analysis, and concludes back on the Thames. Both in the beginning and the end of the novella word repetition becomes critical. The book opens with a depiction of "the *Thames . . .* a *waterway leading to the uttermost ends of the earth*" (Conrad 5-6) where "*Marlow sat* cross-legged . . . he had the pose of a *Buddha . . .* we felt *meditative*" (6, 10; emphasis added). In the book's conclusion, once more "*Marlow . . . sat* apart . . . in the pose of a *meditating Buddha*" (111) with a view of "*the tranquil waterway leading to the uttermost ends of the earth*" (111; emphasis added). Indeed, this cyclical imagery demonstrates the recurring cycle that cruelness and imperialism played in the late Victorian and Edwardian era.

There are more than a few other examples. At the opening, Marlow visits the Brussels, though unnamed, a city is described as "whited sepulchre" (Conrad 14). He penetrates offices, past high houses in a tapered and abandoned street, through doors standing laboriously partly open. When Marlow is in the office, he says "a door open[s]," as if the object itself has agency (14). The building is "as still as a house in the city of the dead" (16). Toward the end, Marlow returns to the "sepulchral city" (102). He pays Kurtz a visit, walking through a weighty door flanked by high homes in a street as calm as a cemetery. In the house is a piano like a sarcophagus. Lastly, "a high door open[s] and [Kurtz's] Intended comes in" (105).

Such repetition comments on the arrangement of the entire book, and we can trace a number of these distributions with a straightforward program. For instance, the words "heart," "dark," and "darkness" come about all the way through the book, although they augment in regularity at the conclusion, when the narrative almost becomes "too dark—too dark altogether" (Conrad 111). The recurrence of these keywords at the conclusion of Conrad's novella signals the repetitive nature of human behavior and European imperialism.

Likewise, the lemmas "dream" and "nightmare" take place throughout the book, although the terms are distributed in different ways. "Dream" crops up twice at the very start, then quite a few times in a cluster about a third of the way through the book. The spreading of the term "dream" shows that Marlow is attempting to inform his loaded vision, signaled by the moderate frequency through the remainder of the narrative. "Nightmare," however, appears only once at the beginning of the novella, where there are "hints for nightmares" (Conrad 21) and then once more in a group near the conclusion (95). Tellingly, all these juxtapositions happen either in association with Kurtz or the wilderness, linking the perceived savagery of man with the locale in which he resides. The distribution of words exemplifies how Marlow's vision develops into a frightening tale.

A more multifaceted, lexico-grammatical case can be seen in the verb "know." Its frequency of 122 occurrences is quite evenly dispersed throughout the book. Many illustrations are pessimistic, either grammatically as in the phrase "I don't know, he did not know" (Conrad 79), or else by inference; as in the sentence "he wanted to know, if only he had known" (79). Surely then, *Heart of Darkness* is about the unreliability and misrepresentation of human familiarity. In the novella's conclusion, there is a modest rupture of optimistic instance: Marlow projects onto Kurtz's Intended that her look says: "I alone *know* how to mourn for him." He records that she told him, "I am proud to *know* I understood him better than any one .

.. You have heard him! You *know*! ... You *know* what vast plans he had" (150). Here, at the conclusion, we have Conrad using the verb as satire, showing that European audiences expected a European colonial agent to behave in a particular way under Victorian ideals, and when it comes to light that he behaved in just the opposite way, one is unable, in a sense of denial, to admit what they really "know."

Joseph Conrad's *Heart of Darkness* is a novella that imprisons the readers' awareness with its unusual setting and darkness. The verbal communication within *Heart of Darkness* diverges from daily speech. However, many repeated expressions in the narrative are noteworthy in that that they take advantage of customary word choices: the words and sentence structures all point toward darkness. A general communication method in the novel is transmuted via the River Thames and the River Congo, using light and dark imagery with nouns and verbs punctuated in placement and frequency in order to comment on the vagueness connecting the poles of Europe and Africa.

Works Cited

Achebe, C. *An Image of Africa: Racism in Conrad's Heart of Darkness*. Ed. Robert Kimbrough. 3rd ed. London: W. W Norton and Co., 1988. 251-261. Print.

Conrad, Joseph. *Heart of Darkness*. Ed. Paul B. Armstrong. New York: W.W. Norton & Company, 2016. Print.

Fellbaum, Christiane. "Co-Occurrence and Antonymy." *International Journal of Lexicography*, vol. 8, no. 4, 1995: 281-303. Print.

Fish, S.E . "What Is Stylistics and Why Are They Saying Such Terrible Things About It?" *Boundry* 2 (Autumn 1979): 129-146. Print.

Halliday, M.A.K. *Linguistic Function and Literary Style*. New York: Holt Rinehart and Winston, 1970. 70-72. Print.

Jakobson, Roman. "Closing Statement: Linguistics and Poetics." *Style and Language*. New York: Holt Wiley, 1960. 350-377. Print.

Jones, Steven. *Antonym*. London: Routledge, 2002. Print.

Justeson, John S. & Salva M. Katz. (1991) "Redefining Antonymy: the Textual Structure of a Semantic Relation." *Literary and Linguistic Computing*, vol. 7, no. 3, 1991: 176-184. Print.

Nofal, Khalil Hassan. "Darkness in Conrad's *Heart of Darkness*: A Linguistic and Stylistic Analysis." *Theory and Practice in Language Studies*. 3.3 (March 2013): 452-458.

Sinclair, J. M. *Corpus, Concordance, Collocation.* Oxford: Oxford UP. 1991. Print.

———. "The Linguistic Basis of Style."*Style and Text.* Stockholm: John Benjamins Publishing Company, 1975. 75-89. Print.

———. "When Is a Poem Like a Sunset?" *A Review of English Literature.* (6. 2) 1965: 76-91.

Toolan, M. "On the Centrality of Stylistics." *The European English Messenger* 6.1 (2002): 19-25. Print.

———. "Stylistics and its Discontents: Getting off the Fish Hook." *The Stylistic Reader.* London: Arnold, 1990. 9-20. Print.

Widdowson, H.G. *Teaching Language as Communication.* Oxford: Oxford UP, 1978. Print.

The Unreadable Sea: Manliness in Joseph Conrad's *Victory: An Island Tale* (1915) and "The Tale" (1917)

Benjamin Bronnert Walker

In the Book of Revelation, when the seas depart the earth, the bitter confusion of human life is ended (Rev. 21.1 NIV). The sea is something through which Christ can sleep, but against which the apostles fearfully sweat in vain (Mark 4.35-41 NIV). In Conrad, the sea and fogs, by contrast, are what make life possible. True clarity for Conrad's characters is utterly paralyzing; whereas "blessed, warm mental fog" and the "unreadable sea" allow men to step forward into action (Conrad, "The Tale" 89). False dreams of moral duty, awareness of the pointlessness of life, and attempts to be good and honest, stop men from truly entering into the murky struggle of active living. This is as much the case for the righteous as the criminal. In *Victory*, both the heroic Axel Heyst and the deathly Mr. Jones, find themselves in isolated stupors when they contemplate too acutely or too objectively the absurd play of life's "shadows" instead of joining in with its dance (Conrad, *Victory* 81; 143). Similarly, the Commanding Officer in "The Tale" only relinquishes his stifling morality when the literal sea fog enables him to send another ship to its death, without truly knowing what he is doing.

It is not only activity but particularly manly activity which requires, in Conrad, types of obscuring fog (including womanly wiles) and deceptive seas. Manliness is constantly in question for Conrad's characters. Their appearances, voices and activities are regularly considered integral to the creation of differing types of masculinity. Men's pursuits and possessions of women especially tend to elicit reflection upon their own genders roles. For example, in *Victory*, the hotelier Schonberg groans that his "possession of Mrs. Schonberg was no incitement to a display of manly virtues. . . . Life was a hollow sham" (Conrad, *Victory* 72). By comparison, Heyst is depicted with his love, Lena, as still being enrapt by the "surprise of novelty, the flattered vanity of his possession of this woman; for a man must feel that unless he has ceased to be masculine" (96). Whereas Schonberg's easy captivity of his wife hollows out his existence, the surprise romance in which Heyst finds himself reawakens his manliness. Crucially, for Heyst it is not Lena's true affection alone that enthralls him; he is even struck and compelled into active love by her smiles for others, which he knows to be fake: "the effect of the mechanical, ordered smile was joyous, radiant. . . . Here was a smile, the origin of which was well known to him; and yet it conveyed a sensation of warmth, had given him a sort of ardor to live which was very new to his experience" (173). Heyst's desire to live and thus to begin to recreate his masculinity, is charged into being by that which he knows to be a deceit but which warms him anyway. In both Conrad's *Victory* and "The Tale," life's "shadows" and fogs, however ephemeral or deceptive, have a power which must be experienced if one is to be masculine.

Through showing how *Victory* and "The Tale" have similar ways of imagining the formations of manliness, it will be argued that Conrad's work emphasizes that the First World War was *not* a profound rupture in ideas about manliness. "The Tale" is the only work of Conrad's that deals with combat during the First World War, and it represents an apotheosis in Conrad's ideas about men. Historical accounts have suggested that whilst the daily realities of psychological breakdown among men during the Great War were different to that which went before, ideas about manliness only had to be slightly rearranged. By splitting men up into private-class (perceived to be mentally weak) and officer-class (perceived to be mentally strong but under huge pressures) older ideas about manliness remained prevalent (Loughran). Moreover, prewar domestic norms were quickly restored after the armistice in 1918 (Lawrence, "Forging a Peaceable Kingdom" 557-589; Lawrence, "The Transformation" 186-216). Though his perspectives on manliness are very different from simplistic forms, Conrad fits well into a narrative that stresses continuity over change in gendered ideas during the war. "The Tale" is continuous with his writing about the formation of manliness in his prewar work, such as *Victory*, which was finished two months before fighting began.

In order to show this and to delve into the complex and unfolding constructions of manliness across Conrad's work, the following analysis will be split into three sections, each examining a different theme: labor, conflict and narration. Each of these is, roughly, a successive stage in the formation of manly activity in Conrad. Incitement to labor delivers the man out of boredom or despair, then conflict results from being drawn into the world of action, and finally, the tale of danger and decision is told, consolidating the manly identity in narrative.

Laboring Bodies

Labor in Conrad can be an invigorating form of active living, connected to the earth and detached from the stupors or lack of feeling in "inert" men, but it can also be lost. In Conrad's "The Idiots" (1896), Jean-Pierre Bacadou, falls apart as each of his children are born severely mentally disabled. His first hope was that he would have "two big sons striding over the land from patch to patch, wringing tribute from the earth beloved and fruitful." As birth after birth results in disappointment, however, Bacadou begins to stalk despondently the "mute earth," which no longer holds any "promise in the fertility of the fields." He slowly loses his desire for life as his dreams of a prosperous laboring future are further extinguished. Even in the way in which Bacadou looks at his children becomes without any "inner fire." Their disability results in Bacadou himself taking on an "indifference which is like a deformity of peasant humanity"—his own mind becomes like that of a malformed body. His thoughts are portrayed as lacking any of the "core" of the life of labor:

> Like the earth they master and serve, those men, slow of eye and speech, do not show the inner fire; so that, at last, it becomes a question with them as with the earth, what there is in the core: heat, violence, a force mysterious and terrible - or nothing but a clod, a mass fertile and inert, cold and unfeeling, ready to bear a crop of plants that sustain life or give death. (Conrad, "The Idiots" 64)

The truth of the peasants' inner lives appear uncertain in the eyes of the narrator. Whether their labor has something of the hot and terrible mystery of the earth or whether it is simply cold and productive is unclear but what is certain is that Bacadou's own mental life is losing grip on the type of labor which is bound to the promise of the earth and which is something more than inert fertility (Conrad, "The Idiots" 265-273).

Though both *Victory* and "The Tale" are not focused on peasant farming, the lack of the power of labor is similarly critical for hindering the formation of characters' masculinities. In these, Conrad's later works, there is a danger in detaching from life's manly labors through overthinking, too much cynicism about activity, or an excess of clarity over meaninglessness. The question which the narrator poses in "The Idiots" over what is inside the core of peasant work, is exactly the sort of question which in Conrad's later writing, is seen to be so hazardous. To constantly question life is to stop oneself from being able to fully enter into its relational possibilities and the joys of manly feeling. In *Victory,* Heyst grapples with the legacy of his father who discarded all beliefs and left Heyst cut off from the normal stream of life. If anything could have destroyed his internal "primeval ancestor" and "original Adam," Heyst explains, it would have been his father: "with his contemptuous, inflexible negation of all effort." Even as Heyst is drawn back into positive laboring life, he suffers when contemplating his father, who would have been hurt by the loss of his son's 'aloofness.' Even on his deathbed, among the "cemetery of hopes" that is London, Heyst's father feared his son believed in "flesh and blood" and that only a "full and equable contempt" would rid him of it (Conrad, *Victory* 149-151).

It is not the restoration of beliefs, however, that creates Heyst's laboring manliness, but the misunderstandings and deceptions of fog and sea into which he chooses to enter. Heyst's "inner fire" is first stoked when he comes into contact with Captain Morrison who, when Heyst agrees to bail him out of some considerable debt, believes Heyst to be the instrument of providence. For Heyst, this baffling and worrying episode simultaneously ignites something in him leading him into a doomed business with Morrison. When it all comes to a sorry end and Morrison dies in England, Heyst is accused by the local hotel crowd on the Indian Ocean of being a murderer. Even though, by this point, Heyst had again departed polite society, his actions stirred up myths and stories around him that would, in part, result in his being pursued to his solitary idyll by a small band of vicious thieves. Not only did entering into the world of labor and action leave Heyst at the whims of its narrations and rumors, it also meant that he would find it more difficult to return to aloofness. Yet, in all this, Heyst is totally aware of the misunderstanding that led to him to be drawn into action; it was not the restoration of that which his father rejected enabling him to become manly, but a something both strangely true and false—just like Lena's smile. It was Heyst's remaining "unattached, floating existence" that allowed him to engage in Morrison's trading ventures in the same moment as having his detachment blighted by a desire to help the poor man. Morrison's perception of Heyst as a vessel for the love of God appeared ridiculous to its object, and yet Heyst also chose not dissuade Morrison, believing it to be a fool's errand to even try. The result of the plunge "after the submerged Morrison" was partnership, as would occur even more deeply with Heyst's great love, Lena, with whom he finds his masculinity fully developed later in the tale. Only in these mysterious seas, bobbing like cork with everybody else, not on the islands to which he attempts to flee, is Heyst's manliness properly formed (*Victory* 11-25).

For the Commanding Officer in "The Tale," the concurrently revealing and deceiving fogs of the seawaters are the environment in which his masculinity is produced. The narrative opens with the night described as a "tide" against which the passionate and intermittent whispering of a man "seemed to plead against the answering murmurs of infinite sadness." As they finish, the man stands over the woman "a moment masculine and mysterious in his immobility." He is described both as a wave over her and among the waves of the night, both as part of a mood which is "the end of all things" and as among the continuous "rhythm of the swelling heart-waves running the circuit of the habitable globe." Through these undulating feelings and active moods of sea-like human life, the woman draws the man into telling her a story, to act again like a fresh wave. The tale he tells is that of his time as a Commanding Officer on the sea during the war. He begins by recounting how naval warfare is a lived mystery, causing one to constantly fear being someday at the mercy of a previously unseen enemy ship or even being killed before the ship is spotted. The waters through which the ship navigates are described as an "unchanged face," and the sea pretends that "there was nothing the matter with the world," leaving sailors who find it "impossible to believe that the familiar clear horizon traces the limit of one great circular ambush." Yet, just as Heyst found after his figurative dives to save Morrison and Lena, the Commanding Officer and his ship, as a "phantom" among phantoms in the "dead luminosity of the fog," is forced into making manly decisions and is led by confusion into conflict (Conrad, "The Tale" 75-89).

Men at War

The result of being drawn into the waters of life is that—both in *Victory* and "The Tale"—the characters, fresh in their manly action, are drawn into war. However, as in the other aspects of life's playing shadows and swirling "convolutions of vapors," these battles are never simplistic and lack a definite distinction between friend and foe. As the narrator of "The Tale" puts it, the ideals of love and war are "so terribly easy, to degrade in the name of Victory" and thus the "noblest activities" become distorted. Equally, in *Victory*, it is the success of greater ideals which are the culmination of the tale, rather than that of any particular side. In "The Tale" the narration spends most its energy in exploring these issues surrounding such conflicts into which men are pulled among the seas, when the Commanding Officer's ship encounters a neutral vessel of which he is incredibly suspicious. The Commanding Officer begins by boarding the ship out of curiosity: "the great motive power of hatred and love." His aim being to detect an "atmosphere of gratuitous treachery" on the neutral vessel; having explained already that he hated such vessels fiercely because they were not open, but stealthy and "murderous."

This "mere vague blot on the fog's brightness" had become the object of the Commanding Officer's fear and disgust. His desire to act had led him to despise those who pretended not to be a part of conflict that, among such seas, he perhaps believed to be an impossible task. Now roped into manly action, the Commanding Officer, just as Heyst, finds himself in the midst of conflict (Conrad, "The Tale" 78-89).

Just as the seas and fogs draw out manly life, they also make men complicit in death through conflict. The "crop of plants" that "sustain life or give death" in Conrad's description of peasants' possible lack of humanity in "The Idiots" captures something of that which is portrayed in life's manly actors in other works. Whilst the manly actors of *Victory* and "The Tale" are fueled by "inner fire," they are drawn nevertheless into the creation of death in a different way. The escape from cold "inert fertility" ensures that they take part in destruction and creation but in manner less detached from feeling and brotherhood (Conrad, "The Idiots" 265-273). War is not an inevitable bad for Conrad's Commanding Officer, is it the deceit of pretending not to take part which is the evil. Thus, when the Commanding Officer becomes complicit in the sinking of the neutral vessel, he does not have a cold or simple solution to its complexity. Furthermore, it is the fog itself that causes the ship's sinking, since they hit rocks, but at the same time, this fog had been what allowed the Commanding Officer to force them out of the bay because he did not know for certain whether they would live or die.

The fog and the sea enable manly life but they also cause a certain type of death. In *Victory*, at the culmination of Heyst's active love for Lena his "fastidious soul . . . even at that moment" keeps "the true cry of love from his lips in its infernal mistrust of all life." Yet, he is able to recognize that in saving his life, Lena has done what no other person could have done for him. Thus, though he is kept from a full declaration of love, he chooses suicide by her side in favor of being apart from her. This is very different from that aspect of death that Mr. Jones, fearing women and descending into immobile boredom, carries around with him (Conrad, *Victory* 339-342). Heyst's death and the kind of death that the Commanding

Officer causes is fueled by the fire of life and is both manly and active.

During these conflicts and wars, the male body is reshaped by the thickening fogs, which are only perceived among increased deception and hostility. As they confront one another, the characters' own prejudices or preconceived notions of their adversaries tend to stop them from understanding accurately. This is particularly an issue with one's judgment of the other's manliness, which is assumed to be totally wretched, whatever new information arrives through conflict. The Commanding Officer in "The Tale" listens to the Northman but has little ability to extend him any trust, he is instead "aware of an inward voice, a grave murmur in the depth of his very own self, telling another tale, as if on purpose to keep alive in him his indignation and his anger." The result of this second internal narrative, which is fueling the conflict and which has detached itself from any objectivity is that the Commanding Officer becomes increasingly disgusted by the Northman. His assessment of the Northman's masculinity for example, degrades him to the level of savage: "Men were like that—moral cannibals feeding on each other's misfortunes." The male body of the Northman is, in the Commanding Officer's eyes, literally sustained by his treacherous consumptions. By contrast, the narrator describes the Commanding Officer (himself) as being "one of those men who are made morally and almost physically uncomfortable by the mere thought of having to beat down a lie." The male body of the Commanding Officer is described as opposite to that of the Northman. The Commanding Officer is physically incapable of supporting deception, he believes his entire form to be fueled by what he thinks to be honest and straight living. As the tension drives to a climax, the Commanding Officer is unable to cope with the "atmosphere of murderous complicity," which he feels to be surrounding him "denser, more impenetrable, more acrid than the fog outside" making him struggle for air. The conflict itself, made possible by the sea fog, has in turn further obscured the Commanding Officer's vision, reshaping and infusing his body, leading him to the concluding act—to send the

Northman on course into the real sea fog, to his death (Conrad, "The Tale" 75-89).

Narrating Manliness

The last stage in the creation of manliness in Conrad is the narration of it, the events' reproduction as tales. The Commanding Officer's fraught story concludes with the narrator revealing that it is he who is the Commanding Officer. The Northman, by steaming out onto the rocks had shown that he was, in some regard, telling the truth; he really was lost at sea in the fog. However, the Commanding Officer hastily points out that the whole truth of the rest of the Northman's story remains undetermined: "it proves nothing. Nothing either way." Yet, the Commanding Officer is not completely certain and instead repeats over and over that he will never know whether he "added to the corpses that litter the bed of the unreadable sea the bodies of men completely innocent or basely guilty." The response of his woman, so aware of his "passion for the truth," is to throw her arms around him in an attempt at comfort, but he quickly retreats. The act of retelling was the culmination of the process, leaving the listener and reader able to understand the intricacies of the Commanding Officer's formation through experience of the sea, but nevertheless we are left blind when trying to unpick the exact truth of story. At the start of "The Tale" it was the woman whose "courage" and love encouraged him to render the formation of his own manliness in compelling narrative: "He dared not make a sound, shrinking as a man would do from the prosaic necessities of existence. As usual, it was the woman who had the courage... 'Tell me something,' she said." Yet, as the narrative ends, he has nothing left to give, and becomes "disengaged." The story-making was his dive back into that unreadable sea, giving himself a role within it. At the culmination, without solution, he tries again to split himself off from active living which had submerged him in the waters of deceit which he so reviled (Conrad, "The Tale" 75-89).

Narration, the last stage in the formation of manliness, in *Victory*, goes beyond death. After Lena, Heyst and their attackers have torn each other apart with guns and knives, and all are dead, the last chapter concludes with their conflict retold in a local court. Some of Heyst's final words are recounted as "'Ah, Davidson, woe to the man whose heart has not learned while young to hope, to love—and to put its trust in life!'" In this, Conrad has Heyst both reflect on his life as a lesson about the best and quickest route to manly living and, at the same time, has Heyst remade in the stories of others as a true man who finally invested himself in love. Davidson then says to his "Excellency," who is reviewing the case, that he supposed Heyst "couldn't stand his thoughts before her (Lena's) dead body," and because "fire purifies everything," he burnt down their house. Again, Davidson is rendering Heyst in a tale in which Heyst ultimately becomes the heroic lover, firmly choosing flames and ashes over the pain of the loss of his dearest woman. The "island tale" is complete, turned from rumors, suspicion and conflict back into dust and simplicity. The response by both the judge and by Davidson, which ends Conrad's novel, is that "'There was nothing to be done . . . nothing.'" In some sense, this is Heyst's highest point of manliness, he has, just before death, become a true man, and he has also become nothing; there is no longer any action to be taken. The story of his life remakes him as a true hero and yet, by simplifying him, takes him out of the complex waters of true life that made it all possible (*Victory* 343-346).

Conclusion

Not only does Conrad challenge the grand biblical narrative of the sea, he does so in ways that are complex and varied. He uses the sea as a way of showing the importance of diving into life's confusion and, through this, forming manliness. He also shows the wild and free outcomes of this process, how they are bound up with life's inner fire, labor, conflict, and death. Along with it all, Conrad is sensitive to the narrations of manliness, the sea and the fog, how these make and break, enliven and freeze, ways of living. His is not a simplistic attack on classical moralities, but more layered and sophisticated, engaging with the struggles of lived male experience in a time where to reject the stream of life seemed, to positivists, to be a possibility. The Great War affected Conrad's thought experiment very little, rather it gave a fresh context for older battles played out among men in imperial locations. Manliness continued to be formed through well-worn routes, strategies, and quandaries. It could also still be, through exiting life and choosing objectivity, rejected in favor of a cold and inert but fertile existence. In such tales, Conrad's heroes are the ones that grapple most ferociously with the tension and choose to live victoriously—to live in manly positive activity, even if that resulted in death.

In Conrad's world, there is little metaphysical or readable truth onto which men can hold tightly. His world is one in which the high seas and islands in South East Asia are where the real action happens, not in the comfortable thoughts of the static. Britain and London are portrayed as ciphers of reality—a "cemetery of hopes"—where (in *Victory*) people go to die of disease or in their beds (11-25). Far-flung colonies and foreign fields of conflict are, by contrast, enchanted, violent, and exciting. Britain is a place where such vivid stories are narrated certainly—where men of action go to tell their tales, to start their dreams and to write their memoirs—but in some sense this is detached from the actual business of true physical living on the seas or in tropical archipelagos. In a sense, Conrad is questioning his own ability to tell his stories of intrigue and empire, without harming something important, without losing the magic of an island's silence to horrible noise. Conrad's writing attempts to free the reader, like Heyst did with Lena, from the roaring, awful theaters of civilized society, but as with Lena, perhaps we are never able to fully escape.

Works Cited

Conrad, J. "The Idiots." *The Secret Sharer and Other Stories.* Ed. J. H. Stape & A. H. Simmons. London: Penguin Classics, 2007. Print.

_____. "The Tale." *Stories from 'The Strand.'* Ed. G. Beare. London: The Folio Society, 1992. Print.

_____. *Victory: An Island Tale.* London: Penguin Classics Edition, 2015. Print.

Lawrence, J. "Forging a Peaceable Kingdom: War, Violence and the Fear of Brutalisation in Post-First World War Britain." *Journal of Modern History* 75.3 (Sept. 2003): 557-89. Print.

———. "The Transformation of British Public Politics after the First World War." *Past and Present,* 190 (2006): 186-216. Print.

Loughran, T. "Masculinity, Shell Shock and Emotional Survival in the First World War" (Review no. 944) *Reviews in History.* Institute of Historical Research, Aug. 2010. Web. 7 January 2016. <http://www.history.ac.uk/reviews/review/944>.

"Mark 4.35-41." *The Bible: New International Version.* London: NIV, 2008. Print.

"Rev. 21.1." *The Bible: New International Version.* London: NIV, 2008. Print.

Showalter, E. *The Female Malady: Women, Madness and English Culture, 1880–1980.* London: Virago, 1987. Print.

Heart of Darkness and the Problem of Faith
Charlotte Fiehn

Man has, as it were, become a kind of prosthetic god.
(Sigmund Freud)

Sigmund Freud could well have had Kurtz in mind when he wrote this in his study *Civilization and Its Discontents* (1930). Through the morally ambivalent narrator of *Heart of Darkness* (1899), Joseph Conrad frames the character Mr. Kurtz as a god-like figure. Reports of his behavior and of the behavior of other characters present Kurtz as exceptional. The language of the text, particularly in relation to Kurtz, is loaded with Judeo-Christian references. Yet, the problem of faith in *Heart of Darkness* depends on much more than a single character's presentation. As this chapter outlines, there are issues of narrative structure and storytelling that pertain to practices of organized religion and to Christianity in particular. Other critics have also recognized Charles Marlow's journey as a kind of spiritual quest, again, heavily loaded with Judeo-Christian imagery and specific references to pilgrimage.

The goal of this chapter is to consider some of the ways that Conrad manages the representation of faith and religion in *Heart of Darkness*, looking particularly at how, in a critical reading, attention to the representation of aspects of faith and religion can generate insights about Conrad's wider discourse on society and the individual.

Faith and Storytelling in *The Heart of Darkness*
When Marlow begins to tell his tale to his audience of sailors, including *Heart of Darkness*'s unnamed narrator, both his posture and his language cast him as prophet-like: he sits "lifting one arm from the elbow, the palm of the hand outwards so that with his legs folded before him he had the post of a Buddha preaching in European clothes and without a lotus flower" (10). As Cedric Watts

suggests, *Heart of Darkness* is a story "told by a British gentleman to British gentlemen" (46), echoing of "social customs of an age of gentlemen's clubs and semi-formal social gatherings at which travelers would meet to compare notes and exchange yarns about foreign experiences" (46).

Marlow speaks historically but hypothetically about human experience: "Imagine the feelings of a commander of a fine . . . trireme . . . ordered suddenly to the north" (Conrad 9). He imagines the experience himself in abstract terms, thinking of "cold, fog, tempests, disease, exile, and death—death skulking in the air, in the water, in the bush" (10). The effect is one of distance and Otherness: Marlow's imagined commander is Roman and civilized but he has to "face the darkness" (10) in a wilderness removed from his homeland. He has to contend with "utter savagery . . . closed around him—all the mysterious life of the wilderness that stirs in the forest, in the jungles, in the hearts of wild men" (10). The commander experiences "regrets" and a "longing to escape" (10) but he also feels "disgust, the surrender—the hate" (10) because of what surrounds him and how it drives at something innate in himself.

Like a priest preparing his audience to hear a sermon, Marlow begins with this abstract example of how civilized man is vulnerable to the wilderness. Marlow even explains the nature of salvation, what it is that "saves" (Conrad 10) the civilized man: the idea of "efficiency—the devotion to efficiency" (10). Preaching a doctrine of imperialism, Marlow justifies it as "[a]n idea at the back of it, not a sentimental pretense but an idea; and an unselfish belief in the idea—something you can set up, and bow down before, and offer a sacrifice to. . ." (10). Yet, as Conrad's readers gradually appreciate, this justification is also an explanation of why Kurtz acted as he did.

Consistent with the structure of an effective oral presentation—and again the comparison to a Church sermon is obvious—Marlow shifts to talk about his own experiences by becoming self-effacing, insisting that "I don't want to bother you much with what happened to me" (Conrad 11), trying to suggest something offhand about his narrative as a whole. His own experiences, though, are precisely what his story will be about and the self-effacement is a tactic that even the unnamed narrator is aware of and able to expose: Marlow shows, he says, "the weakness of many tellers of tales who seem so often unaware of what their audiences would best like to hear" (11).

Marlow is not unaware, though, and he has no intention but to relate his own experiences. He proceeds to justify himself and his topic by outlining how, "to understand the effect of it on me you ought to know how I got there, what I saw, how I went up that river to the place where I first met the poor chap" (Conrad 11). He then proceeds to follow this plan, beginning with an account of his return to London "after a lot of Indian Ocean, Pacific, China Seas" (11). Like a true orator, he engages his audience again, suggesting that they will "remember" (11) certain of the details about his return to London and that they will recall him, perhaps, "loafing about, hindering you fellows in your work and invading your homes, just as though I had got a heavenly mission to civilize you" (11). The simile comparing his behavior to a missionary seeking to "civilize" (11) is both ironic and a compelling instance of foreshadowing.

The nature of the idea and its effects are what Marlow presents to his audience as he frames his account of receiving his instructions to search for Kurtz. Like a lost soul, Marlow wandered aimlessly. He had a "passion for maps" (Conrad 11) and wanted to explore the "blank spaces on the earth" (11), betraying his imperialist mindset and his rather childish enthusiasm for adventure, which becomes a source of temptation. Childhood and innocence allowed him to perceive "a blank space of delightful mystery" (12), but with experience, he sees "a place of darkness" (12) and images of a snake, a creature so obviously associated with sin, the Devil, and temptation. What becomes snake-like, though, is the "mighty big river" (12). Marlow perceives it as "an immense snake uncoiled, with its head in the sea, its body at rest curving afar over a vast country and its tail lost in the depth of the land" (12).

Marlow's temptation evokes the story of Eden and man's fall from Paradise: "it fascinated me as a snake would a bird—a silly little bird" (Conrad 12). Seeking the opportunity to pursue his underlying desire, Marlow turns to "the women" (12) to help him find a job that will enable him to explore the region he finds so tempting. The role of these women in enabling Marlow's pilgrimage offers an intriguing counter to the role of Kurtz's Intended, mirroring the role of women, specifically the Virgin Mary and Mary Magdalene in the foundation of the Church but also, perhaps, echoing the role of Eve in the Fall of Man. An "aunt" (12) of Marlow's, "a dear enthusiastic soul" (12) assists him in securing a position with a "Company" (13), which, again, can stand for the church and equally represent something more sinister. Its capitalization throughout the text supports both interpretations.

The name of the Company and its exact function is omitted, except to suggest that they are involved in trade and "had received news that one of their Captains had been killed in a scuffle with the natives" (Conrad 12) and "a glorious idea" (12) that relates clearly to Marlow's discussion about conquest and the importance of having a strong idea behind it. Marlow's visit to the Company in Europe takes him to "a city" (13) and a "white sepulcher" (13), a physical rendering of civilization that hints at spiritual emptiness. Marlow describes "narrow and deserted streets in deep shadow, high houses, innumerable windows with venetian blinds, a dead silence, grass sprouting between the stones, imposing carriage archways right and left, immense double doors standing ponderously ajar" (13). The environment suggests opulence married with spiritual decay, as does the language. The deserted streets marry to the images of windows covered with blinds, suggesting a lack of perspective, the inability to see. Referring also to a "dead silence" (13), Conrad embeds the sense of decay at a textual level to reinforce the imagery.

Heart of Darkness As A Pilgrimage Narrative

When Marlow first arrives in Africa, Conrad refers to the journey as being "like a weary pilgrimage amongst hints for nightmares" (17). From the first moments of the adventure, however, Marlow represents it as a pilgrimage of various dimensions. As Deborah Gurth notes, the narrative supports two "interwoven mythical structures" (155): the Quest, which is "Marlowe's [*sic*] initiatory journey and *descencus ad inferos* leading to Kurtz" (155) and "the mythic structure of a creation set in some primordial past and portraying how, through the actions of a quasi-legendary figure, an original world was destroyed and suspended by another"(155).

Considering the Quest framework specifically, Gurth relates Marlow's "call to adventure" (156), his journey to Brussels, to various aspects of the classical quest: "the image of a vast snake uncoiled, symbolic of earth's mysteries, emerges from the depth of his childhood and impels him to leave behind the familiar world and enter the unknown" (156). Gurth also identifies the "headquarters of the Company" as a "mythical gateway to the underworld, with the Fates guarding the door" (156). Yet, the people who employ Marlow and those who work for the Company support a comparison between to the Church as well as the underworld. The secretary is "white-haired" (Conrad 14) and "in a sanctuary" (14), in "pale plumpness" (14), Marlow meets his employer, a "great man" (14) who "had his grip on the handle-end of ever so many millions" (14). The comparison depends on the reader recognizing conventions for representing churchmen as aging, on the one hand, and seemingly gluttonous on the other, but the language also supports the comparison, with "sanctuary" (14) directly comparing the inner offices of the Company to the inner space of a church building. Marlow also refers to his encounter with the two women and the signing of his contract as "ceremonies" (14) and Conrad describing the women as plainly dressed, one even wearing "a starch white affair on her head" (14), the two women together, nun-like in appearance. Although the presentation of the women "guarding the door of Darkness" (14) and the capitalization of "Darkness" (14) mark direct allusions to hell, framing the beginning of Marlow's journey as metaphorical descent into the underworld, as Gurth suggests, the layering of images allows for the second and specifically Christian reading, that positions the Company as representative of the Church, the allusions to hell thus suggestions of Church corruption.

Traveling, then, to the "edge of a colossal jungle so dark green as to be almost black, fringed with white surf . . . far, far away along a blue sea whose glitter was blurred by a creeping mist" (Conrad 16), every aspect of the landscape, as Marlow perceives it, is dramatic but somehow unnatural, oversized or exaggerated in its scope. It is a "God-forsaken wilderness" (16) and Marlow finds himself "isolated" (17) from everyone around him. A striking aspect of Marlow's isolation is that the men around him are "black fellows" (17) and he perceives them as grotesque or at least as distorted and exaggerated, like the environment they live in. To Marlow, though, the natives also appear rather elemental: "their eyeballs glistening. They shout, sang; their bodies streamed with perspiration; they had faces like grotesque masks—these chaps; but they had bone, muscle, a wild vitality, an intense energy of movement that was as natural and true as the stuff along their coast" (17).

The subtle allusions to a background of awareness also frame the context in which these men might have a function. The "man-of-war anchored off the coast" (Conrad 17) testifies to an ongoing French war, and Conrad expands the image to an epic scale with his diction, describing the background as an "empty immensity of earth, sky, and water," where the warships are "incomprehensible, firing into a continent" (17). The "incomprehensible" and the "insanity in the proceedings" (17) also frame the first impressions of Africa and its people as alarmingly Other. The "somebody on board" (17) refers to the "camp of natives" (17) as "enemies—hidden out of sight" (17), though, and this suggests how they are like a people somehow without knowledge of God. Their energy and the chaos of their experience, coupled with the chaos and energy of their environment, suggests the void that Kurtz fills as self-appointed leader. He sees them and the environment as raw materials at his disposal, his self-justification aligning to Marlow's earlier dialogue about just how colonialists and imperialists justify their actions.

Although Marlow journeys "upwards of thirty days" even before he "saw the mouth of the big river" (Conrad 18), undertaking an extended pilgrimage to find Kurtz, he sees much of the chaos and despair that Kurtz seeks to rework for his own ends. Marlow's language constantly emphasizes desperation and ungodliness. Even the Swede who "hanged himself on the road" (18) anticipates the justification for Kurtz's actions, his death implying that the despair of the land is contagious, the brutality of the environment unbearable without some sense of higher purpose. Ironically, Marlow's response to hearing of the Swede is an exclamation: "Why, in God's name?" Yet, it is the precise absence of God, the "scene of inhabited devastation" (18), which leads to the stranger's despair: "The sun too much for him, or the country perhaps" (18).

The closer Marlow comes to Kurtz, the sharper the Christian language within the story's text becomes, further expanding the value system that words like "high" and "just" appeal to. Marlow himself defines the men he sees in power over the natives, distinguishing them from "the devil of violence, and the devil of greed, and the devil of hot desire" (Conrad 19) and describing them instead as somehow more innately hellish. No particular motive compels them, not violence, greed, or desire, as Marlow mentions. Instead, "strong, lusty, red-eyed devils . . . swayed and drove men" (20). One in particular he describes, too, as "a flabby, pretending, weak-eyed devil of a rapacious and pitiless folly" (20), whose "insidious" (20) nature Marlow will not even appreciate until "several months later and a thousand miles father" (20), suggesting the vast and terrible scale of the man's cruelty.

Marlow's various encounters with men who are slaves to "red-eyed devils" (Conrad 20), representing the mechanisms of colonialism and imperialism, establish horror and shame at what is being done. Although he persists in describing "[b]lack shapes" (20), he insists that the natives are "men" and that "they were not enemies, they were not criminals" (20). Marlow's reaction to these scenes suggests his own development as a Christ-figure, too. He sees and responds to suffering; on some level, he wants to fight the injustice of men treated as machines, "dying slowly" (20). Conrad also makes clear that it is a descent into hell that Marlow has undertaken, describing how he "had stepped into the gloomy circle of some Inferno" (20). Like Dante, his pilgrimage takes him further down into the circles of hell, each one more gruesome than the next. The Company's accountant, too, reveals Kurtz's position in the hellish landscape as being very much at its center. "In the interior you will no doubt meet Mr. Kurtz" (22), he says, and he also tells Marlow to pass on a message to Kurtz that everything is "very satisfactory" (22), as if Kurtz is a person to whom he is accountable.

The deeper Marlow enters into the wilderness, the more significant Kurtz's name becomes. The meeting with the accountant suggests his importance, even that "[h]e will be somebody in the Administration before long" (Conrad 22) because "[t]hey, above . . . mean him to be" (22). The Manager, too, speaks of Kurtz with an odd but striking reverence, repeating his name and inspiring Marlow to do the same with a striking emphasis: "There were rumours that a very important station was in jeopardy and its chief, Mr. Kurtz, was ill. Hoped it was not true. Mr. Kurtz was . . . Hang Kurtz, I thought. I interrupted him by saying that I had heard of Mr. Kurtz on the coast" (25). Having mentioned "rumours" (25), too, the Manager then proceeds to call Kurtz "the best agent" (25) and "an exceptional man, of the greatest importance to the Company" (25). The painting attributed to Kurtz of the woman, "draped and blindfolded carrying a lighted torch" (27) also implies the kind of sacrificial honoring that Kurtz receives from those around him; although the Manager clearly suspects that Kurtz has had an "unfortunate accident" (26), he persists in representing him as heroic and exceptional.

The "brickmaker of the Central Station" continues the trend of praising Kurtz as exceptional. He describes him as "a prodigy . . . an emissary of pity, and science and progress, and devil knows what else" (Conrad 28). Since Kurtz still has not appeared by this point in the story, these repeated praises of an unknown figure, a figure without form, expand his presence, suggesting him as god-like before the reader learns that he is indeed, recognized as a local deity. This sense of his influence is important to realizing why the natives attack Marlow's steamboat, why the "glimpse" of it "had for some reason filled those savages with unrestrained grief" (44).

God, Christ, and the Anti-Christ: Representations of the Divine Self

Recognizing that both Kurtz and Marlow function as a Christ figure in Conrad's narrative is vital to an effective reading of the textual schema. Distinct from god-figures, Rowan Williams suggests that Christ-figures in literature are "a possible impossibility" (2), that they demonstrate not what it is to be Christ but what it is to not be like him, to lack his essence. Drawing attention to the "gaps" (Williams 2), the distinction between the actual Christ and the human Christ parallels, Christ images emphasize the perfection of Christ's actual incarnation. They stress a Christ indistinguishable from God, a rendering of God in human form. Characters that represent Christ inevitably fall short because they cannot imitate Christ's perfection. However, this "gap," as Williams calls it, shifts the comparative emphasis to the ways in which Christ figures, in fact, are imperfect and the ways our own understanding of Christ fall short.

Ludwig Wittgenstein writes that "Christianity is not based on a historical truth; rather, it offers us an (historical) narrative that says: now believe!" (32). The imperfection of Kurtz as a Christ figure draws particular attention to this idea: to the importance of historical narrative in relation to representations of truth. Following the natives' attack of the steamboat, Marlow believes Kurtz is dead and feels disappointment that he will not have the opportunity of "a talk" (Conrad 48). Marlow is "cut to the quick at the idea of having lost the inestimable privilege of listening to the gifted Kurtz" (48), only to realize that the opportunity still remains, that the "voice" (48) of Kurtz has a transcendent power. As Watts suggests, Conrad's narrative anticipates Freud and Jung's exploration of "the divine self" (50). The narrative and the characterization of Kurtz represent a study of "the striving, lustful, anarchic id seeking gratification despite the countervailing pressure of the ego or superego" (50). Kurtz is a powerful figure. He is charismatic and a prominent personality in the environment he finds himself in. He attracts loyalty from the natives, from the Russian, and even, to a degree, from Marlow. He navigates an environment that Marlow describes as "unearthly" (Conrad 32); an environment that people customarily perceive, Marlow suggests, as "a thing monstrous and free" (32). Kurtz's capacity to thrive in this type of environment, though, the extent to which he lures Marlow into his sphere of influence, implies something very much more sinister about Kurtz and his role within the novel.

Marlow meets Kurtz after the attack on the steamboat, realizing that Kurtz ordered the attack. Their first encounter is all the more striking because it has been so dramatically anticipated and because Conrad has made Kurtz physically threatening to his would-be rescuer. Marlow, however, appears entirely enraptured, unable to remain objective in his narrative, recognizing Kurtz as "a gifted creature and that of all his gifts the one that stood out preeminently, that carried with it a sense of real presence, was his ability to talk, his words" (Conrad 48). The significance of Kurtz's language is paramount when it comes to recognizing the basis for this apparent infatuation. From Marlow's perspective, it is "the gift of expression, the bewildering, the illuminating, the most exalted and the most contemptible, the pulsating stream of light or the deceitful flow from the heart of an impenetrable darkness" (48). Kurtz's speech, the power of his expression, is striking, particularly with the repetition and exclamation ("Absurd! Absurd be—exploded! Absurd!" [48]) and the short, emphatic sentences ("And I was right too. A voice" [48]) that convey the apparent energy and charisma of Kurtz that Marlow otherwise describes. Perhaps to suggest his instability, too, Conrad has Kurtz begin speaking "suddenly" (49) and in a somewhat incoherent manner, though his speech is fundamentally powerful. He talks about his "Intended" (49) and about "my ivory" (49), claiming possession of everything and speaking of extravagant ideas. Marlow also recognizes that Kurtz has taken "a high seat amongst the devils of the land" (49) and thus immersed himself so absolutely in the "region of the first ages" (49), absorbing its primordial power.

Kurtz's experience in the jungle becomes all the more troubling as Marlow discovers the report that Kurtz was charged to write for "the International Society for the Suppression of Savage Customs" (Conrad 50). The irony conveyed through the name of the organization, particularly the words "Suppression," "Savage," and "Customs," exposes the imperialist dynamics and values foundational to the operations of the company that employ both Kurtz and Marlow. The language also suggests that Kurtz is very much interested in suppression and suggests the kind of language and ideas in the report, parts of which are revealed to the reader. Listening to Kurtz and reporting his speech to his audience, Marlow provides a voice for Kurtz within the narrative. Initially, Kurtz speaks about "the women" (49) and then comments on the ivory, with Marlow again describing Kurtz as "gifted" (49).

Marlow's response to the report creates a dilemma for the reader, though, because he reacts to evidence of Kurtz's barbaric racism and his megalomania but ascribes it to illness: the report is "too high-strung" (Conrad 50). The reader expects Marlow to condemn the destructive effect of colonialism, but by suggesting that Kurtz is mentally unstable, Marlow begins to mitigate the destruction Kurtz has caused and the violence of his opinions. Elsewhere, Marlow also describes the report as "a beautiful piece of writing" (50), apparently ignoring the comments about how "we whites, from the point of development we had arrived at, 'must necessarily appear to them [savages] In the nature of the supernatural beings we approach them with the might as of a deity,' and so on" (50).

Far from offering an outright condemnation of Kurtz, with reluctance, Marlow betrays the violence of Kurtz's opinions and exclamations. He reveals Kurtz's possessiveness and a sense of the darkness that Kurtz has embraced in the jungle. He describes how Kurtz claims everything for himself: "[e]verything belonged to him—but that was a trifle. The thing was to know what he belonged to, how many powers of darkness claimed him for their own. That was the reflection that made you creepy all over" (Conrad 50). Yet, even as the syntax of this expression is distancing, it is the "reflection" (50) that is "creepy" (50), not Kurtz himself or even what he believes. Marlow creates distance by insisting that those "surrounded by kind neighbours" (50) cannot understand it. The rhetorical question, "You can't understand?," distances Kurtz from his own language and his actions. It frames the circumstances of his experience as removed from civilization and thus free from its moral constraints. The repeated reference to the "kind neighbor" (50) has the same effect but suggests that it is a collective conscience that prevents people from acting as Kurtz has done: the presence of "kind neighbors" (50) prevents the need for violence. Even as Marlow insists "I am not trying to excuse or even explain—I am trying to account to myself for—for—Mr. Kurtz" (50), he does both, allowing Kurtz to remains an enigma to him. In one particular instance, the natives become excited and a woman rushes out "to the very brink of the stream" (66). When Marlow asks what the reaction is for, Kurtz gives a "smile of indefinable meaning" (66). He also, to Marlow, responds with "Do I not?" that appears compelled by "supernatural" (66) forces.

Even as Kurtz's powers seem "supernatural" (Conrad 66), though, the journey out of the jungle doubles as a rapid progression towards death: "[t]he brown current ran swiftly out of the heart of darkness, bearing us down towards the sea with twice the speed of our upward progress. And Kurtz's life was running swiftly too, ebbing, ebbing out of his heart into the sea of inexorable time" (67). Kurtz is not just ill but dying, and Marlow's alignment of Kurtz's life to the natural world, the "ebbing, ebbing" (67) suggests the almost romantic way in which Marlow regards him. This depiction is particularly conspicuous because Conrad gives little sense of Kurtz's physical appearance; the grand language associated with Kurtz makes him seem ethereal. Marlow mentions few details in passing, such as that Kurtz has a "bony arm," is "not much heavier than a child," and has "colorless lips" (66) but even these details hardly seem to fit with the personality of a man whose influence and presence is supernatural. The frailty of his physical form, in the end, suggests a transcendence of the body.

The prospect of death raises concerns about Kurtz's "reputation" (Conrad 62), with Kurtz mentioning that he has not yet finished all he intended and the Manager insisting that that "Mr. Kurtz has done more harm than good to the Company" (61). Concern for "the Company" (61), however, creates a jarring focus on institutions rather than individuals. Given that Conrad has presented the Company using religious imagery—likening the headquarters to church buildings and the men and women inside them, within the Company hierarchy, to priests and nuns respectively—its contrast with Kurtz suggests an allusion to opposition or at least disparity between Christ and the Church.

Like a true disciple, however, Marlow demonstrates enduring loyalty to Kurtz, even as he struggles to reconcile Kurtz's gospel, his words, to his own moral perspective. Kurtz dies crying out, "a cry that was no more than a breath" (Conrad 68) and the ambiguity of his words is striking, "The horror! The horror!" (68). Given his earlier statements, his obvious racism, what Kurtz declares a "horror" (68) may well be the endurance of native populations. Marlow himself meditates on the possible meaning: "He had summed up—he had judged. 'The horror!' He was a remarkable man. After all, this was the expression of some sort of belief" (69). As in other such statements about Kurtz, Marlow's language is elegant and suggestive of the influence that Kurtz exerts. The adjectives, "remarkable," "vibrating," "appalling," and "strange" particularly render the range of qualities that Kurtz demonstrates. The nouns, too, "expression," "belief," "candour," "conviction," "revolt," "truth," "desire," "hatred," "contempt," and "evanescence" (69), have the same effect, cataloguing the diverse reactions that Kurtz inspires but also really legitimizing him by further establishing the power of his performance. Finally, Conrad's verb choices articulate the profundity of Kurtz's ideas. Kurtz "summed up" and "judged" (68), characterize Kurtz as truly considering what he is saying; such word choices lend weight to his thoughts. He has the means to make a judgment, in the end, which causes Marlow, his principle audience, to "remember" (69); to value the insight.

Although Marlow does later question the "summing up" (Conrad 69), the impression of this initial language overpowers any sense that Marlow even can condemn Kurtz. His own language, "I like to think my summing up would not have been a word of careless contempt" (69-70) is both fundamentally weak, especially with the use of the hypothetical, and is strikingly vague. He does not want to use a word of "careless contempt" (70), but he does not say that Kurtz does this either. He accepts Kurtz's language as the more acceptable: "Better his cry—much better" (70) and validates it by calling it "an affirmation, a moral victory paid by innumerable defeats, by abominable terrors, by abominable satisfactions. But it was a victory" (70). Other characters also affirm this by declaring that Kurtz had "the faith" (71) and "could get himself to believe anything" (71); his victory comes through belief in himself and the durability of that belief through those he influenced, including Marlow.

The conclusion of the narrative and the lasting effect of Kurtz is ambiguous, though, like Kurtz's dying declaration. Considering Marlow's perspective, Agata Szczeszak-Brewer suggests that "[e]ither the pilgrimage from the profane world of arbitrary social roles towards the ultimate knowledge and self-formation remains incomplete or, if [he] does reach its telos, it turns out to be empty" (102). The issue, really, emerges after Kurtz's death, when Marlow visits the Intended, a woman who is unnamed but to whom Kurtz apparently was engaged. The loaded meaning of "Intended" is particularly poignant to a reading of Kurtz as a Christ figure because it echoes of both the Old Testament language of "Chosen people" and the New Testament foundation of the Christian Church through those chosen from among Christ's disciples. Conrad is yet more direct with his allusion to a Christian context, however, by having Marlow speak to the Intended about Kurtz's final words to convince her that his last thoughts were of her. The Intended's language, in fact, is full of allusions to her faith in Kurtz and her devotion to him. She speaks of how it was impossible not to "love" him and how she had "all his noble confidence. I knew him best" (Conrad 73). Although Marlow appears to doubt this, her sense of being "very happy—very fortunate—very proud" (74) implies that she drew considerable value from her relationship with Kurtz, as Marlow did. Like Marlow, the Intended perceives Kurtz as a god-like figure though in the form of a prospective spouse, echoing the idea of a marriage between Christ and the Church. The Intended begs, however, to know the "last words" of Kurtz because she wants "something—something—to—to live with" (75). The syntax and particularly the aposiopesis or gap suggested by the dashes, imply a spiritual longing here, too; something that is rather spontaneous. Marlow's decision to lie to her, to insist that the last word he pronounced was "your name" (75), is also indicative of the way the Gospel of Christ, his words, were rendered through the Church, the Church often misinterpreting or editing, as Marlow does, the most striking language. The Intended's response, her "exulting and terrible cry" (76) give a final sense of spiritual release, of exultation that is profoundly connected to a sense of "religious" truth.

Works Cited

Conrad, Joseph. *Heart of Darkness*. Ed. Robert Kimbrough. New York: W.W. Norton & Company, 1988. Print.

Freud, Sigmund. *Civilization and Its Discontents*. Trans. & Ed. James Strachey. *The Standard Edition of the Complete Psychological Works of Sigmund Freud.* Vol. 21. London: Hogarth Press, 1973. Print.

Murphy, Francesca Aran & Rowan Williams. "Imagining Christ in Literature." *The Oxford Handbook of Christology*. Ed. Francesca Aran Murphy. Oxford: Oxford UP, 2015. *CrossRef.* Web.

Szczeszak-Brewer, Agata. *Empire and Pilgrimage in Conrad and Joyce*. Gainsville: UP of Florida, 2011. Print.

Wyatt, Cedric. "Heart of Darkness," *The Cambridge Companion to Joseph Conrad*. Ed. J. H. Stape. New York: Cambridge UP, 1996. 45-62. Print.

RESOURCES

Chronology of Joseph Conrad's Life

1857	Józef Teodor Konrad Korzeniowski is born on December 3, in Berdyczów, the Polish section of Russian occupied Ukraine.
1862	Due to his father's political ideologies and anti-Russian sentiments, Conrad accompanies his parents, Apollo Korzeniowski and Ewelina Bobrowska, in exile to Vologda, Russia.
1865	Conrad's mother dies of tuberculosis, contracted under the harsh conditions of exile. Conrad begins to learn English. He will not become fluent in English until he is in his late twenties.
1869	Conrad and his father are permitted to leave Russia and migrate to the Austrian-occupied section of Poland.
1869	Conrad's father dies of tuberculosis in Kraków. Orphaned, Conrad is placed under the guardianship of his maternal uncle, Tadeusz Bobrowski.
1874	Conrad drops out of formal schooling. Flees Poland in order to avoid conscription into the Russian military. Joins the French Merchant Marines in Marseilles.
1876	Conrad serves aboard the *Sainte-Antonie*, where he meets Dominic Cervoni, the inspiration for his character Nostromo. Sails Caribbean.
1877	Conrad is involved in a Carlist plot to smuggle weapons to Spanish rebels.
1878	Conrad attempts suicide with a self-inflicted gunshot wound to the chest. His uncle pays the gambling

	debts Conrad accrued during the Carlist plot. Conrad transfers to the British merchant fleet in order to avoid possible conscription, once again, into Russian service had he stayed in the French merchant fleet. Sails Australia and the Mediterranean.
1880	Conrad is aboard the sinking ship *Palestine*, inspiring story "Youth." Sails Southeast Asia and India.
1886	Conrad becomes a subject of the British Crown. Injured on board the *Highland Forest*, he jumps ship after a hospital stint in Singapore.
1887	Conrad visits the Malay Archipelago, having been made first officer of the ship *The Vidar*.
1888	Conrad is appointed master command of the ship *Otago*. Sails Australia and Mauritius. In less than five months, Conrad makes six voyages across the globe. These travels inspire the settings for *Almayer's Folly*, *An Outcast of the Island*, *Lord Jim*, and the worlds of many of his short stories.
1889	Conrad resigns his command of the *Otago* and returns to London, where he begins writing *Almayer's Folly*.
1890	Conrad returns to the sea as second-mate on a river steamer and sails up the Congo River on a four-month expedition. He temporarily becomes captain of *Roi des Belges*. His journey and journal, *The Congo Diary*, become the inspiration for "An Outpost of Progress" and *Heart of Darkness*.
1894	Conrad's uncle and guardian, Tadeusz Bobrowski dies. Conrad ends his nautical career. Meets future wife Jessie George.

1895	*Almayer's Folly* is published under pen name "Joseph Conrad."
1896	*An Outcast of Islands* is published. Conrad marries Jessie George. Settles in Essex, United Kingdom. Befriends H. G. Wells and Henry James.
1897	*The Nigger of the 'Narcissus'* published. Conrad befriends R. B. Cunninghame Graham and Stephen Crane.
1898	Conrad's oldest son, Borys, is born. "Karain: A Memory," "The Idiots," "An Outpost of Progress," "The Return," and "The Lagoon" are published in the collection *Tales of Unrest*. Conrad befriends his soon frequent collaborator, Ford Madox Ford, and moves family to Kent, United Kingdom.
1899	*Heart of Darkness* is published in serial form.
1899	*Lord Jim* published in serial form.
1901	*The Inheritors*, written in collaboration with Ford Madox Ford, is published in bound book form.
1902	Bound book version of *Heart of Darkness* is published; "The End of the Tether" and "Youth" are published under the collection *Youth: A Narrative*.
1903	Bound book version of "Typhoon," "Amy Foster," "Falk," and "To-morrow" published under the collection *Typhoon and Other Stories*. *Romance*, written in collaboration with Ford Madox Ford, is published in bound book form.

1904	*Nostromo* is published in serial, then book form. Conrad's wife suffers knee injuries that leave her permanently disabled.
1906	Conrad's second son, John, is born. *The Mirror of the Sea* is published. *The Secret Agent* is published in serial form.
1907	*The Secret Agent* is published as bound book form. Conrad and his family move to Bedfordshire, United Kingdom.
1908	Bound book version of "Gaspar Ruiz," "The Informer," "The Brute," "An Anarchist," "The Duel," and "Il Conde" is published under the collection *A Set of Six*.
1909	Conrad has a falling out with Ford Madox Ford over Conrad's contributions to *The English Review*. Moves family to Kent, United Kingdom.
1910	Conrad suffers nervous breakdown after writing *Under Western Eyes*. *Under Western Eyes* is published in serial form.
1911	*Under Western Eyes* is published in bound book form.
1912	*Some Reminiscences* is published. This autobiographical account is later republished as *A Personal Record*. "A Smile of Fortune," "The Secret Sharer," and "Freya of the Seven Isles" are published under the collection *'Twixt Land and Sea*. *Chance* is published in serial form.
1914	*Chance* is published in bound book form and meets with critical acclaim. It becomes Conrad's first financially successful publication. Conrad and his family travel to Poland, under Austro-Hungarian control, and become

	trapped in the country due to the outbreak of World War I. Return to England weeks later.
1915	"The Planter of Malata," "The Partner," "The Inn of the Two Witches," and "Because of the Dollars" are published in the collection *Within the Tides*. *Victory* is published in bound book form.
1917	*The Shadow-Line* is published in bound book form.
1919.	Conrad and his family move to Bishopsbourne, United Kingdom. *The Arrow of Gold* is published in bound book form.
1920	*The Rescue*, a book Conrad began writing in 1898, is published in bound book form.
1921	Conrad visits Corsica to research material for *Suspense*. *Notes on Life and Letters* is published in bound book form.
1923	*The Rover* is published in serial, then bound book form.
1924	Conrad declines offer of knighthood. On August 3, at the age of sixty-six, Conrad dies of a heart attack. He is buried in Canterbury cemetery.
1925	"The Warrior's Soul," "Prince Roman," "The Tale," and "The Black Mate" are posthumously published in the collection *Tales of Hearsay*. Conrad's unfinished novel *Suspense: A Napoleonic Novel* is published posthumously.
1926	*Last Essays* is posthumously published in bound book form.

Works by Joseph Conrad

Long Fiction
Almayer's Folly, 1896
An Outcast of the Islands, 1896
The Nigger of the 'Narcissus,' 1897
Heart of Darkness, 1899
Lord Jim, 1900
The Inheritors, 1901
Typhoon, 1902
Romance, 1903
Nostromo, 1904
The Secret Agent, 1907
Under Western Eyes, 1911
Chance, 1913
Victory, 1915
The Shadow Line, 1917
The Arrow of Gold, 1919
The Rescue, 1920
The Nature of a Crime, 1923
The Rover, 1923
Suspense: A Napoleonic Novel, 1925

Short Fiction
"The Black Mate," 1886/1908
"The Idiots," 1896
"The Lagoon," 1897
"An Outpost of Progress," 1897
"Karain: A Memory," 1897
"The Return," 1898
"Amy Foster," 1901

"Youth," 1902
"The End of the Tether," 1902
"To-morrow," 1902
"Falk," 1903
"Gasper Ruiz," 1906
"An Anarchist," 1906
"The Informer," 1906
"The Brute," 1906
"The Duel: A Military Story," 1908
"Il Conde", 1908
"The Secret Sharer," 1910
"Prince Roman," 1911
"A Smile of Fortune," 1911
"Freya of the Seven Isles," 1912
"The Partner," 1915
"The Inn of the Two Witches," 1915
"Because of the Dollars," 1915
"The Planter of Malata," 1915
"The Warrior's Soul," 1917
"The Tale," 1917

Nonfiction

The Congo Diary, 1890/1978
"The Autocracy and War," 1905
The Mirror of the Sea, 1904–1906
A Personal Record, 1912
The First News, 1918
The Lesson of the Collision: A Monograph Upon the Loss of the "Empress of Ireland," 1919
The Polish Question, 1919
The Shock of War, 1919
Notes on Life and Letters, 1921

Notes on My Books, 1921
Last Essays, 1926

Bibliography

Achebe, Chinua. "An Image of Africa: Racism in Conrad's 'Heart of Darkness'" *Massachusetts Review* 18 (1977). Reprinted in *Heart of Darkness: An Authoritative Text, Background and Sources Criticism.* Ed. Robert Kimbrough. London: W.W. Norton and Co., 1988. 251-261. Print.

Acheraïou, Amar. *Joseph Conrad and the Reader: Questioning Modern Theories of Narrative and Readership.* Basingstoke, UK: Palgrave Macmillan, 2009. Print.

Baines, Jocelyn. *Joseph Conrad: A Critical Biography.* London: Weidenfeld, 1993. Print.

Batchelor, John. *The Life of Joseph Conrad: A Critical Biography.* Oxford: Blackwell, 1994. Print.

Berthoud, Jacques. *Joseph Conrad: The Major Phase.* Cambridge, UK: Cambridge UP, 1978. Print.

The Cambridge Companion to Joseph Conrad. Ed. J. H. Stape. Cambridge, UK: Cambridge UP, 1996. Print.

Conrad, Jessie. *Joseph Conrad as I Knew Him.* London: W. Heinemann, 1926. Print.

Crankshaw, Edward. *Joseph Conrad: Some Aspects of the Art of the Novel.* New York: Russell & Russell, 1963. Print.

Darras, Jacques. *Joseph Conrad and the West: Signs of Empire.* Trans. Anne Luyat & Jacques Darras. London: Macmillan, 1982. Print.

Dowden, Wilfred S. *Joseph Conrad: The Imagined Style.* Nashville: Vanderbilt UP, 1970. Print.

Fleishman, Avrom. *Conrad's Politics: Community and Anarchy in the Fiction of Joseph Conrad.* Baltimore, MD: John Hopkins UP, 1967. Print.

Ford, Madox Ford. *Joseph Conrad: A Personal Remembrance.* New York: Ecco Press, 1989. Print.

Frederick, Karl R., ed. *Joseph Conrad: A Collection of Criticism.* New York: McGraw-Hill, 1975. Print.

Goonetilleke, D. C. R. A. *Joseph Conrad: Beyond Culture and Background.* Basingstoke, UK: Palgrave Macmillan, 1990. Print.

Gurko, Leo. *Joseph Conrad: Giant in Exile.* London: Fredrick Muller Ltd., 1965. Print.

Hamner, Robert D. *Joseph Conrad: Third World Perspectives.* Boulder, CO: Lynne Rienner 1990. Print.

Hampson, Robert. *Joseph Conrad: Betrayal and Identity.* Basingstroke, UK: Palgrave Macmillan, 1992. Print.

Hawthorn, Jeremy. *Joseph Conrad: Language and Fictional Self-Consciousness.* Lincoln: U. of Nebraska P, 1979. Print.

_____. *Joseph Conrad: Narrative Technique and Ideological Commitment.* London: Edward Arnold, 1990. Print.

Jones, Susan. *Conrad and Women.* Oxford: Clarendon Press, 1999. Print.

Knowles, Owen & Gene M. Moore. *Oxford Reader's Companion to Conrad.* Oxford: Oxford UP, 2000. Print.

Lothe, Jakob, Jeremy Hawthorn, & James Phelan, eds. *Joseph Conrad: Voice, Sequence, History, Genre.* Columbus: Ohio State University Press, 2008. Print.

Martin, Ray. *Joseph Conrad: Memories and Impressions, An Annotated Bibliography.* New York: Rodopi, 2007. Print.

Meyer, Bernard C. *Joseph Conrad: A Psychoanalytic Biography.* Princeton, NJ: Princeton UP, 1967. Print.

Moser, Thomas C. *Joseph Conrad: Achievement and Decline.* Cambridge, MA: Harvard UP, 1957. Print.

Najder, Zdzisław. *Joseph Conrad: A Life.* Trans. Halina Najder. Rochester, NY: Camden House, 2007. Print.

Peters, John G. *Conrad and Impressionism.* Cambridge, UK: Cambridge UP, 2001. Print.

Panichas, George A. *Joseph Conrad: His Moral Vision.* Macon, GA: Mercer UP, 2005. Print.

Ray, Martin. *Joseph Conrad and His Contemporaries, An Annotated Bibliography of Interviews and Recollections.* London: Joseph Conrad Society (UK), 1988. Print.

Saveson, John. E. *Joseph Conrad: The Making of a Moralist.* Amsterdam: Rodopi NV, 1972. Print.

Seymour-Smith, Martin. *Joseph Conrad.* London: Greenwich Exchange, 1995. Print.

Sherry, Norman. *Conrad's Eastern World*. Cambridge, UK: Cambridge UP, 1966. Print.

―――――. *Conrad's Western World*. Cambridge, UK: Cambridge UP, 1971. Print.

―――――, ed. *Joseph Conrad: The Critical Heritage*. London: Routledge, 1997. Print.

Simmons, Allan H. *Joseph Conrad*. Basingstoke, UK: Palgrave Macmillan, 2006. Print.

―――――, ed. *Joseph Conrad in Context*. Cambridge, UK: Cambridge UP, 2009. Print.

Spittles, Brian. *Joseph Conrad: Text and Context*. Basingstoke, UK: Palgrave Macmillan, 1992. Print.

Stape, J. H., ed. *Notes on Life and Letters*. Cambridge, UK: Cambridge UP, 2002. Print.

Stape, John. *The Several Lives of Joseph Conrad*. London: William Heinemann, 2007. Print.

Watt, Ian. *Conrad in the Nineteenth Century*. Berkeley: U of California P, 1979. Print.

White, Andrea. *Joseph Conrad and the Adventure Tradition: Constructing and Deconstructing the Imperial Subject*. Cambridge, UK: Cambridge UP, 1993. Print.

Zins, Henryk. *Joseph Conrad and Africa*. Nairobi: Kenya Literature Bureau, 1982. Print.

About the Editor

Jeremiah J. Garsha is a postgraduate researcher in the Faculty of History at the University of Cambridge. He is a social and cultural historian of bodies and objects. His research focuses on visual and material cultures of imperialism, framed in a world history context. He specializes in comparative colonial genocide, with broader interests in violence and postcolonial memory, specifically the positioning and repositioning of physical memory structures within landscapes of atrocities. He received his BA from the University of California at Santa Barbara in history and Germanic literature. He holds an MA degree in modern European history from San Francisco State University as well as an MPhil in African studies from the University of Cambridge.

His research on Joseph Conrad's writings began with his MA thesis, which uses an interdisciplinary focus to explore the intertextuality and internationalism of early twentieth-century intellectual protests against colonization, heralded by and organized around *Heart of Darkness*. His published chapter "Brutish Behavior: Joseph Conrad, Mark Twain, and Anticolonial Protests, 1899–1905" in *Critical Insights: Literature of Protest* (2013) builds upon Conrad's central themes of colonialism as a corruption of personal morality and universal values by analyzing the historical context and biographical life experiences of the authors. Conrad's writings pertaining to the representation of subjection and narrative depictions of colonial violence continue to influence Jeremiah's work. His MPhil dissertation documents the shifting narrative rhetoric used in colonial monuments and genocide memorials in Namibia, Zimbabwe, and South Africa. His PhD dissertation moves firmly into the realm of transnational history in its exploration of German and British colonial occupation in East and Southwest Africa (modern day Tanzania, Kenya, and Namibia) by unpacking the global history of the anthropological tradition of collecting and displaying indigenous body parts; the cultural, social, and political transformation of these body parts into objects of scientific inquiry; and the framework of postcolonial corporeal repatriation. Conrad's use of colonial violence, specifically scenes of decapitation and display can be found in Jeremiah's most recent scholarship, which focuses exclusively on the long twentieth-century transnational history of Wahehe Chief

Mkwawa's severed head. His publications have appeared in a global range of formats, including *Genocide Studies and Prevention: An International Journal, Przegląd Zachodni* (*Journal of Polish Western Affairs*), and the Canadian *Eugenics Archive.*

Contributors

Fitrilya Anjarsari is a graduate student in Gadjah Mada University, where she focuses on postmodernism literary critiques. Her research bridges the fields of literature and history. She is currently conducting research on history with the Wageningen University and Research Centre on "Gender, Household and Labour Relations in Postcolonialism 1800–Present." Her other research interests include the historical position of farming in Indonesia. She also writes for ISRSF in partnership with Northwestern University. Her work on literary criticism had also been published for Gadjah Mada University Press and several publishing house in Indonesia. She is currently finishing her thesis and preparing for a doctoral degree.

Peter Arnds is Director of Comparative Literature and Literary Translation at Trinity College Dublin. He was Visiting Professor at Middlebury College, the University of Kabul, JNU Delhi, and the J. M. Coetzee Centre for Creative Practice at the University of Adelaide. He is the author of *Intertextuality in Wilhelm Raabe and Charles Dickens* (Peter Lang, 1997); *Representation, Subversion and Eugenics in Günter Grass's 'The Tin Drum'* (Camden House, 2004); and "Lycanthropy in German Literature" (Palgrave 2015). He has also edited *Translating Holocaust Literature* (Vandenhoeck & Ruprecht, 2015) and translated Patrick Boltshauser's novel *Stromschnellen* (*Rapids*, Dalkey Archive Press, 2014, nominated for the Dublin International Literary Award). A member of the PEN Centre, he has published prose and poetry in literary journals around the globe and was a writer-in-residence at the Heinrich Böll Cottage on Achill Island (Mayo). His collection of poetry, *A Rare Clear Day*, appeared in RedFox Press in 2015.

Francesco Buscemi teaches media studies in various European cities (Bournemouth, Milan, Stirling, and others). He earned his PhD at Queen Margaret University, where he focused on Bourdieusian and a semiotic analysis of how food in the media supports national ideologies. Another strand of research involves meat, cultured meat, and the links to living animals, death, religion, blood, gender, and the relationships between nature and culture. In 2012, Francesco was awarded the Santander Grant Fund for his research *Edible Lies: How Nazi Propaganda Represented Meat to Demonise the Jews* and has also investigated meat representations in the propaganda of the Italian regency of Fiume, Italian Fascism, and the East German regime. He has published a book on the Italian film director Liliana Cavani and various articles and book chapters on food and media studies. Francesco is currently a member of the Semiotic Society of America and the International Society for Cultural History. He writes for his blog *Behind Food*.

Stefania Elena Carnemolla is an Italian freelance researcher specializing in the history of discoveries, the history of Portuguese and European expansion, sea voyages, seafaring, sea trade, travels and explorations, and the history of maritime, nautical, and oceanic sciences. She received her degree in humanities at Pisa University and has held scholarships at the Fundação Calouste Gulbenkian as well as at other Portuguese institutions. She has published two books, numerous academic articles, and essays on maritime subjects, such as on shipwrecks along the Portuguese Carreira da Índia. As a contributor of the Italian Navy journal, she focuses most of her work to the relationship between science and technology in the maritime world. She is also a freelance journalist with interests in foreign affairs, geopolitics, economy, culture, science, technology, defense issues, and shipping.

Taryn B. Cornell holds an MPhil in African studies from the University of Cambridge and a BA in history, politics, and international relations (Combined Honours) from Durham University. Her research areas focus on Southern Africa, technology, and postcolonial and feminist theories, with projects including digital media use in South African LGBTI communities and the disconnection between public and private approaches to gendered violence. Taryn is also a researcher on a collaborative project between Cambridge's Centre of Governance and Human Rights and the UN Special Rapporteur on extrajudicial, summary or arbitrary executions, compiling research on armed violence reduction programs across the African continent. An Anglo-American, Taryn currently lives in London, United Kingdom.

Lydia Craig is a graduate student at Loyola University Chicago, where she pursues a PhD in Victorian studies with an additional focus on Early Modern drama. In particular, she studies nature imagery, class issues, and early modern influence in Charles Dickens' novels. She holds an MA in English literature from Loyola University Chicago and a BA in English and history from the University of Georgia. She served as the 2015 McElroy Memorial Shakespeare Celebration's Publicity Assistant and volunteers as a social media/writing intern at the Chicago Metro History Education Center. Recently, she received the 2015 Anthony Ellis Award for Best Graduate Paper at the Thirty-Ninth Comparative Drama Conference. Her essay "Politic Silence: Female Choruses in Lochhead's Medea and Wertenbaker's The Love of the Nightingale" recently appeared in the Fall 2015 issue of *Text & Presentation*.

Gerardo Del Guercio is formerly of the Royal Military College of Canada (St-Jean), Collège Jean-de-Brébeuf, and l'université de Montréal. He is the author of *The Fugitive Slave Law in The Life of Frederick Douglass, an American Slave and Harriet Beecher Stowe's Uncle Tom's Cabin: American Society Transforms Its Culture* (Edwin Mellen, 2013). Additionally, he has published essays on Benjamin Franklin, Henry James, Nathaniel West, and Jean Toomer. His works have appeared in several journals—including *Southern Studies*, *College Language Association Journal* as well as *The Early America Review*. He holds a BA from Concordia University, an MA from l'université de Montréal, and a TESOL from York College, CUNY. At present, he is teaching English in Montréal, Québec, Canada, completing his teacher training at Binghamton University, SUNY, as well as completing a collection of essays on Edgar Allan Poe that is under contract with McFarland.

Kieran Dodds is a social historian interested in southern African audiences, performances, and popular cultures. He is a graduate of the University of Cambridge African studies program. His dissertation centers on soccer in late colonial Lesotho and apartheid South Africa and especially on the social identities that actors came to fashion and fasten around sport. He has also conducted research into orality and the public sphere in post-1994 South Africa and the theme of sacrifice in the classic African novel.

Charlotte Fiehn studies English at Lucy Cavendish College at the University of Cambridge. Her research interests include George Eliot and the nineteenth-century British novel, British modernism, medieval and Renaissance literature, and English romantic poetry. Her recent publications include articles on Shakespeare and George Eliot and chapters on the political rhetoric of Elizabeth I, on Henry James as an American writer in exile, and on D. H. Lawrence. She has presented at several conferences, including the South Atlantic Modern Language Association Conference 2015, Senses and Spaces: II International Conference in Transatlantic Studies Real Colegio Complutense at Harvard University, and at the 2016 annual conference of the British Association for Victorian Studies.

Phillip A. Lobo is a PhD candidate enrolled in the University of Southern California's Department of Comparative Literature. He specializes in the study of subjectivity and formal realism, particularly as they pertain to novels and games, as well as the practice of world-building. He has been a regular contributor to *Open Letters Monthly*, an online arts and literature review, writing chiefly on games and associated media.

Joshua Pritchard is a doctoral candidate in the Faculty of History, University of Cambridge. His PhD focuses on the relationship between race and nationalism in colonial and postcolonial Zimbabwe. He has written previously on the history of European imperialism in Africa more broadly but has particular interest in the interactions between colonizer and colonized in the Southern African context. He holds an MA in African history from the School of Oriental and African Studies, University of London, and a BA (Hons) in modern history from Aberystwyth University.

Fouzia Reza is a lecturer in the Department of English at Southeast University, Bangladesh. She holds a BA in English and an MA in English literature from the University of Dhaka. Her areas of interest are creative writing, gender and body politics, memory, migration and space studies, stereotypes, and performance art. She is a member of *Brine Pickles*, a creative writing group. Being a Bangladeshi immigrant of Saudi Arabia for the majority of her life, she relentlessly supports many issues regarding immigrants, women, and representations. *Lord Jim*'s preoccupation with the issue of dislocation and Conrad as a writer has always fascinated her since her creative language is, generally, English. She can be reached at fouzia.reza10@gmail.com.

Vikarun Nessa is a senior lecturer in the Department of English, Southeast University, Bangladesh. She has completed her BA (Hons) and MA in English literature from the Department of English, University of Dhaka. Her areas of interest are adaptations, gender studies, and postcolonial literature. She has published several articles in national and international journals. She has been a panel speaker in a seminar on "International Mother Language Day and Bangla," organized by the Department of Linguistics, University of Dhaka. She became interested in *Lord Jim* because of her interest in colonial and postcolonial literature. Moreover, Conrad's portrayal of female characters has always intrigued her. As a practicing Hijabi she also feels a close affinity within the post-9/11 Muslim/terrorist discourse and ideas related to identity crisis and stereotyping.

Hatice Övgü Tüzün received her BA in English language and literature from İstanbul University. Her MA (thesis titled "Hamlet and Conrad") and PhD (thesis titled "Naipaul's East: The Portrayal of India and non-Arab Muslim Societies in V.S. Naipaul's Travel Narratives") were completed at the University of Kent, United Kingdom. She has published articles on multiculturalism, modern literature, travel writing, and the political novel. Her recent interests include posthumanism and emotions in literature. She is currently Chair of the Department of American Culture and Literature at Bahçeşehir University, İstanbul.

Benjamin Bronnert Walker is a Wellcome Trust doctoral student at the University of York in the Department of History where he works on international health and Ghana in the twentieth century. He received his BA in History at Gonville and Caius College, Cambridge where he was given the Scholar's Award and Book Prize. He then moved to Peterhouse College, Cambridge to complete an MPhil in African Studies on a grant from the Newton Trust and the college itself. He is a keen short-story writer and enjoys analyzing the intersection between historical and literary disciplines.

Index

Achebe, Chinua x, xv, 16, 23, 24, 25, 50, 156, 182
Agamben, Giorgio 48
Ahmed, Jimmy 92, 93, 94
Allen, Jerry 123
Almayer, Kaspar 10, 114
Almayer, Nina 127
Anderson, Walt 173
Arendt, Hannah 37, 47, 84
Armstrong, Robert 181
Avellanos, Antonia 72
Avellanos, Don José 89

Bacadou, Jean-Pierre 196
Bacon, Francis 172
Barron, Joseph 8
Bennett, Andrew 59
Benson, Gale Ann 92
Bento, Guzman 87
Bhabha, Homi K. 48
Blackwood, William 71, 181
Bobrowski, Tadeusz xxv, 223, 224
Bower, Tom 47
Brantlinger, Patrick 28
Brillat-Savarin, Anthelme 163
Brooke, Rajah James 124, 127

Caillois, Roger 63
Captain Lingard xxviii
Casement, Roger 13, 41, 42, 45
Cervoni, Dominique xxvi
Césaire, Aimé 51, 61, 64
Chamberlain, Joseph 13
Chaudhary, Mukhtar 16
Chopra, Priyanka 107
Christensen, Tim 51
Clifford, Hugh 118

Cohen, Leonard 92
Coleridge, Samuel Taylor 110
Conrad, Sebastian xiv
Cook, James 5
Counihan, Carole 169
Croft-Cooke, Rupert 153
Crusoe, Robinson 158
Curle, Richard 124

Davies, Laurence xxii, 48, 49, 83, 176
Davis, Mike 168
Decoud, Martin 72, 89, 160
De Freitas, Michael 92
Deleuze, Gilles xiii, 43, 48
Derrida, Jacques xiii, 47, 63
Dickens, Charles xxiv, 239, 241
DuPuis, Melanie 169, 177

Eliot, T. S. 110

Fernando, Lloyd 119
Firchow, Peter 22, 27
Fish, Stanley 187
Flaherty, Captain 136, 138
Fleishman, Avrom 55
Ford, Ford Madox 23, 225, 226
Forster, E. M. 22, 186
Foucault, Michel xiii
French, Jennifer 159
Freud, Sigmund 24, 206, 220
Fussel, Paul 116

Galsworthy, John 148, 171, 172, 176
Garnett, Alf 57
Garnett, Edward 14, 21, 22, 64

Goldie, George Taubman 12
Golding, William 187
Goodman, David 169
Goodman, Michael 169
Gould, Charles 72, 74, 81, 87
Gould, Emilia 72
Graham, R. B. Cunninghame 55, 64, 225
Guattari, Félix 43, 48, 49
Guerard, Albert J. 24
Guisan, Henry 47
Gurth, Deborah 209

Hakluyt, Richard 124
Halliday, Michael 187
Hamid, Rose 106, 108
Hawkins, Hunt 28
Hawthorn, Jeremy 30, 170, 234
Heart of Darkness viii, ix, xi, xii, xviii, xix, xx, xxi, xxii, xxv, xxix, xxxi, 3, 5, 9, 10, 11, 12, 13, 14, 15, 16, 17, 18, 19, 20, 21, 23, 24, 25, 26, 27, 28, 29, 30, 31, 32, 33, 34, 35, 36, 41, 42, 43, 45, 47, 49, 50, 51, 52, 53, 54, 56, 57, 58, 62, 63, 64, 65, 69, 83, 160, 169, 170, 177, 179, 180, 181, 182, 183, 184, 188, 189, 191, 192, 193, 206, 207, 209, 211, 213, 215, 217, 219, 220, 224, 225, 229, 233, 237
Heyst, Axel 194
Hiddleston, Jane 63
Hinrichs, C. Clare 169
Hitler, Adolf 36, 39, 40, 47, 48, 49, 61
Hochschild, Adam 48

Hölderlin, Friedrich 44
Hugo, Victor xxiv
Hulse, Michael 48, 49

Ingram, Billy 174
Ismay, J. Bruce 132, 133, 139
Ismay, Thomas 132

Jakobson, Roman 187
Jeffers, Thomas 157
Jim, Tuan 102, 105

Karl, Frederick R. xxii, 48, 72, 83, 176
Keppel, Henry 124
Kimbrough, Robert xxxi, 34, 181, 192, 220, 233
Kipling, Rudyard 10
Knowles, Owen 20, 31
Korzeniowski, Apollo xxiv, xxv, 42, 223
Korzeniowski, Ewa 4
Korzeniowski, Józef Teodor Konrad xxiv, 4
Koutonin, Mawuna Remarque 102
Kurdi, Aylan 99, 101, 110, 111

Lacan, Jacques xiii
Lazarus, Emma 106
Leavis, F. R. 23, 186
Lee, Paula 172
Lennon, John 92
Lingard, William 126
Livingstone, David 5

Magdalene, Mary 209
Magnet, Shoshana 154
Malik, Michael Abdul 92
Marcus, Miriam 8

Marlow, Charles xxv, xxix, 3, 69, 136, 206
Marlowe, Christopher xxv
Maroola, Dain 114, 127
Marx, Karl 11
Masefield, John 21
Mickiewicz, Adam xxiv
Mirror of the Sea, The xxvi, xxvii, xxxi, 6, 145, 226, 230
Mishra, Pankaj 97
Monet, Claude 23
Moore, Gene 15
Muschg, Adolf 47

Nail, Thomas 104
Naipaul, Vidiadhar Surajprasad 84
Najder, Zdzisław xxvi, xxvii, 149
Nigger of the 'Narcissus', The ix, xvi, xvii, xxii, 8, 50, 225
Nixon, Rob 86
Nofal, Khalil Hassan 182
Novick, Peter xiii

Olmeijer, Willem Carel 9
Olmeijer, William Charles xxviii
Ossipon, Comrade Tom 77

Park, Mungo 5
Peters, John G. 70, 83
Petrini, Carlo 163, 167, 178
Pirrie, William James 132

Range, Thrushcross 92
Rhodes, Cecil 12
Ribiera, Don Vincente 88
Rime of Ancient Mariner, The 110
Robertson, J. M. 152
Rousseau, Jean-Jacques 40

Said, Edward 15, 27, 56, 65, 84, 86, 107
Schmirhahn, Anselm 35, 40
Schneider, Lissa 70
Sekimizu, Koji 143
Selous, Frederick 9
Shakespeare, William xxiv
Sherry, Norman 126
Shields, Matthew 158
Shire, Warsan 99, 100, 112
Sinclair, John 183, 187
Sinclair, Upton 171
Singh, D.S Ranjit 129
Singh, Frances B. 26
Skerritt, Joseph 92
Slow Food movement xi, 162, 164, 169, 170, 171, 172, 174, 175
Soutine, Chaim 172
Spivak, Gayatri Chakravorty 62
Stanley, Henry Morton 184
Stone, Robert 84
Straus, Nina Pelikan 70
Szczeszak-Brewer, Agata 219

Tate, D. J. M. 118
Tennyson, Alfred 100
Thompson, Gordon W. 70
Toolan, Michael 187
Torgovnick, Marianna 30
Turgenev, Ivan 57

Unwin, Fisher 118, 129

Verloc, Adolf 77
Verloc, Winnie 77, 78, 81, 82
Von Ranke, Leopold xiii

Waheed, Nayyirah 101
Waite, R. G. L. 48
Wait, James xvii, 8, 56
Wait, Jimmy 8
Wallace, Alfred 124, 128
Warren, Robert Penn 86, 98
Watt, Ian 23, 186
Watts, Cedric 206

Westerweel, Bart 170
White, Andrea xx, 5, 124
Widdowson, H. G. 183
Widmer, Urs 35, 47, 49
Williams, Rowan 213, 220
Wittgenstein, Ludwig 214
World War I xxx, 227
Wyk, Van 59